EXPERIMENT IN OCCUPATION

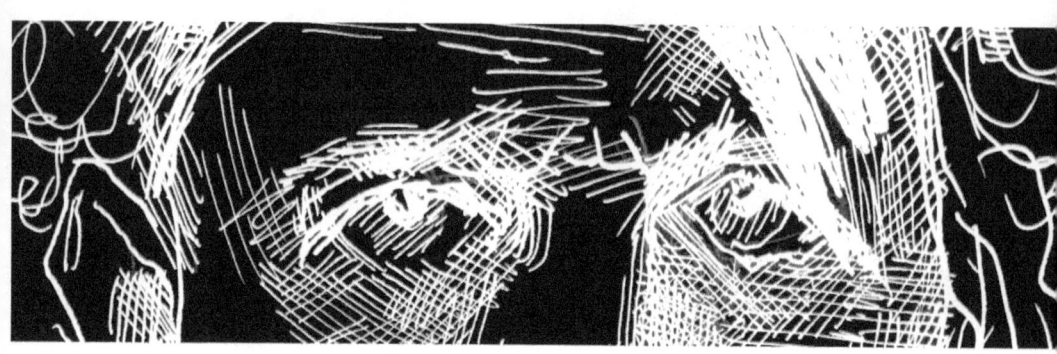

Experiment in OCCUPATION

WITNESS TO THE TURNABOUT
Anti-Nazi War to Cold War, 1944–1946

ARTHUR D. KAHN

THE PENNSYLVANIA STATE UNIVERSITY PRESS ■ UNIVERSITY PARK, PENNSYLVANIA

Library of Congress Cataloging-in-Publication Data

Kahn, Arthur David.
    Experiment in occupation :
    witness to the turnabout,
    anti-Nazi war to Cold War, 1944–1946 /
    Arthur D. Kahn.
         p.   cm.
ISBN 978-0-271-05852-8 (pbk :alk. paper)
1. Germany—History—1945–1955.
2. World War, 1939–1945—Personal narratives,
American.
3. Kahn, Arthur David.
4. Cold War.
5. Military government—Germany.
I. Title.

D842 .K25 2003
943.087'4—dc22
2003022421

Copyright 2004 THE PENNSYLVANIA STATE UNIVERSITY
All rights reserved
Printed in the United States of America
Published by The Pennsylvania State University Press,
University Park, PA 16802-1003

The Pennsylvania State University Press is a member of the
Association of American University Presses.

It is the policy of The Pennsylvania State University Press to use acid-free paper. Publications on uncoated stock satisfy the minimum requirements of American National Standard for Information Sciences—Permanence of Paper for Printed Library Material, ANSI Z39.48 1992.

We will not accept a Hitler-dominated world. And we will not accept a world, like the postwar world of the 1920's, in which the seeds of Hitlerism can again be planted and allowed to grow.
—FRANKLIN DELANO ROOSEVELT
from worldwide radio address, 27 May 1941

We shall not be able to claim that we have gained total victory in this war if any vestige of fascism in any of its malignant forms is permitted to survive anywhere in the world.
—from message to Congress, 14 September 1943

. . . the mere conquest of our enemy is not enough. We must go on to do all in our power to conquer the doubts and the fears, the ignorance and the greed, which made this horror possible.
—from the Jefferson Day address written the night before he died

Contents

Preface	ix
List of Abbreviations	xiii
Introduction: An OSS Recruit Despite Himself	xv

PART I: WHY WE FIGHT!

1	*Soviet Partisans and Soviet Suspicions* SUMMER 1944	3
2	*"We Do Not Call Upon the Germans to Revolt"* FALL 1944	13
3	*The Capture-Liberation of Metz*	21
4	*The Battle of the Bulge* WINTER 1944–1945	27
5	*Mainz: Investigating a Pre-VE Day Military Government* SPRING 1945	35
6	*Interrogating Victims of Nazism and Nazis*	51
7	*Wuerzburg: Another Military Government Experience*	59
8	*"What We Russians Like to Consider as a Typical American"*	69

PART II: POLICY CLASH IN MILITARY GOVERNMENT

9	*"Crack Patton's Military Government Wide Open!"* SUMMER 1945	79
10	*"If Only You Americans Weren't Here . . . !"*	91
11	*Patton's Last Stand*	107
12	*Elections, the American Cure-All* FALL 1945	113
13	*Rehearsal for McCarthyism*	119

PART III: TRIUMPH OF THE COLD WARRIORS

14	*A Military Government in Crisis* WINTER 1945–1946	131
15	*Elections: The American Panacea II*	141
16	*Democracy, American Zone Style!*	149
17	*Summing Up and the Collective Guilt Issue* SPRING 1946	155
18	*Demoralized GIs*	161

Epilogue: 1946–1947	171
Appendices	183
Index	217

Preface

IN JUNE 1946, little more than a year after VE Day, I returned to the United States from Germany, bringing with me hundreds of pages of documents accumulated during two years of service initially as an Office of Strategic Services (OSS) operative attached to psychological warfare units and finally as Chief Editor of Intelligence for the Information Control Division (ICD) of the Office of Military Government—U.S. (OMGUS). At home I recouped letters I had mailed regularly to my mother and to a friend.[1] I immediately set to work on a book entitled *Betrayal: The American Occupation of Germany*. Published in 1949, *Betrayal* appeared among a spate of books by disillusioned mid-level Military Government (MG) officials challenging the conventional wisdom both about the nature of the American occupation of Germany and about the sources of the intensifying conflict with the Soviet Union.[2]

Publication of such books ceased with the onset of McCarthyism and the tensions of the Cold War, and during the next several decades the insights in these books were forgotten or ignored. With the fiftieth anniversaries of Pearl Harbor and of VE Day, Americans experienced a revived interest in the exploits of a wartime generation denominated by a television anchorman "the Greatest Generation." Missing from the new flood of books, television programs, and films, however, was any attempt at a retrieval of the buried history recounted in the books by disillusioned MG officials a half-century earlier.

Republication of *Betrayal*, I determined, was not appropriate. In the first place, writing back in 1946, I did not, could not, foresee the abandonment of the wartime alliance with the Soviet Union and the outbreak of a Cold War that would bring with it unrelenting tensions in international relations for a half-century. Nor did I in *Betrayal* exploit the wealth of material in the documents I brought home exposing what had been unique in my varied war and postwar experiences: familiarity with German politics at the local level

---

1. Cited without distinction as "letters home."
2. *Betrayal* (New York: Independence Publishers, 1949) was directed to a popular readership, and I made no attempt to provide a comprehensive apparatus; as a result many excerpts from *Betrayal*, which, indeed, form the basis for the final chapter and the epilogue of this book, lack documentation. In addition, the intelligence reports upon which a substantial portion of the text were developed as tactical documents often assembled in haste and with no concern for future historians' exigencies. First names of individuals were only rarely included in these reports, and most such first names are irretrievable at a lapse of sixty years.

and knowledge of how high-level Military Government policies were translated into actual practice.

I set out to write a personal memoir of my wartime and postwar experiences. As I sorted through the documents preserved in my files—reports and memoranda, correspondence with American officials and with German public-opinion makers, along with additional miscellaneous source materials—it became clear that this trove of documents provided a unique chronicle of events leading to a historical development of critical import for the remainder of the twentieth century:the Cold War. In such context a chronology of a twenty-three-year-old's confrontation with a series of significant events serves merely as a vehicle for tracing the evolution of the themes represented in the titles of the three divisions of this book. In Part I, "Why We Fight!" (the title of a series of World War II Army orientation films), I describe intimations of a shift in American policy in opposition to the war aims proclaimed by President Roosevelt and the Supreme Commander in the European Theater, Dwight D. Eisenhower. Until the fall of 1944, however, at the Twelfth Army Group Psychological Warfare (PW) unit we had no inkling of a policy conflict among top officials in Washington and at Supreme Headquarters of the Allied Expeditionary Forces (SHAEF) in Europe. Only slowly, step by step, did we begin to suspect that not only top officials but second-level Army brass and military government officials as well were not dedicated to the war aims proclaimed by Franklin Roosevelt and Dwight Eisenhower. A first indication of such policy division came with a blunt admonition from SHAEF:"W e do not call upon the Germans to revolt." We experienced clear evidence of rejection of the FDR war aims when two PW Intelligence operatives exposed the appointment by an MG commandant of Nazis and war profiteers to high posts in Aachen, the first major German city captured by Allied troops. A third evidence of this trend became apparent in the crushing of anti-Nazi committees, which in the last weeks of the war organized revolts to assist the Allied troops in "liberating" a number of German cities. Thereafter, in blatant violation of directives, MG officials refused to appoint to positions of authority proven anti-Nazis, including political prisoners liberated from concentration camps.

In Part II, "Policy Clash in Military Government," I describe the emergence, particularly after Roosevelt's death, of an overt clash within American MG over our war aims. Investigations I conducted in Munich revealed the open defiance by Gen. George S. Patton, military governor of Bavaria, of directives for denazification and democratization.

In Part III, "Triumph of the Cold Warriors," I recount the rout of the pro-FDR faction in the American occupation zone and the unabashed sabotage by top officials in the American Zone of policies agreed upon by the Big Three Occupation Powers at the Potsdam Conference in August 1945. Though professing his dedication to our wartime goals, Eisenhower proved incapable of resisting the anti-Soviet policies of his subordinates. By the fall of 1945 an atmosphere of anti-Soviet conformity, a forerunner of McCarthyism, pervaded the American Zone of Germany. By May 1946, a year after VE Day, all pretense at carrying out our original war aims had disappeared. (This is a story that was ignored in the "Greatest Generation" publicity of the last ten years.)

The overwhelming proportion of *Experiment in Occupation* is based on the documentation I brought home from Germany. I have also drawn upon *Betrayal* for events still fresh in my memory in the mid-forties and for material in documents I did not retain in my files. I also refer to official histories published late in 1945 for distribution solely among former Psychological Warfare staffers (ignored as sources in *Betrayal*), one by the Twelfth Army Group Publicity and Psychological Warfare Branch and the other entitled *The Psychological Warfare Division Supreme Headquarters Allied Expeditionary Forces [SHAEF]: Account of Its Operations in the Western European Campaign, 1944–1945*.[3] For a chronicling of Soviet occupation policies and of Soviet responses to actions and pronouncements of the Western allies, I turned to Marshal Gyorgy Zhukov's *Reminiscences and Reflections* (a copy of the 1974 English edition was presented to me during a 1990 visit to the Soviet Union as a guest of the Soviet Veterans of the War). I also cite Dwight D. Eisenhower's 1950 *Crusade in Europe*, which though a more impressionistic account of war and postwar events nevertheless helps to illuminate post–VE Day developments in Germany.[4]

For material brought to light since the opening of Soviet and East German archives I turned to Melvyn P. Leffler's *The Specter of Communism: The United States and the Origins of the Cold War*; the German translation of Soviet archives on the Potsdam Conference released in the 1980s; an analysis by Russian historian Alexei Filitov of the minutes of three Soviet wartime commissions established to draft proposals for postwar Soviet policies in Germany; and *Russians in Germany: A History of the Russian Zone of Occupation, 1945–1949*, by an American scholar, Norman M. Naimark, an analysis of Russian occupation policy and actions in postwar Germany. In *America's*

---

3. Hereafter cited, respectively, as "12th Army Group History" and "PW Div. SHAEF History."
4. Marshal Gyorgy Zhukov, *Reminiscences and Reflections*, English ed. (Moscow:Progress Publishers, 1974), chapter titled "The Potsdam Conference:The Control Council for Governing Germany," 429–73; Dwight D. Eisenhower, *Crusade in Europe* (1950; reprint, Baltimore:J ohns Hopkins University Press, 1997).

Strategic Blunders, Willard C. Matthias, who served in the Military Intelligence Division of the War Department General Staff, presents an insider's account of Cold War strategic planning in U.S. inner councils.[5]

Stateside publications were unavailable in Germany during and immediately after the war, and in verifying dates and other details for Experiment in Occupation through the *New York Times Index* and other sources, I discovered that members of the American press corps in Germany as well as newspaper pundits at home had arrived at conclusions similar to mine about the process of transformation in military government policies. I quote extensively from their dispatches.

This investigation is of a policy conflict within the American Military Government and the Army of Occupation between those who sought to fulfill the war aims enunciated by Franklin Roosevelt and those who even during the war were preparing for a further conflict with the Soviet Union. The declaration signed at Potsdam in August 1945 by the United States, the United Kingdom, and the Soviet Union, and later ratified by France, provided a charter for the joint administration of Germany and, in effect, ratified the Roosevelt war aims. In this book I adjudge the policies and actions of the Soviet Union as well as of the United States by the fidelity with which they carried out or violated the provisions of the Potsdam Declaration.

---

5. Melvyn P. Leffler, *The Specter of Communism: The United States and the Origins of the Cold War, 1917–1953* (New York:Hill & Wang, 1994); *Teheran, Jalta, Potsdam: Konferenzdokumente der Sowjetunion*, herausg. Ministerium fuer Auswaertige Angelegenheiten der UdSSR, 3 vols. (Cologne, 1956); (3) Alexei Filitov, "Stalins Deutschlandplanung und -Politik waehrend und nach dem zweiten Weltkrieg," in *50 Jahre sovietische und russische Deutschlandpolitik sowie ihre Auswirkungen auf das gegenseite Verhaeltnis* (Berlin, 1999), 43–54; Norman M. Naimark, *The Russians in Germany: A History of the Soviet Zone of Occupation, 1945–1949* (Cambridge:Harvard University Press, 1995); and Willard C. Matthias, *America's Strategic Blunders: Intelligence Analysis and National Security Policy, 1936–1991* (University Park:Pennsylvania State University Press, 2001).

Abbreviations

BVP	Bavarian People's Party
CDU	Christian Democratic Union
CIC	Counterintelligence Corps
CSU	Christian Social Union
DP	Displaced Person
FFI	Forces françaises de l'intérieur
FTP	Franc tireurs et partisan
G-2	Army tactical intelligence
HJ	Hitler Jugend (Hitler Youth)
ICD	Information Control Division
ICIS	Information Control Intelligence Survey
KPD	Communist Party of Germany
Kzler	Former concentration-camp inmates
MG	Military Government
NDP	National Democratic Party
NSDAP	National Socialist Workers Party of Germany (Nazi Party)
OMGUS	Office of Military Government (US)
OR	Other Ranks
OSS	Office of Strategic Services
OWI	Office of War Information
Pgs	*Parteigenossen* (Nazi Party members)
POW	Prisoner of war
PW	Psychological Warfare
PWD	Psychological Warfare Division (at SHAEF)
PWE	Prisoner-of-war enclosure
SA	Brownshirted storm troopers
SD	German National Security Service
SHAEF	Supreme Headquarters of the Allied Expeditionary Forces
SPD	Social Democratic Party of Germany
UNRRA	United Nations Relief and Rehabilitation Agency

Introduction: An OSS Recruit Despite Himself

"What could they possibly want me for?"

It was February, 1944, and I was replying to a suggestion from the owner of a shop where I rented Russian-language records that I submit an application for a position at the newly established military intelligence agency, the Office of Strategic Services (OSS). A recruiter had urged the shopkeeper to recommend individuals with foreign-language skills for possible appointment to the agency.

What could the OSS want, indeed, with an unwarlike twenty-three-year-old rejected a year and a half earlier for military service, the son of impoverished shopkeepers in a provincial New Jersey town, a graduate of a state teachers college with a brief experience as a high school English teacher. As for competence in foreign languages—I could claim three years of high school and four years of college French, three years of college German and six months of intensive Berlitz private lessons in Russian (which I had hoped would prove advantageous in the event of my being drafted into the Army). But I had never held an extended conversation in any of these languages!

After Pearl Harbor I responded without reservations to FDR's call to a mobilization of all Americans. When in August 1942 my mother clapped her hands and burst into tears of joy upon my being classified 4F, I had mixed feelings about being excluded from participation in a decisive moment in history.

As a child in New York City I feared to go to school before Easter because the Italian and Irish boys jeered at Jewish classmates and even attacked us as Christ-killers. In Somerville, New Jersey, where we moved after the Crash, our next-door neighbor was a high muck-a-muck in the local KKK klavern; he stored its paraphernalia in his barn. As a senior in a teachers college, I was never called out of class for an interview. "The principals and superintendents are not necessarily anti-Semitic," the president of the college assured me, "but they would just as soon not have any problems with their school boards." When after obtaining a master's degree at Rutgers University I informed the head of the English department of my desire to continue on to a doctorate in order to teach in college, he warned me that heads of college English departments preferred candidates with Anglo-Saxon backgrounds.

As a Jew, I had a special responsibility to participate in this war.

"What have you got to lose by applying?" insisted the owner of the language-record store, thrusting the OSS recruiter's business card into my hand.

I wrote to the recruiter and received an application form by return mail. I solicited letters of reference from the principal of the high school where I had served two years as an English teacher and from Arnold Forster, executive director of the Anti-Defamation League, a friend from my childhood. He was at the time collaborating with the FBI in conducting investigations of pro-Nazi organizations and, in fact, hired me briefly as a researcher.

Summoned to Washington for an interview, I was asked no questions about my 4F classification and subjected to no tests of my language abilities. A few days later I was instructed to report to OSS headquarters to await an opening at the OSS training school.[1]

Although in drills with a variety of weapons at the OSS training school I was uniformly the most incompetent in my group, I was apparently not to be permitted to fail! In June 1944 I was dispatched overseas to England. A week after D-Day I was detached to a psychological warfare unit awaiting orders to cross the Channel to France. Among my new colleagues were professors from Ivy League universities, as well as German and Russian émigrés with degrees from prestigious European universities, some fluent in several languages.

A SHAEF directive dated 10 May 1944 defined as the mission of the Psychological Warfare (PW) subbranch: "the conduct of Psychological Warfare . . . for the purpose of undermining the enemy's will to resist, demoralizing his forces and sustaining the morale of our supporters to include (1) combat propaganda against enemy forces in the forward areas and toward the civil population behind the lines and (2) consolidation activities in the combat zone."

During the four weeks that we awaited orders to depart for France we received no training or other preparation for these responsibilities. When late in July we were ordered to prepare for imminent redeployment across the Channel, the German refugee at the German desk, a man in his mid-forties, panicked at the prospect of possible capture on the battlefield. Catching Al Toombs, the acting head of the Psychological Warfare Intelligence unit, just as Toombs was running off for a train to London, he requested transfer to a desk job at OSS headquarters. Nonplused, Toombs summoned me. "Do what you can at the German desk until I return," he instructed.

---

1. At OSS headquarters I worked intensively on my languages, listening to Linguaphone records. During the next months overseas I continued to work on improving my mastery of these languages. I encountered no difficulty at all in communicating in French or Russian. My German improved under the tutelage of a German refugee colleague and from lessons at the Berlitz school in Brussels during three months I served as a liaison officer at Montgomery's headquarters. To my surprise when I first ventured to interrogate Germans, though handicapped by a pedantic concern for correct grammar and syntax, I communicated with fluency.

The German desk was charged with evaluating intelligence on morale conditions inside Germany and among the German troops opposing our forces. I had no knowledge of Germany and was ignorant of order of battle and military matters generally. I possessed a pathetically limited command of the German language. I worked late into the night poring over intelligence materials accumulated since D-Day—PW and G-2 (military intelligence) reports, extracts from captured documents, and monitorings of Wehrmacht and German civilian radio transmissions. I set up a filing system, breaking down the piles of data under subject headings and according to German Army units. When Toombs returned from London, distraught at his failure to find a qualified candidate for the German desk, he discovered, or so I recounted to my mother, that by working "like a dog I had so completely reorganized what my predecessor had done that it was necessary that I be given the position permanently." In fact, Toombs, a former president of the Washington press corps, a gentle man in his mid-thirties who displayed boundless trust in members of his staff, shook his head and declared, "We'll see how things go."

On 30 July the order for departure for France arrived.

PART I: WHY WE FIGHT!

Soviet Partisans and Soviet Suspicions
SUMMER 1944

The enclave captured by the Allied troops during nearly two months of fighting encompassed an area only a few miles deep along a restricted portion of the Channel coast, and we had not far to travel before reaching our encampment in a pasture about twenty miles south of the port of Cherbourg, liberated two weeks earlier. My task was to brief PW interrogators on questions to pose to prisoners of war (POWs). As the 12th Army Group history reports, as late as May 1944,

practically nothing was known about the processes of gathering intelligence for Combat Psychological Warfare Operations. . . . Psychological Warfare Intelligence became a miniature G-2 [Army tactical intelligence]. The section kept a situation map, an order of battle file and an intelligence log, and followed closely the reports made by tactical interrogators and by G-2 officers at all levels. Psychological Warfare interrogators were seeking from prisoners information which would reveal weaknesses in enemy morale.

On a large blackboard I displayed the enemy order of battle, listing each division and its commanding general along with its subsidiary units and officers down sometimes to company level. In a card file I assembled details gathered by our psychological warfare interrogators. Particularly impelling anecdotal data I transmitted to our Operations unit as possible material for tactical leaflets, for PA broadcasts across the lines, or for inclusion in *Frontpost*, a propaganda newspaper distributed by air drops and artillery shells to the German troops.[1]

Our commanding officer, Col. Clifford R. Powell, a former lieutenant governor of New Jersey, was a tough old bird with a military clipped haircut that seemed as appropriate to his personality as his curt and often racy language. One of his favorite expressions was "Watch out or you're goin' to get your tit caught in a wringer." It was rumored—and later confirmed—that he had accepted demotion from his World War I rank of major general in order to serve in this war. Two of his sons, junior officers, were attached to combat units in France.

---

1. "How did you know to broadcast across the lines," a prisoner exclaimed, "that our captain was snug in bed with a French whore while we were shivering in the trenches?" "Over a period of weeks," as the 12th Army Group history was later to report, "a rather complete picture was built up of the personalities and morale of all the enemy divisions facing First Army."

On 17 August Gen. George S. Patton's newly deployed Third Army captured the key coastal town of St. Malo, compelling the enemy to abandon Brittany and a vast area of western France to the south. Meeting up with Canadian troops battling down from the north, the Third Army bottled most of the German divisions in northern France within the Argentan-Falaise pocket. German units catalogued in my files disintegrated or retreated in disorder, and my task of assembling, analyzing, and reporting prisoner-of-war intelligence came to an abrupt end. On 19 August the Communist franc tireurs et partisans (FTP) issued a call for an uprising in Paris, and on 25 August the city fell to the Resistance, the French 2nd Armored Division, and the American 28th Infantry Division.

That day, too, our unit was transferred from First Army to Twelfth Army Group, the umbrella command over the U.S. First and Third Armies.[2] While we awaited orders for following the armies further to the east, Colonel Powell sent me out to investigate the attitudes of the recently liberated population of southwestern France.[3] Although I heard complaints about shortages of food and of what some condemned as unnecessary destruction by Allied bombings, generally welcoming crowds gathered about my jeep. Abruptly, on a secondary road in west-central France I came upon what had once clearly been a village, but where I saw nothing more than scattered heaps of brick and lumber, and roadways destroyed by shell craters. I questioned a passerby. "Mais c'est Oradour, monsieur," she replied, assuming that the name would invite immediate recognition, for this was the village where in retaliation for local partisan harassment the Germans massacred more than 600 people. They shot the men and set fire to the church after locking the women and children within. *Why we fight!*

On Friday, 1 September, upon returning to our new headquarters at Versailles, at Al Toombs's instruction, I set out for the Third Army prisoner-of-war enclosure (PWE) "to find out why no reports had been received for almost two weeks from the psychological warfare interrogators stationed there." At the compound I discovered that during the confusion of the rapid advances at the front our team had received no directives from headquarters. They were despondent at learning that their reports had not arrived at head-

---

2. Twelfth Army Group PW deployed interrogators with American armies and additional special investigators in areas occupied by these armies. SHAEF PW was dependent for PW Intelligence upon these Army Group operatives, having none of its own.

3. The 12th Army Group history described this aspect of our mission:

By an adequate service of news, information, and guidance about the requirements of the military authorities, it [Psychological Warfare] assisted in the establishment and maintenance of law and order, combated the spread of rumors and instructed the civil population with respect to what was expected of them. By the gathering of the intelligence as to the morale, opinions and conditions of life among the civilians . . . it assisted in apprising the military as to civilian reactions to measures taken by the authorities and as to the existence of tension points and frictions.

quarters. Having no vehicle of their own, they had been unable to dispatch a valuable prisoner to a higher echelon for further interrogation.

The interrogators quoted prisoners as echoing the Nazi propaganda line directed to raising domestic morale that America would soon join with Germany in fighting Russia. "One POW declared," I noted in my report, "that an American major had asked him whether he would be willing to fight with the Americans against the Russians"—a piece of intelligence that seemed to me at the time too outlandish to warrant a comment.

On my way back to headquarters I made a detour to visit a First Army POW enclosure (PWE), where, informed of the recent capture of a company of Russians in German uniforms, I saw an opportunity to obtain unique intelligence and had the first of what was to prove to be a series of interrogations of Soviet citizens. Most of these young men, representatives of many Soviet nationalities, had served under General Vlassov, who during the chaotic days immediately following the German invasion of the Soviet Union brought an entire army across the lines to fight alongside the Wehrmacht. To compel Soviet deserters and captured soldiers to put on Wehrmacht uniforms, the Germans, these men reported, applied harsh pressure through starvation and torture. All expressed fear of execution for violating their oath to Stalin to use the last bullet on themselves rather than to surrender.

One young man requested that he and his comrades be given guns and allowed to attack a heavily fortified hill from which American units had been unable to dislodge the enemy. The standard American tactic was to soften enemy strongpoints with artillery and aerial bombardment before launching an infantry attack.

"Many of you would die in such an action," I exclaimed.

The admonition struck them as curious. "Men are dying all over Europe," one replied. The others nodded.

I reported their offer. It was rejected.

In a report I drafted in collaboration with Sgt. Boris Krass, the Russian-language interrogator on our First Army interrogation team, I noted:

if it could be found out definitely that the Soviet Union . . . is willing to repatriate POWs who violated the oath [to die rather than to accept capture], it is conceivable that there would be mass desertions and perhaps even mass uprisings among the Russians. (POWs reported instances of Russians shooting their German officers.) In any case, with the probability of up to 100,000 Russian POWs falling into our hands in the near future, this problem would appear urgent.

German propaganda played upon the fears of the Russians, warning that the Americans, faced with overflowing POW camps, had orders either to shoot any Russians they captured or to turn them over to Negro troops, who would cut them up. On the other hand, it was clear that our Russian-language leaflets and public-address broadcasts across the lines were effective. "The very fact," I noted in my report, "that the Russians are singled out to be addressed makes them happy." Some did express criticisms of our leaflets. The offer of asylum in America included in our leaflets, they insisted, provided no incentive to desertion since the men wanted to return home and not to be sent across the ocean. One man became incensed at reading in a German propaganda sheet that a Vlassovite had been offered asylum in the United States, while he who had been condemned to serve in a German punishment battalion after successfully resisting donning a Wehrmacht uniform now found himself in a POW cage alongside German prisoners.

On 6 September I set out again, assigned to transport the Third Army interrogation team eastward to catch up with Patton's advancing divisions. Early the next day we arrived in a drenching downpour at the newly established Third Army PWE outside the village of Toul. The compound extended across a vast meadow bordered by dense woods from which German stragglers were emerging almost hourly to surrender. On all sides as far as I could see, thousands of prisoners huddled under rain-soaked blankets or, without cover, shivered beside sputtering campfires. (The Allied armies had nearly doubled the number of prisoners captured during August—to a total of almost 300,000.)

"Can you speak kraut?" a GI guard asked. A crowd of German officers, many wearing iron crosses, pressed toward the fence of an officers cage. Some spoke unaccented English and boasted of connections in England. One reminded me that they had borne the brunt of bolshevik aggression for us as well as for themselves.

"Was wollt ihr?" (What do you want?), I demanded.

Two officers advanced supporting a third under his armpits. The man murmured, "Ich muss zum Arzt" (I have to see a doctor).

I searched along the line of anxious faces. "Ich bin Jude" (I am a Jew), I replied. The bemedaled officers turned and slunk off.

My exchange with the German officers attracted attention at neighboring cages, and as I proceeded down the passage, I was assailed by a cacophony of voices in various languages, "We are Yugoslavs . . . Russians . . . Italians . . . Spaniards . . . partisans. We do not belong here." Men in shabby civilian garb or in makeshift uniforms waved documents identifying themselves as members of the French Resistance.

"How many of you are Soviets?" I asked in Russian. The show of hands indicated that they formed the largest contingent. "Who can serve as your spokesman?" I asked. A young man in civilian clothes wearing a black beret rakishly tilted on his head stepped forward.

Once in my tent, Andrei Tsibikov exploded into a tirade:"We are Soviet soldiers escaped from German captivity. We took to the Vosges mountains as partisans and engaged in guerrilla warfare with the fascists. When we came out of the forests to greet our liberators, we were rounded up, forced to surrender our arms and marched into this camp. We should be fighting Germans, not sitting next to them."

As an eighteen-year-old recruit in a training regiment, Andrei had been captured in Byelo-Russia on 7 July 1941, a mere two weeks after the Germans burst across the Soviet frontier. During his first months of captivity he was sent from one prisoner camp to another in Germany, subjected to routine nazi brutalities. After striking a German guard in a fit of desperation, he was sent first to a prison near Caen in Normandy and then to a labor battalion working on the Atlantic Wall. On 9 July 1943 he escaped with a comrade and made his way to Paris with the help of French railway men. Knowing no French, they decided to continue on to Yugoslavia to join Tito's partisans and boarded a train to Dijon. Realizing that with their ignorance of languages they would not succeed in crossing the Swiss border, they returned to Paris. Desperate with hunger, they addressed a stranger in the Bois de Boulogne. He proved to be a Serb. He took them to the commander of the Soviet underground in France, and the commander, in turn, arranged for them to be sheltered in the home of two elderly French ladies who had previously hidden more than fifty refugees. After seven months spent perfecting their French, the two were sent to join partisan units in the Vosges mountains of eastern France. In short order Andrei was appointed commander of a detachment fighting alongside French maquis (the Communist-led franc tireurs et partisans—FTP).

"Colonel," I announced to the camp commandant after interviewing representatives of other partisan groups, "you are holding Allied soldiers in this enclosure."

"I haven't fuel to haul in food, medicines, tents and other supplies for this horde, get the local Resistance to take them off my hands," the colonel declared. (In his swift advance Patton had overextended his supply lines and run out of gas.)

Entrusted by the Americans with the task of mopping up nests of Germans in the forests, the commander of the Gaullist forces françaises de l'intérieur (FFI) in Bar-le-Duc, the departmental administrative seat, was enthusiastic at the possibility of obtaining reinforcements. But in retreating the Germans had seized the local foodstuffs, and I shuttled back and forth between the FFI commander and the camp commandant until they reached an agreement on rations for the liberated guerrillas.[4]

The afternoon of 10 September 1944 a truck convoy carrying Soviet partisans arrived at Bar-le-Duc. They were immediately provided with rifles and sent into the woods to round up German stragglers. The following morning a further group, including eighteen Yugoslavs, were evacuated from the POW camp. Eventually more than 300 were turned over to the French.

Andrei presented me with issues of "Sovietsky Partizan, the Organ of the Soviet Partisans in France," which, hand- or typewritten, was mimeographed for distribution at irregular intervals.[5] A document containing an order appointing commanders of Soviet partisan units was signed by "Nik" as supreme commander of the battalions. Andrei gave me the address of a Frenchman in Paris who, he said, would be able to put me in contact with Nik.

In an ancient six-story building within sight of the Hôtel de Ville (the town hall), Andrei's friend, a hearty and burly butcher and a Communist, reported that during the hectic days of the liberation of Paris Nik had been caught in a general roundup of suspicious individuals. Following the butcher's directions, I drove to the detention center. Without asking to see any official document or demanding a receipt, the warden ordered Nik to be brought from his cell and turned over to my custody.

"Though certainly a good and brave soldier," I wrote in my subsequent report, Nik was "no intellectual." Sensing my frustration with his meager responses to my questions, Nik volunteered the address of his superior, Vladimir. Vladimir proved to be articulate and showed no restraint in offering information. Since mid-1943, he reported, Soviet agents who parachuted into France had been collaborating with the FTP in assembling escaped Soviet POWs into partisan units. They also collected data on hundreds of Soviet citizens brought to France as forced laborers, information that would be used in determining the treatment these people would be accorded after the war.

Shortly before D-Day through leaflets and clandestine encounters, Vladimir recounted, Soviet agents circulated a warning to Soviet troops serving in the Wehrmacht of a last chance to redeem themselves in the eyes of their country. Indeed, among the documents Andrei Tsibikov had given me was a leaflet with such a message directed to Vlassovites and signed by "The Commander of the Soviet Partisans in France."[6]

---

4. One problem could not be resolved:the few dozen Spanish Republicans who had escaped from French internment camps to continue their war against fascism, which for them had begun in 1936. Since they had no government to assume eventual responsibility for them, the French commandant would not accept them.

5. See appendix 1, p. 183, for the text.

6. See appendix 2, p. 183, for the text.

Vladimir urged me to seek a meeting with the newly arrived Soviet chargé d'affaires, and on Friday morning, 16 September, I drove to the Soviet embassy. "We made an agreement in London regarding liberated Soviet troops and forced laborers," Chargé d'Affaires Alexander Gusovski exclaimed. "Now you inform me that our citizens were huddled in a camp next to German prisoners. Outrageous!"

In North Africa, where until recently he had served as Soviet plenipotentiary, Gusovski related, liberated Soviet citizens were assembled by the Americans into camps maintained at Soviet expense while they awaited transportation back to the Soviet Union. Recently, however, the Soviet ambassador in London had informed him that the Allies were dawdling in setting up a similar liaison mechanism in France. My report, he noted, confirmed the apathy of the Allies in face of a mounting crisis. He dismissed as a nazi canard the allegation that the Soviet government did not recognize the existence of any Soviet prisoners on the basis of the Stalin oath.[7]

Upon my return from my meeting with Gusovski, Colonel Powell instructed me to prepare with several carbon copies a report on my experiences with the Soviet partisans for circulation within SHAEF.

"My" Russian partisans, their numbers augmented by some fifty women and children, now billeted in St. Mihiel, about twenty miles from Bar-le-Duc, reported that after they flushed the Germans out of the forests, the French officers' attitude toward them underwent a disquieting change. At the suggestion of the camp leaders, on 18 September I drove Andrei Tsibikov back to Paris to inform Alexander Gusovski of the deteriorating conditions. At the Soviet embassy, Gusovski reported that Moscow had made representations to Washington and London regarding the treatment of Soviet citizens liberated by the Allied armies in France. He maintained hope that measures similar to those taken in North Africa would soon be implemented in France.

I discovered that in the two days of my absence relations between the Soviets and the French at St. Mihiel had further deteriorated. The French charged the Russians were disorderly. The Russians, who had suffered years of Nazi captivity, resented taking orders from FFI (Gaullist forces françaises de l'intérieur) officers, men who, they charged, had suddenly blossomed forth as Resistance captains and majors after never displaying even minor hostility toward the Germans. When a French officer expressed chauvinist contempt for the men and women in the camp, I retorted, "Some peoples, monsieur, have contributed more toward victory than others."

---

7. It did not occur to me that Gusovski's additional statement that Soviet citizens were not to serve in any other army than the Red Army might apply to partisans associated with the French FTP. As I was to learn forty-five years later upon a visit to the Soviet Union, such men were to suffer humiliation and even imprisonment upon returning home, winning amnesty for their "crime" only under Mikhail Gorbachev.

In response to my appeal, the departmental prefect called a meeting of local officials and camp leaders. He declared his desire that the Russians consider themselves as welcome and honored guests. The Russians nodded in comprehension at his report of the local food crisis. They joined him and the local officials in urging me to seek assistance, especially in obtaining a supply of shoes and soap, from the American displaced persons' assembly point established only days earlier at nearby Verdun.[8]

At an immense army barracks at the outskirts of Verdun, I found Captain Paul E. Middleton and a small unit of officers and enlisted men staring in dismay at a horde of men, women, and children disembarked only minutes earlier from a train arriving from the front. "Yesterday and today I received a mob of Soviets," exclaimed the captain. "I have no one who speaks a word of their language."

By coincidence as the captain and I were talking, two Russians whom Middleton had sent off to Paris two days earlier arrived. (In desperation at receiving no directives or additional personnel from his superiors, Captain Middleton, risking disciplinary action, had sent the men to seek assistance from the Soviet embassy.) Gusovski instructed the men to see to it that liberated Soviet citizens were entrusted with organizing and policing themselves. They were to maintain a precise record of supplies provided by the Americans and French to enable eventual Soviet reimbursement.

At Captain Middleton's request I mounted a platform and called out, "Zdravstvuitye soyiuzniki!" (I greet you, Allies!). I followed with what was to become a message I would employ often in similar situations. "You are now free," I declared, "free from captivity, free from fear. From us Americans you will receive treatment that people of a brave ally deserve. Until we can arrange your return to your homeland," I continued, "you must organize yourselves into disciplined units so as to travel with minimal disorder from stop to stop on the way to Marseilles, where you will disembark for Odessa and your homeland."

Since the French authorities held ultimate responsibility for the assembly center and had to be consulted on all matters relating to displaced persons, Captain Middleton said that he required a capable interpreter for discussions with both the French and the Soviets. In addition, the Soviets currently in

---

8. The Soviet citizens at St. Mihiel were subsequently transferred to an assembly point at Châlons-sur-Marne, where I visited them frequently, bringing gifts of captured German cigarettes and candy. On one occasion I had the first of what would be a series of disillusioning experiences with Soviet citizens when during a political discussion I stated, "We can help you now, but after the war you must join in helping the rest of the world in building a better social order." I awaited a reply, expecting responses couched in standard Soviet Party jargon, something like, "We are aware of our responsibility to history. You may count on us to provide an example . . . and to assist our comrades in all other countries in the glorious endeavor." My remark met, however, with grim silence. I waited until certain that I was not to receive a reply and took my leave.

the barracks would soon be departing on the next stage of their homeward journey, and he would be forced to deal with new contingents arriving in their place. As I typed on my portable typewriter, Middleton dictated a memorandum addressed to Colonel Powell requesting my continued services at the assembly point.

The colonel's response was to the point:"Hell, since nobody else is doing the job, go down whenever he sends for you."

On 8 October at Colonel Powell's instruction I drafted a memorandum to be forwarded to SHAEF:"Subject: Report on Soviet Refugees in France with suggestions for American action to aid them." After briefly describing my experiences with the Soviet partisans and subsequent developments at the St. Mihiel and Verdun assembly centers as well as my conversations with the Soviet chargé d'affaires, I described the difficulties encountered by American liaison officers "forced to work through slow military channels because of the absence of direct liaison with the French and the Soviet authorities." I noted also that because of the absence of clear directives and administrative procedures among their liberators, the Soviet citizens were developing hostility toward Americans. I suggested the appointment of an American official fluent in both French and Russian to assist overburdened French officials in establishing better relations with the Russians and closer contact with American authorities.[9]

I sent Gusovski a report of recent developments at St. Mihiel and received a prompt reply expressing his gratitude for my efforts.[10] SHAEF sent a single-sentence response to my memorandum:Headquarters saw no reason for revising its procedures for dealing with Soviet refugees.

"All right, Arthur," commented Colonel Powell, nonplused by SHAEF's brusque reply to the memorandum, "it's been left to you to do it on your own."

A Second Encounter with Russians: The Red Guard Medal

On 23 October, shortly after a heroic rescue of the powerful transmitter of Radio Luxembourg from destruction by the retreating Germans, PWD/SHAEF (Psychological Warfare Division) designated Lt. Col. Samuel R. Richman as commanding officer of PW personnel at the station. That very day I was dispatched to Luxembourg to discuss with officials at the station the kinds of broadcasting materials they desired from the Twelfth Army Group PW Intelligence unit. At the outskirts of the city I found my way blocked by a convoy of American Army trucks transporting several hundred

---

9. For further extracts from this memorandum, see appendix 3, pp. 183–84.
10. Reprinted in appendix 4, p. 184.

recently liberated Russians. I followed the trucks to an abandoned school, where the Russians were welcomed by an elderly man named Schneider, the head of the Luxembourg Communist Party and the newly appointed duchy's liaison with the Soviets. In pigeon German Victor (Mischa) Kriushchuk, a captain in his mid-twenties, overwhelmed the Luxembourger with daunting demands for the relief of the horde of demoralized men, women, and children jumping from the trucks, a few gripping small bundles wrapped in kerchiefs, the rest with merely the clothes on their backs. At an impasse in the discussion, I addressed Mischa and his colleague, the political commissar Semyon (Seenya) Lvovsky, in Russian, offering to supply items about which the Luxembourger expressed the greatest concern.

Ludwig Mahler, the 12th Army Group PW commissary sergeant (and a nephew of the famous composer), urged me to seek the assistance of the American Red Cross. At Red Cross headquarters, my requests were welcomed, and the next day I appeared at the school with a truck loaded with captured German camp beds, medical supplies, and foodstuffs as well as a supply ("organized" by Mahler) of captured cigarettes, candy, and cans of marmalade. In gratitude Mischa pinned on my jacket a Red Guard medal and invited me to participate in the 7 November celebration of the anniversary of the 1917 Russian Revolution, and, indeed, on that day I drove to Luxembourg for the occasion. Before a vociferous holiday crowd of some 500 men, women, and children, Mischa introduced me as a representative of the American Army. I corrected him, asserting that I was merely an American who wished our Russian friends and allies well. Familiar with the grandiloquent clichés familiar to Russian audiences, to repeated applause I proclaimed them one by one:' 'the first Socialist state . . . the glorious revolution . . . the fascist barbarians, the unity of the peace-loving peoples of the world."

When I concluded the crowd rose and stamped their feet and clapped in the rhythmical measure customary among the Russians, overjoyed, as some later informed me, that an American understood so well and understood the thoughts and aspirations of Soviet citizens.[11] These people had a desperate desire for lasting peace after the end of the current war. They believed that I as an American shared this desire. I did share this desire, but many of my countrymen, as I was yet to discover, had other aspirations.

11. Mischa and Seenya presented me with a photograph of the two them sitting in their office. On the back they wrote, "A memento to our dear American friend from Soviet citizens Mikhail Kriushchuk and Semyon Lvovsky, Luxembourg, November 7, 1944, on the day of our great people's holiday." In a June 1946 covering letter to a packet of documents I was mailing home I noted that I was including a copy, since lost, of "the speech of the leader [Kriushchuk] of the camp in a Luxembourg broadcast in a program which I directed."

"We Do Not Call Upon the Germans to Revolt"
FALL 1944

In 1943 General Walther von Seydlitz, a scion of a distinguished Junker family and one of the generals captured at Stalingrad, announced the formation of a Free Germany Committee composed of German POWs of all ranks as well as anti-Nazi exiles living in Russia. In broadcasts over Moscow radio and through leaflet drops, the committee called upon their countrymen to halt the slaughter on the battlefield and from air bombardments on the homefront—sacrifices suffered, they insisted, solely for the benefit of the *Bonzen* (Nazi bigshots). After the abortive 20 July 1944 putsch, in which high-ranking Wehrmacht officers joined anti-Nazi civilian personalities in an attempt to overthrow Hitler, the Free Germany Committee issued an appeal to German generals, industrialists, and the Catholic Church to promote a popular uprising against the Nazi regime. On 14 August, Field Marshal Friedrich von Paulus, the German commander at Stalingrad, who had hitherto refused to participate in Free Germany activities, addressed an open letter to the German nation that was broadcast over Radio Moscow. He declared:

At Stalingrad the Sixth Army under my command executing a command from Adolf Hitler fought to the last possibility, hoping that in sacrificing itself it would give an opportunity to the Supreme Command to finish this war with no unfavorable results for Germany. These hopes failed. . . . Supremacy of the enemy in the air and on the sea is so overwhelming as to make the situation even more desperate. For Germany the war is lost. Germany came to such a position in spite of the heroism of her Wehrmacht and her people because of the political and military leadership of Adolf Hitler. To this must be added that the methods by which some of his trusted colleagues have treated the populations is a matter of disgust for every true soldier and every true German. . . . In such circumstances I consider it my duty to say to all the German people and to my comrades who are prisoners of war the following: Germany must rid itself of Adolf Hitler and establish a new state leadership which will bring the war to an end and create conditions to secure for our people a future life and restore friendly relations with our enemies of today.

Early in September north of Luxembourg the U.S. First Army burst across the German frontier. In response, Field Marshal Karl Rudolf Gerd von Rundstedt issued an order of the day to his troops: "I expect you to defend the sacred German soil with all your might and to the last man."

With Allied troops confronting fierce resistance at the Siegfried Line, SHAEF requested of 12th Army Group PW Intelligence a proposal for a PW approach to undermine the sudden and costly opposition.

Since in my new capacity as editor of the 12th Army Group PW daily intelligence digest I kept abreast of reports from the front, Colonel Powell assigned me the task of drafting a reply to the SHAEF request. In my memorandum I noted that Wehrmacht troops now faced enemies in both directions, an enemy in front prepared to accept their surrender and afford them good treatment under the Geneva convention and an enemy in the rear prepared to kill them if they fell back in face of our murderous artillery and air bombardment. I suggested as a propaganda slogan, "The enemy is behind you!"

Colonel Powell sent the memorandum up through channels. SHAEF rejected the proposal with a single-sentence message: *"We do not call upon the Germans to revolt."*

Cracking enemy resistance, the American First Army advanced on Aachen, the first German city threatened by the Allied forces. An ancient Roman outpost, Charlemagne's capital and the site of his tomb, Aachen was a city of legend and a shrine of German military glory.

All over the Reich, Germans awaited Hitler's decision—to spare the city from devastation or to turn it into a symbol of German last-ditch resistance. On 9 September Hitler ordered the evacuation of the population throughout Gau Cologne–Aachen and a scorched-earth policy in face of the Allied advance.[1]

On 18 September General Eisenhower broadcast a statement of Allied objectives in the advance into Germany:

The immediate task of Allied Military Government will be to secure the lines of communications, to suppress any activities in the Allied occupied territories of Germany that would impair the speedy conclusion of the war. Simultaneously the Military Government will begin the task of destroying National Socialism. It will remove from responsible posts all members of the Nazi Party and of the SS Elite Guard and others who have played a leading part in the National Socialist regime. This process begins immediately on the arrival of the Allied armies in each area and the inauguration of the Allied Military Government *[emphasis added].*[2]

---

1. A Gau was a Nazi administrative district governed by a Gauleiter.

2. On 23 September, affirming Eisenhower's declaration and his own impatience with those who would be "soft" on Germany, President Roosevelt proclaimed, "The whole German people must be made to understand that they have been defeated so that they will never again attempt to perpetrate a monstrous crime upon humanity."

In an editorial welcoming the president's pronouncement, the *New York Times* declared:"The forma-

With leaflets dropped from the air or fired from artillery and with broadcasts over Radio Luxembourg and from public-address trucks that inched up to the frontlines, PW units issued an appeal to the Wehrmacht commanders: "Save Aachen from useless destruction. Further resistance is hopeless. Eisenhower promises conquest without oppression. Prisoners will receive good treatment."

On 18 October, Hitler issued a "total war" decree for the mobilization of a *Volkssturm*, a home guard to be composed of old men, the infirm, and boys under seventeen years of age. SHAEF requested a 12th Army Group PW Intelligence proposal for a propaganda response to Hitler's new "miracle weapon," which was supposed to guarantee final Nazi victory now that his V-bombs had failed to do so, and Colonel Powell entrusted me once again with the preparation of a response.

Baffled by the categorical rejection of the Siegfried Line memorandum, in the Volkssturm document I once again recommended a propaganda line aimed at awakening Germans, both soldiers and civilians, to a realization that they now confronted two foes—the irresistible Allied forces in front of them and a more menacing enemy in their midst and in their rear.

SHAEF did not acknowledge receipt of this memorandum.

A week later, confronting hordes of refugees clogging the roads as Allied troops expanded their breakthrough into Germany, SHAEF requested a recommendation for a psychological warfare response to Hitler's 9 September order for the evacuation of populations in the path of the Allied advance.

From reports of G-2 military intelligence and PW interrogators, as well as captured documents and SHAEF's weekly digest of the German press and radio broadcasts and articles in the Swedish press, it was clear that the potential for a call to Germans to revolt was clearly at hand. I resolved in this new memorandum to focus on developments demonstrating irrefutably that the time had arrived for a call to revolt.

I opened my memorandum with a brief summary of recent events in Aachen, noting first that on 10 September Heinrich Himmler, chief of the Gestapo and commander of the SS, made a one-day visit to Aachen. The next day at an air-raid alarm the citizenry was herded into shelters. No air raid followed, but when the all-clear sounded people discovered that leading Party members had vanished with their families. The German press ex-

---

tion of American policy toward defeated Germany which had been developing tortuously from the ground up in various departments without any success at merging conflicting views into a solidified policy is now being made under specific direction from the top."

On 29 September as First Army poised for an assault into Aachen, Eisenhower broadcast a further proclamation defining Allied war aims:"W e shall overthrow the Nazi rule, dissolve the Nazi party and abolish the cruel, oppressive and discriminatory laws and institutions which the Party has created. We shall eradicate the German militarism which has so often disrupted the peace of the world."

horted the remaining Aacheners to obey the Fuehrer's order to evacuate the city.[3] On 14 September detachments of SS and SA (brownshirted storm troopers) men arrived to enforce the evacuation. "The Evacuation Order for Gau Cologne–Aachen" posted throughout the city and its environs threatened punishment for disobedience and presented detailed instructions for carrying out the evacuation.[4]

"We have visited [the evacuees'] assembly camps," reported the *Westdeutscher Beobachter* on 14 September. "Nowhere was there any haste, nervousness or irresolution. The Aacheners left their beloved town with complete calm and resolve." But in a captured document dated 25 September addressed to the 246 Volksgrenadier Division by the Army High Command 7, General of Tank Forces Brandenberger complained of "members of the Armed Forces who have advised the population not to heed the order." Such actions, he warned, would "constitute an act of sabotage against the High Command." In fact, Wehrmacht resistance reached into the highest echelons. After expressing his intention to declare Aachen an open city and advising the population against evacuation, Graf von Schwerin-Krosigk, CO of the 116 Panzer Division, was removed from his command.

On 27 September a correspondent of the *Svenska Dagbladet* recorded a grim picture of the evacuation:

Life in Cologne is increasingly affected by the approaching war. . . . Confusion reigns at the railway station. Trains carrying refugees and evacuees from the frontline areas arrive at all hours . . . and meet other trains full of troops bound for the front. The number of airraid alerts is increasing, and refugees and evacuees from the western territories report growing Allied air activity, including attacks on trains and everything moving on the roads.

An order issued by an SS Obersturmbannfuehrer and police lieutenant colonel revealed stubborn resistance to evacuation:"I give notice once again that at least the male inhabitants of the areas to be evacuated must be re-

---

3. An undated entry in the captured notebook of a political officer of the 11th Panzer Division gave evidence of priority treatment accorded Party members and of Nazi mistrust of the civilian population: "Evacuation has been ordered by the Fuehrer. It's an order. Relatives of political leaders are to be the first evacuated. Caution is required in dealing with civilians of evacuated areas because of the danger of espionage." On 13 September, under the headline, "The Aachen Slogan: We Will Return," the Cologne newspaper *Westdeutscher Beobachter* proclaimed with typical nazi bombast:
The evacuation . . . is prompted by the wish to clear civilians from the range of the Wehrmacht in anticipation of the time when the enemy's assault of Fortress Germany will begin. As naturally as the population has heeded the call of its leaders and evacuated for reasons of military expediency, so would they have stayed ready to defend their city house by house against the invaders. . . . It is Aachen's glory to be the town in the Reich most destroyed by the enemy.
4. Grohe, the local Gauleiter and Reich defense commissioner, issued a monitory proclamation: "Whoever interferes with evacuation measures and resists evacuation not only mortally endangers himself but must also be regarded as a traitor to the community and treated accordingly."

moved, if necessary, by force." A captured unsigned order dated 3 October warned that "civilians traveling through our frontlines into 'No man's land' are helping the enemy knowingly or unknowingly. Civilians loitering in and in front of our battle zone area will be shot."

On 9 October German radio announced that the evacuation of Aachen had been completed. In reality, some 10,000 of the 160,000 Aacheners remained in hiding within the city. Widespread looting followed an SA halt to distribution of foodstuffs. Posters headed "Warning against Looting" were displayed throughout the city threatening summary shooting of looters.

On 10 October two American lieutenants accompanied by an enlisted man carrying a white flag advanced through the smoldering rubble-strewn streets to present an ultimatum:

The city of Aachen is now completely surrounded by American forces equipped with both air power and artillery to destroy the city if necessary. . . . You will either unconditionally surrender the city with everything in it thus avoiding needless loss of German blood and property, or you may refuse and await its complete destruction. The choice and responsibility are yours.

In response, as a captured diary of a leading Aachen citizen recounted, a delegation of citizens appealed to the SS commanding officer to surrender the city. Colonel Wilck dismissed them with a curt announcement that in obedience to the order of the Fuehrer Aachen would be defended to the last man. Riots broke out among civilians and Wehrmacht troops, and in a bunker at Hansemann Platz eight civilians who exhorted their fellow citizens to take up arms against the SS were shot. There were rumors of soldiers routing civilians out of shelters in order to find safety for themselves. During the night civilians hiding in the outskirts of the city made their way to the safety of the American lines.

On 19 October, with the American forces about to launch a final assault into Aachen, the Berlin correspondent of *Stockholms Tidningen* reported: "The SS in Aachen has started a regular battle against people hiding in the ruins and cellars. Large placards have been put up proclaiming a traitor anyone hiding to await the arrival of the enemy."

On 21 October units of the U.S. First Army completed the investment of the city. The next day, raising the Stars and Stripes in the center of the city, an American officer proclaimed the dedication of the victorious troops to the war aims enunciated by FDR and General Eisenhower, declaring, "Nothing of Nazism will be allowed to remain. The keynote of our policy towards the Germans is one of strict justice."

On a one-day visit to Aachen, I saw on a heap of rubble a professionally lettered poster recording in both English and German the Fuehrer's boast of twelve years earlier:

GIVE ME TEN YEARS AND YOU WILL NOT RECOGNIZE GERMANY AGAIN.
—ADOLF HITLER

On 30 October 1944 I completed a fourteen-page memorandum headed "The Evacuation Order." To demonstrate even further that even without an Allied call Germans were rebelling against Nazi authority, I summarized reports of resistance to the evacuation order in numerous rural communities around Aachen where Wehrmacht troops sided with the civilians in resisting the evacuation order, even threatening the Nazi Party brownshirts with violence.[5]

Finally, in an "Analysis of German Orders and Propaganda on the Evacuation Decree," I called attention to the harsh language in the posters and leaflets ordering evacuation and to the violence mounted by Party functionaries and SS troops against civilians and Wehrmacht soldiers resisting the evacuation. I ended the memorandum with an undisguised attempt to persuade people at SHAEF that the time had come for a call to revolt:

With the evacuation decree the war has entered a new phase as far as German civilians are concerned. Now the Nazis have declared war against them just as they had previously done against people in the occupied territories. . . . Germans are experiencing . . . sufferings undergone by millions of Russians and other peoples formerly under the Nazi yoke.

Supreme Headquarters acknowledged receipt of the memorandum and praised it but took no note of its recommendation.[6]

(At 12th Army Group Psychological Warfare headquarters we were not furnished with copies of the SHAEF PW directives, and not until late fall of 1945, a year after these events, upon publication of a history of psychological actions during 1944–45, did we learn the rationale for the "we do not call upon the Germans to

---

5. I reprint the description of such incidents in appendix 5, pp. 184–85. A poll of fifty-eight POWS conducted at my request by PW interrogators revealed that "the soldiers displayed resentment and fear at the decree. They exhibited definite anti-Party attitudes." Asked why they thought many civilians were refusing to obey Hitler's evacuation order, seventeen expressed the opinion that people feared losing their homes and belongings after having worked lifetimes to obtain them; sixteen thought that people were reluctant to leave their places of birth; five thought that people resisted because they had no fear of the Allies; one remarked that, if evacuated, people would continue to suffer repression under the Nazi Party. Asked whether they themselves would have attempted to evade the order, forty-four replied in the affirmative, only two in the negative.

6. See appendix 6, p. 185.

revolt" directive.[7] *It read: "The evidence clearly showed that there was little inclination on the part of either German soldiers or civilians to revolt, and that in any case, they both were under too much restraint to make this line of propaganda even remotely effective."*)

While conducting air bombardments on German cities that inflicted thousands, even hundreds of thousands of casualties, SHAEF continued to express concern about German casualties resulting from a call for revolt against the SS and the Party authorities. Uprisings—even if abortive— would, of course, have weakened the enemy and shortened the war.

SHAEF was apparently less concerned about saving the lives of Allied soldiers than about saving German lives.

At our PW headquarters we were not alone in our resolve that every psychological approach be pursued in order to speed the end of the war and to save Allied casualties. Indeed, an editorial in the Army newspaper *Stars and Stripes* of 10 November echoed the "why we fight" sentiment of nearly all Americans in the European Theater of Operations:"The Americans have come to Germany not to pat childslayers on the head or to feed SS scoundrels with spam. The Americans have come to this land of gangsters in order to bring the villains to justice. It is not only American divisions that have entered Germany. Justice has entered Germany and not a single German will venture to cry welcome to justice. For justice carries a sword."

Subsequent events would further expose different war aims among influential figures at SHAEF and in Washington.

---

7. The copy of the directive appeared in *The Psychological Warfare Division Supreme Headquarters Account of Its Operations in the Western European Campaign, 1944–1945,* a volume issued for distribution solely to former PW staffers and never released to the press or to the public.

3

The Capture-Liberation of Metz

Immediately upon my completing the Aachen-Evacuation report, Capt. Hans Habe, head of German editorial in the Operations section of the Twelfth Army Group Psychological Warfare branch, requested that PW Intelligence provide a detailed account of events in a German town in the days immediately preceding and following its capture for broadcasts to German cities in the path of the advancing Allied armies. Since First Army rejected repeated requests to permit PW investigators to enter Aachen, Habe suggested Metz, which had just fallen to American troops, as an acceptable substitute. (A hilltop fortress city with a population of almost 100,000, Metz along with the rest of the province of Lorraine had been incorporated into France during the eighteenth century, transferred into the Reich in 1871 after the Franco-Prussian War, returned to France after World War I, and then reincorporated into "Greater" Germany in 1940.)

For three days, 26–29 November, I conducted interviews with a varied group of Metz citizens, including, among others, an Army officer, a vicar, a printer, the deputy mayor, clerks in the police headquarters, and a fishmonger. I opened the report with material providing a sense of the atmosphere after the capture of the city:

The city of Metz has suffered no major damage though many buildings are windowless, and a few were hit by shells. As yet there is no electricity in the town. The CO of the American troops has imposed a 6 p.m. curfew as the result of breaches of discipline on the part of our soldiers and because of a danger from snipers. . . .

The people of the town go unconcernedly about their business. . . . [M]any citizens of Metz are not yet convinced that the Germans have gone forever and fear exhibiting too much enthusiasm for us prematurely.

I went on to sketch a history of events at Metz beginning with the fall of France in June 1940:

In July 1940, after a month of German military administration, Gauleiter Buerckel arrived and established a civil government. The first nazi terror measure was instituted on 16 August, the day after the Feast of the Virgin, when the citizens prayed for the deliverance of the city. Buerckel declared this a provocation and expelled all the important citizens, including the bishop.

In October 1940 the Ortsgruppenleiter called for the formation of the DVG

(*Deutsche Volksgemeinschaft*—*an organization of members of the German "community"*), *the initial step toward the formation of branches of the NSDAP [Nazi Party]. At first men were invited to join voluntarily, but when no one presented himself, pressure was applied.* . . .

A mass expulsion to France of Frenchmen not native Lorrainers occurred on 21 November. . . . *The Nazis claimed that they were de-Gallicizing the region.*

The period between 1942 and 1944 was one of continued repression, expulsions and clumsy German attempts at Germanization.

31 August 1944 turned out to be a crucial date in the city's recent history, and the details I assembled provided impressive material for broadcasts to demonstrate to Germans what to expect both from the Wehrmacht and the Nazi officials as the Allies advanced into Germany:

Terrified at the approach of American troops, Gauleiter Buerckel ordered the evacuation of the city. All the Germans fled in disorder, taking with them whatever they could carry. A Gestapo man was heard to shout in the street: "Hurry, hurry, all is lost, the Americans are coming!"

Only a few soldiers, three or four to each fort, were left behind to guard the industrial equipment of the town which had been sheltered in the forts to escape air bombardment. Informants reported that these men were exclaiming: "Ach, wenn die Amerikaner kommen wuerden!" (Oh, if the Americans would only come!)

[Running out of gas, the Americans withdrew, abandoning temporarily the siege of the city.]

After a few days, the Nazis stole back to Metz, the Gestapo and the Party people leading the way. . . . *The first decree of the Kreisleiter, Schubert, was for the mobilization of men for digging [trenches]. Men sixteen to sixty were forced to register each week, a different color identity card being issued every week or ten days. Families of men who failed to register were denied ration tickets. The Nazis were unsuccessful in this effort, for most of the men of the city hid. The Nazis did not have enough police to search them out and were rarely able to assemble more than a thousand men for trench work. Trench diggers sabotaged the effort. There was a notorious instance in which during two consecutive nights two men finished a single foxhole. Nevertheless, a trench fifteen kilometers in length and four meters in width was dug between Thionville and Metz.* . . . *No sooner were the trenches dug than they filled with water. Soldiers were heard grumbling: "Alles Quatsch!" (It's all nonsense!).*

In order to enforce nazi control of the population, the people of the surrounding towns were forced to move into Metz. The men immediately went into hiding, and from the middle of September until the day the Americans entered the city, adult male civilians were nowhere to be seen in Metz. . . . *Passages were bored from one cellar to another so that men could flee at the approach of the Schupo (Schuetzpolizei—security police) or the Gestapo. Some hid on roofs, in closets or in wardrobes. One man took refuge under the eaves of his roof. A builder constructed a double wall and hid his son in the intermediate space for a period of six months. The deputy mayor's cousin remained concealed in a dark room built behind a closet. . . .*

The Nazis conducted systematic looting in the villages from which they had expelled the inhabitants. Every soldier and Nazi official was permitted to send home packages of booty weighing up to fifteen kilos. One soldier was known to have mailed sixteen such packages in one day.

The evacuation program instituted by the Nazis during the weeks before the fall of the city was chaotic:

No one knew exactly when the order for evacuation would be issued, but everyone was determined to follow the advice of the BBC not to leave the city. . . . Older Wehrmacht soldiers told Metz citizens: Die Amerikaner kommen bald, macht nur, dass ihr hier bleiben koennt. (The Americans will arrive soon, see to it that you are able to remain here.)

Preparations for evacuation did not get underway until Saturday, 11 November. . . . Faced with the task of evacuating thousands, the Nazis made a distinction between Lorrainers and the Reichsdeutsche, in contradiction to their previous pretensions. On this first occasion, only fifteen families, a total of sixty people divided into Lorrainers and Reichsdeutsche, left. . . .

The evening of Sunday, 12 November, a PA truck went through the city announcing that everyone was to evacuate the city by the next evening. . . . When the suffragan bishop protested against the order to an officer attached to the German HQ, the officer replied: "I know nothing. Es ist diese Schweinepartei!" (It's this party of swine). . . .

At five p.m., Monday, 13 November, the Kreisleiter gave the order for immediate evacuation. No attempt was made to round up the inhabitants, however, until about 7 a.m. Tuesday. . . . When the Schupos failed to round up a substantial number for evacuation, the Gestapo followed with the Feldgendarmerie [military police] and seven hundred police hastily summoned from the Rhineland. Gestapo agents marched a crowd to the railroad station, where they remained all day until a train was sent off with the old and the infirm—ten cars full. This train succeeded in getting through before the Americans closed the ring about the city. Parents were separated from sick children, and hundreds of families were broken up. In the evening, the Gestapo reported that there were no other trains available, and the rest of the civilians were sent back to their homes.

Wednesday morning, 15 November, Gestapo agents again rounded up the citizenry. . . . A long line of women pushing baby carriages or carrying infants in their arms was sent out of the city on foot. It was raining and very cold. People were moved to tears. A Lorrainer asked a Gestapo man the meaning of the action. "Everyone must leave, hurry, we are leaving within an hour," was the response. "And what do you say to this woman pushing a carriage with her infant? Suppose that was your own little Gretchen? This is not humane," insisted the Lorrainer. "Yes, it is cruel, I cannot look at it, but it must be," replied the Gestapo man.

"Those who didn't want to leave their homes were forced out with blows of rifle butts and with threats of being shot," reported the deputy mayor (he had been appointed to his post in a Free French broadcast over BBC) in an account he drafted for me. "People were given at most an hour to prepare themselves.... Once the population had been evacuated, robbery and pillage took place in an organized fashion. Clothing, food, pigs, poultry, etc. were stolen."

In the next attempt at evacuation, I went on to recount, people were marched on foot for long distances and then returned to the city when it was discovered that the Americans had cut off retreat. Nevertheless, the Gestapo assembled the populace once again and held them in a local barracks for an entire day. When American shells hit trains in the railway yards and word arrived of destruction of railway bridges, the people were sent home. The next day all the Reichsdeutsche except some units of troops left the city. On Saturday, 18 November, the Germans blew up the bridges over the Moselle. The next day, the Americans entered Metz, and the many people who had been hiding came out to the streets for the first time in months.

The attempt to mobilize a Volkssturm (the people's militia) afforded good material for broadcasts to Germans. On 1 November all men between sixteen and sixty in Metz were ordered to register into two groups, Reichsdeutche and Lorrainers. Lorrainers were invited to volunteer for a battleline contingent, but none responded. A woman who signed a receipt for a registered letter, however, discovered that she had also signed on the carbon copy a statement in which her husband volunteered for that frontline contingent. On 12 November some two hundred Reichsdeutsche (no Lorrainers), among whom were thirty cripples, were sworn into the Volkssturm. "When two soldiers on horseback encountered a line of marching VS," an informant reported, "one turned to the other and scoffed:' DEUTSCHLANDS LETZTE HOFFUNG!'" (Germany's last hope!). Only seventeen VS responded to an order to report for frontline duty.

Brawls erupted between Wehrmacht soldiers and the SS fanatics. A Wehrmacht officer exclaimed in a loud voice in a Metz tram when an SA man passed him, "We will settle accounts with you after the war." At a railway station a chaplain on his way to Metz from Germany slapped the face of a

Hitler Youth leader who insulted him, declaring, "That's from me, a priest." After displaying his Wehrmacht leave pass, he exclaimed, "For you I've broken my head in Russia." He slapped the Nazi once again. Everyone at the station applauded.

"Wehrmacht soldiers, fearing the SS, used to say to us," reported one of my informants:" 'We poor devils sit in the muck, and don't know for whom or for what. They force us to attack and prevent us from retreating. They stay behind us with machine guns.'" All units complained that Party men were not at the front.

During the last days of the battle:"Confusion reigned. . . . Members of the Wehrmacht were willing to pay any price for civilian clothing or to rob to obtain it. . . . Even SS men were reported to have forced women to provide them with civilian clothes. . . . SS patrols sought out deserters and turned them over to the Gestapo, who forced them at the point of a gun to make a last-ditch fight in the center of the city." Civilians, police, and troops demanded an end to the fighting:

At night women shouted from the windows: ERGEBEN SIE SICH UND RETTEN SIE UNSERE STADT! *(Give up and save our city!). Schupos ordered to the front declared that they would not fire but would allow themselves to be taken prisoner.*

In the St. Vincennes quarter of the city an officer was killed by his enlisted men when he refused to surrender. When a unit of twenty men guarding the prefecture, many of whom had previously tried to desert, asked their officer to surrender, he telephoned divisional HQ for instructions and was told that a German officer does not surrender. . . . A Lorrainer eager to save the historic structure from destruction assured the soldiers that they had nothing to fear from the Americans, and they refused to continue resistance. Whenever SS men saw a white flag exhibited by Wehrmacht troops, they fired at the surrendering unit.[1]

I concluded the report with some general observations about the attitudes of the people of Metz:

Devout Catholics, the Lorrainers resented the nazi hostility to the Church. All the interviewees, without being asked, expressed indignation at the German treatment of the Jews. All except the FFI lieutenant stated that they admired the exploits of the Red Army. A tailor said that he felt that people in France had never been properly informed about the Soviet Union. Attitudes regarding the post-war treatment of Germany differed. Everyone was in agreement that nazi criminals should be severely punished. The deputy mayor suggested that it would be sufficient to force

---

1. For further details of particular interest to the Psychological Warfare staffs both at Twelfth Army Group and at SHAEF, see appendix 7, pp. 185–86.

Germany to endure the treatment that had been inflicted on Lorraine. Some people noted that German anti-nazis deserved special treatment.

Although some of the intelligence I obtained at Metz merely confirmed what had been learned from POW reports and from miscellaneous intelligence documents (including the possible effectiveness of a call to revolt), the Metz interviews also afforded an unprecedented insight into what life was like under the Nazis and into the demoralization of Wehrmacht troops facing the overwhelming power of the advancing Allied troops.

Because of its history of alternate French and German domination, Metz, of course, provided only a limited model for what American military government would face as we advanced into Germany. Nevertheless, the investigation offered indication of the superficiality of the Nazi hold on the minds of a populace under their domination for a full five years of Hitler's dictatorship.

I left Metz with a sense of confidence that we would be able to accomplish the denazification and democratization of Germany. In subsequent experiences in the coming spring and summer I would learn that such confidence was not fully warranted.

4

The Battle of the Bulge
WINTER 1944–1945

On 5 December, PW Intelligence moved from Verdun to Luxembourg, and I was no longer able to visit the Russians in Châlons-sur-Marne. On the other hand, I was now within walking distance of the Luxembourg assembly point. Mischa and Seenya had no compunctions about sending a messenger to summon me whenever any problem, no matter how petty, arose.[1] Responding to one such call, I found the two of them in conference with a taciturn, stylishly dressed young man, an émigré from Russia in the early twenties. He had been dispatched, he declared, from OSS headquarters in Paris to recruit volunteers to cross enemy lines to post stickers with the message "Macht Schluss!" (Make an End). The Soviet embassy, he asserted, approved of his mission. Offering no comment, I rose, shook hands with the stranger, and left.

That evening I climbed the stairs to the command room, resolved not to express judgment on a mission authorized by my own agency, the OSS. Did not the Soviet embassy insist, I asked Mischa and Seenya, that all assembly centers be administered by Soviet officers? Was it then likely that the embassy would authorize a White Russian émigré to undertake a mission in the service of an American intelligence agency? Would the embassy permit American officers, unsupervised by Soviet officials, to dispatch Soviet citizens behind enemy lines? "What chance is there," I asked, "of the volunteers escaping capture and what will happen to them if caught?" As happened with the Vlassovite POWs when I questioned their offer to attack a heavily fortified hill, this final question evoked a contrary response to what I expected. Both the captain and the commissar remarked that thousands were dying every day on the battlefield, and millions of Soviet soldiers regularly accepted dangerous missions without posing questions. *(While SHAEF refused to risk German lives by issuing a call for a revolt against Hitler, the OSS was prepared to sacrifice Russian lives in a perilous and dubious stratagem!)*

I asked Mischa and Seenya their opinion of the effectiveness of "Macht Schluss!" stickers. "Stickers or no stickers," responded Commissar Lvovsky categorically, "the Germans won't surrender until their armies and their cities are annihilated."

---

1. It may be difficult for anyone who did not enjoy contact with the people in these assembly points to appreciate the depth of their desperation, far away from home, fearful of their future, and traumatized by their recent past. They were grateful to anyone who offered them help. In 1990 a Ukrainian who had been at the school in December 1944 related that whenever I appeared, people whispered to each other, "Our American is here. There is nothing to worry about."

Mischa and Seenya found it difficult, nevertheless, to reject any opportunity to strike a blow against the enemy. I proposed, therefore, an alternative action:their drafting Russian-language leaflets to promote desertions among Soviets in German uniform and sabotage among forced laborers. They seized eagerly at my suggestion. German war industry, they assured me, could not continue to function without Russian labor. That very evening, they declared, they would draft leaflets for me to transmit to SHAEF.

The next day Mischa informed the White Russian that they were not sufficiently persuaded of the usefulness of the sticker mission to risk the lives of men and women under their charge. They dismissed his insinuation that they were yielding to my influence. They were capable, they assured him, of arriving at such a decision on their own.

But my association with the Luxembourg Soviets soon came to an end.

On 18 December, Field Marshal von Rundstedt launched a massive surprise attack against thinly held American positions in the Ardennes forest, just to the north of Luxembourg. Caught off guard and demoralized by the infiltration of English-speaking German special forces in American uniforms, green American troops suffered heavy casualties. Entire units surrendered. Press reports termed the battle "the worst defeat ever suffered by American Armies." The 12th Army Group PW history recounts that "during the counteroffensive the city of Luxembourg itself was under immediate threat by the enemy . . . 12th Army Group personnel had been alerted for possible departure." At PW Luxembourg headquarters orders were given to prepare to burn documents. Some of the German refugees, aware of the treatment they could expect if captured, panicked. The Germans veered north, however, into Belgium, and on 22 December Luxembourg radio, which had gone off the air, resumed transmission.

If the Americans evacuated Luxembourg, Red Guard Captain Victor Kriushchuk insisted, he and his people would remain to fight, and he asked me to obtain arms for him. The afternoon of 28 December, however, the Red Cross informed me that the Russians had been ordered to prepare for transportation westward as soon as a train became available.[2]

The evening of 1 January 1945 I was summoned to a conference with Toombs, Colonel Powell, and a visiting major. The American First and

---

2. For prisoners of war and forced laborers in German captivity, every move meant a transfer to a more terrifying site of suffering and exploitation, and when I arrived at the railway station at 6 A.M. on Sunday morning, 31 December, I found hundreds of Russians already loaded into the cars, grimly silent. As I walked down the platform, tossing handfuls of captured German cigarettes into the open windows, I caught sight of a woman who often at my request had sung my favorite Soviet popular song:"Ah, Odessa, on the wonderful Black Sea, you have suffered much sorrow." "You!" I cried, pointing with mock menace, "how about my song!" She began to sing in the characteristic reedy Russian female singing voice, and the Russians up and down the train joined in. As the train pulled out, hundreds of Russians waved and shouted, "Do zvidanye, Artoor!"

Ninth Armies having been cut off from the rest of Twelfth Army Group by the German offensive and transferred into the British Twenty-First Army Group, our contact with our PW interrogators at those armies would have to be made through the British Army Group. Accordingly, I was to depart the next morning to serve as liaison officer for Psychological Warfare Intelligence at Field Marshal Montgomery's headquarters in Brussels.

During my six months in Europe I had been living in an isolated world among American-born and émigré intellectuals in the Twelfth Army Group PW unit, enjoying only occasional transient contact with the French, Luxembourgers, and Germans. I rarely asked the Russians, whom I came to know more intimately, about their prewar lives or their wartime experiences. In effect, apart from my brief experience at Metz, I had little more sense of what the war meant to Europeans who had endured years under nazism than I had of the emotions and struggles of combat troops.

In my association with the British and the Belgians, however, I was to become more conscious both of my Americanness and more aware of the reasons why we were fighting. More than my previous experiences, my three-month sojourn in Brussels was to shape the attitudes with which I would confront events in Germany during the last weeks of the war and the year following VE Day.

On our second day in Brussels the five GIs in my team announced, "We're not going to eat the slop they feed the British Other Ranks." The British brigadier, Colonel Powell's counterpart in the Twenty-first Army Group PW branch (I subsequently was informed in a tone of condescension that he had been a "mere" headmaster at some "public school") listened to the complaint with no expression of resentment and instructed me to have my sergeant arrange with the British mess sergeant for the establishment of a separate mess for himself and our four enlisted men.

Assigned to one of the numerous headquarters officers' messes, I discovered that British officers dined in comfort and ceremony hardly to be imagined or tolerated at an American headquarters. Individual messes were like Mayfair clubs. Served by Other Ranks (ORs) in tails, the twenty or so "members" assembled for a "happy hour" before dinner. Many of the field marshal's staff officers, some titled (titles were never mentioned), and others, in any event, "gentlemen"—seemed to know each other, having attended the same "public schools" or the same colleges at Oxford or Cambridge. I encountered no other anomalous character—not even a single German refugee—who had slipped into their company to provide me with company and to coach me how to behave in this exalted company. Here I was a twenty-four-year-old son of impoverished shopkeepers in a backwater New Jersey town, a graduate of an obscure teachers college—and, in face of British upper-class anti-Semitism, a Jew!

Upon my first appearance at the door to the mess, officers broke off conversation to glance at me and immediately resumed their socializing. At table no word was directed toward me. In my discomfort I began taking a forty-five-minute streetcar ride to a transient American officers' mess in downtown Brussels. For breakfast, however, I had no choice but to venture into the imperial lion's den, always hoping to find a seat at a vacant table. One morning, to my dismay, I discovered that every table was occupied except one at which a lone captain was reading a newspaper. He closed the paper, saw who it was, and walled me off again. When he rose to leave, I put my hand on his arm. "You know," I murmured, "in my country your behavior would be considered utterly boorish."

He looked askance for a moment, muttered, "in my country, too," and hurried off.

At noon as I opened the door, the captain advanced with hand outstretched and introduced himself. Then he took me by the arm and led me about the room, introducing me to each of the other officers. All responded with gracious warmth as though utterly unmindful of cutting me consistently during the previous days. (Years later, an Englishman assured me that, according to British upper-class custom, a stranger simply does not exist until formally introduced.)

The British officers rarely worked. They conversed, drank tea, and busied themselves in social activities. Both they and the ORs were astonished at my working as hard as the enlisted men, clear evidence that I was not a gentleman.

I often had the impression of having passed through Alice's looking glass. One evening at dinner, for example, a captain exclaimed in a high-pitched but gravely respectful tone, "How old is Old Norway?" He was talking about the king! Again at a general briefing in the large auditorium, Field Marshal Sir Bernard Law Montgomery strode back and forth across the broad stage, slapping his thigh with his stick and reporting on the exploits of "the duke of So-and-so's grenadiers and the duke of So-and-so's fusiliers." Shakespeare redivivus! Indeed, I had no difficulty in making the transition at a special showing of Laurence Olivier's newly released film of Henry the Fifth.

Officers displayed contempt for the Continentals. When one evening at dinner someone reported that the Belgians were panicking at a German black radio announcement of supposed new Wehrmacht advances into their country, the brigadier sneered, "I don't care what these people say in their coffeehouses." An officer who had served as a journalist in Spain during the civil war opined that the people on neither side in that conflict had the slightest idea what they were fighting about.

Wonderland, indeed! From the moment that I was formally introduced, the officers not only included me in their social life but refused to go anywhere without me, and the "gentlemen" conducted me into the highest circles of Belgian society. When at a banquet at the home of White Russian aristocrats I addressed the countess in her native language, she insisted that I sit at her right hand to the delight of my British mentors. The brigadier thereafter employed me in appeasing disgruntled Russian liaison officers who could not understand why women were not permitted to share their billets. I could not resolve their problems, but I could mollify their anger and relieve their boredom, for they seemed to have few responsibilities to occupy them, and the British officers simply ignored their presence. Their commanding officer, a major, a big-boned, generously mustachioed peasant in his late forties, a character out of Sholokhov's *Quiet Flows the Don*, exclaimed with delight when I appeared at his door and hastily put aside the work he pretended to be engaged in. He was overjoyed when I joined him in applauding Moscow broadcasts of war communiqués of Red Army victories, then following one upon another.

From the Belgian aristocrats to whom I gained access through my British colleagues I achieved little insight into the war experience of the ordinary Belgians, for many of these wealthy and titled individuals had suffered little more than inconveniences during the years of German occupation. Indeed, at dinners in their homes I was always amazed at the delicacies they served, brought either from their country estates or bought on the black market. I did gain insight, however, into the other side of Brussels society in the company of a group of young creative people with whom I developed intense wartime friendships. I became particularly close to the Slusznys—Marcel, a half-Jew and a lawyer employed in a government ministry and as a university professor, and his wife, Nicole, a painter; and Marcel's brother Naum, a concert pianist, and his Jewish artist and art critic wife, Esther. Marcel had been imprisoned for several months by the Germans until liberated by the British. Naum, a distinguished pianist and a judge in the Belgian Queen Elizabeth international piano competition, and Esther had spent four years in hiding, protected by the Belgian queen mother.[3] Naum's playing suffered because he lacked energy. He had difficulty in eating, his stomach having shrunk from famine. "There isn't enough meat, nor fats," I wrote home. "They have had no citrus fruits for five years."

3. For a brief period the Slusznys were sheltered by Paul de Man, the literary theoretician who suffered obloquy in the eighties when his wartime pro-Nazi writings were discovered.

The Slusznys introduced me to the Rabuses. Carl was an accomplished painter; his Jewish wife, Erna, a professional photographer. After Carl's brief imprisonment in a concentration camp, they fled from Munich to Brussels, where, like the Slusznys, they lived through the war in constant fear of arrest. As a German Carl was banned from local art galleries, and the couple existed on Erna's photography. Also in our group was Lucien André, the official poet of the Belgian resistance, who earned his living as a school inspector. During the war his fiancée, Gertrude, daughter of a Parisian painter of some renown, dressed as a nun and brought Jewish children to safe refuges.

The central figure about whom this group of young people revolved was Madame Cerf, a widow in her mid-forties. My friends called her Tante Marcelle. In March 1942 her son Roger had been the first Belgian to be parachuted into Belgium from England, where he had fled during the German invasion. Upon arriving in Brussels, Roger brought greetings to the father of one of his comrades. A Rexist (a Belgian collaborator), the man betrayed Roger to the Nazis, and Roger's arrest became a cause célèbre. The Queen Mother and the Roman Catholic cardinal interceded for him with the Wehrmacht commander, but Roger was turned over to the Gestapo, and appeals proved vain. Tante Marcelle believed that Roger was executed by a firing squad. In fact, as his friends learned, he died in the Dachau concentration camp. She subsequently recovered an eight-week segment of his prison diary, recording the period from 7 June through 3 August. Written in English in an extraordinary literary style, the diary was addressed to his English fiancée. It is rich in pathos, humor, and exudes modest heroism. Madame Cerf let me copy the diary, a significant document, exposing why members of "the Greatest Generation" in many countries rallied to ensure a victory for "why we fight!"[4] Tante Marcelle and I discovered that Roger and I were born within days of each other, and, like me, he would have been twenty-four years of age if he had survived.

With the British officers I had an experience with the kind of people that would serve in a British military government, people whose dedication to democracy differed from mine. I wondered whether we could cooperate with them in carrying out the war aims enunciated by FDR and by the Supreme Commander in the European Theater, Dwight D. Eisenhower. It did not occur me then that Americans in high position at SHAEF might be no more dedicated to the FDR war aims.

---

4. In appendix 8, pp. 186–90, I reprint extracts from this diary.

With my young Belgian friends I had my first insights into what German occupation meant in the lives of citizens, particularly of Jews and confirmed anti-nazis.

I matured considerably during my three months in Brussels, personally and politically. I was more prepared to enter Germany.

5

Mainz: Investigating a Pre–VE Day Military Government
SPRING 1945

By the end of January, after suffering 80,987 casualties, including 19,000 dead, American troops recaptured all the territory overrun by the Germans during the Battle of the Bulge. Their manpower exhausted after a loss of 100,000 men, the Germans could no longer replenish their shattered divisions or withdraw forces from the West to stem the advance of the Red Army, which on 26 January after capturing Warsaw, Breslau, and Poznan launched the final and most massive offensive of the war.

With the crushing of the German assault into Belgium, First Army was transferred from Montgomery's Twenty-first Army Group back to Gen. Omar Bradley's Twelfth Army Group, and it was clear that Ninth Army would soon follow. The Brussels PW Operations and Intelligence units were ordered back to Luxembourg, except for me and a single sergeant.

On 24 March, after Ninth Army, following First Army and Patton's Third Army, broke across the Rhine, I set out with a British civilian colleague for a tour of Ninth Army territory, traveling as far as Muenchen-Gladbach, an industrial city on the west bank of the river. At an outdoor army mess I discovered a hand-lettered sign reading, "Russians welcome here!" an expression of GI admiration for allies whose spate of victories on the Eastern Front was guaranteeing a prompt conclusion to the war. With my intense hostility against the Germans, I gazed with satisfaction at the vast acres of rubble in the cities and felt no pity for the misery of people huddling in bunkers by the thousands. Writing home I expressed my resentment at the air of prosperity in undamaged villages where people looked better fed and clothed than people in England, France, and Belgium. Clearly, the Germans had benefited from plundering all Europe. In obedience to the nonfraternization order, GIs on the streets, often arm in arm with liberated foreign workers, ignored the Germans, who made way for them. Groups of foreign workers, laughing and smiling in their newly regained freedom, displayed pits of cloth indicating their nationality. This was victory, I thought. The future was hopeful!

On 28 March the American First and Ninth Armies (now also restored to 12th Army Group command) commenced a massive assault into the Ruhr, the German industrial heartland and center of war production, threatening to encircle hundreds of thousands of German troops. Arriving at my office the following morning, I discovered Colonel Powell at my desk. He had come to call me "back home."

With German resistance collapsing and tens of thousands of enemy soldiers surrendering every day, SHAEF had little need of psychological warfare intervention to undermine enemy morale, and Toombs dispatched me into Germany to gather intelligence for formulating leaflets and radio broadcasts addressed to the thousands of displaced persons swarming down the highways to greet our troops. I was also to question Russians about German civilian attitudes in order to enable SHAEF to refine its policies for the forthcoming occupation of the defeated nation.

Before setting out, however, I caught up on intelligence documents that had accumulated during my three-month absence in Brussels. In January two of my colleagues, Paul Sweet and Saul Padover, distinguished history professors (Padover had also been an assistant to Harold Ickes, Roosevelt's secretary of the interior), carried out an investigation in Aachen, which as the first important German city to fall to the Western Allies afforded a test of American Military Government policy and procedures. After a week of intensive investigation, they produced a scathing exposé of rampant Nazi influence in the city administration. They reported that upon taking up his duties as MG commandant, Lieutenant Colonel Swoboda conducted the local bishop to civilian evacuation camps and asked him to select administrators for the city. For mayor the bishop recommended an official of the local Veltrup armaments plant, which had profiteered during the war on a steady supply of slave labor and of materials pillaged from occupied countries. On the plea that he could not restore order without competent associates, the mayor appointed Party members to twenty-two of the seventy-two key positions in his administration. (Individuals with such backgrounds were excluded under a SHAEF directive from appointment to high positions.) When a Social Democrat distributed a mimeographed leaflet attacking the antidemocratic orientation of the municipal administration, the mayor denounced him as a "communist" and expressed chagrin that the Americans had "misled" the population with "propaganda" promises to remove Nazis from power.

In response to the Sweet-Padover report, General Eisenhower ordered a shake-up in the Aachen MG and a purge of Nazis from the city administration.[1] But in April 1945 my colleagues and I did not appreciate how ominous a precedent this first military government experiment would prove to be.

---

1. I observed in *Betrayal*:

Swoboda's reliance upon the advice of a bishop in this first significant American Military Government experience in Germany was to set a pattern repeated throughout the American zone of occupation. Coming from a nation with an unmatched church attendance, many MG officers, upon assuming their responsibilities, turned eagerly to the clergy for direction and advice. If, as often was the case, they were ignorant of the ignominious role of both the Roman Catholic and Protestant churches during the Hitler years, they were also deaf to warnings about that shabby record. (64)

We had not yet been informed, either, that in the industrial Ruhr, where American forces were mopping up after crushing a huge German army, MG officers following after the troops were suppressing anti-Nazi resistance organizations, in effect, extending to a logical conclusion the SHAEF ban on appeals for anti-Nazi rebellion. As vituperative denunciations in the Nazi press and radio broadcasts attested, Germans were responding to the appeals to revolt that were broadcast by the Soviet-sponsored Free Germany Committee. At word of the approach of American troops, in Wuppertal,[2] for example, the Antifa (the abbreviation adopted for these antifascist resistance organizations) seized strategic buildings and communication centers and rallied Wehrmacht troops to the revolt. After bloody street battles, the rebels overwhelmed the SS and captured the Gauleiter, the chief of the Gestapo and other prominent Nazis. The Antifa then formed an antifascist municipal council, organized an antifascist police force, and prepared to welcome the advancing Americans.

American troops entered the city, encountering only minimal resistance.

But after the troops came MG. "We do the appointing and administering here," the chief MG officer announced. He disarmed the police, dissolved the Antifa, and proceeded to appoint the Aachen kind of Germans to administrative posts.[3]

Mainz

On 10 April I hitchhiked from Luxembourg to the nearby city of Mainz, a major city at the confluence of the Rhine and Main rivers. By the time of my arrival, less than three weeks after the capture of the city, the original MG detachment of twelve overworked officers had been reduced to four, eight having been sent to take command in newly captured localities. Assisted by a mere ten GIs, these officers could not react to reports from outlying rural areas of rampant nazi gangs, of attacks on Americans by Werewolves (a shortlived guerrilla movement mounted primarily by members of the Hitler Youth) and of lynchings of displaced persons (DPs).

An MG officer who joined me at breakfast my first morning in the city badgered me for my loyalty to "my" president. He muttered with indignation at what he called Roosevelt's capitulation to Stalin at the recently con-

---

[2]. A textile center of 400,000 a short distance across the Rhine from Cologne, Wuppertal was a hotbed of anti-Nazism. After 1933 thousands of Wuppertalians were condemned in mass trials to long terms at hard labor. At VE Day more than 7,000 Wuppertal anti-Nazis were being held in concentration camps and prisons.

[3]. Four months later the MG-appointed police president in Wuppertal was being investigated by the British for war crimes against Russian forced laborers. If, as never happened to our PW unit's knowledge, MG officers were asked to justify their disbandment of the German resistance committees, MG officers could point to a SHAEF directive forbidding the formation of German organizations of any kind.

cluded Yalta Conference. "After we crush the Germans," he insisted, "you wait and see, we'll finish the job with the Reds." Two days later he greeted me with the announcement, "Well, fella, your man's dead!"

"That's a helluva joke," I replied.

"It's been on the radio since early morning," he declared.

The previous afternoon, at the request of the American colonel in charge of the nearby mammoth Gonsenheim Displaced Persons assembly point, I had instructed Soviet officers to assemble their people in the central parade ground at an early hour to prepare for a general clean-up of their barracks. "Brooms, mops and pails are to be collected at the administration building by volunteers from each floor," I announced. As the crowd prepared to disperse, I raised my hand for silence and announced:"T oday we Americans have received sad news. One of the leaders of the freedom-loving peoples of the world is dead. *Oomyer, Pryezidyent Roosevelt.*" There was a hush. Then a sigh welled up in the crowd, turning into a continuous, half-repressed wailing. A man cried, "Shapky!" and the men removed their caps. Women sank to their knees and crossed themselves, rocking back and forth in shock and grief.

Stunned, the men and women made no attempt to leave, and I thought to myself that it was neither Churchill, embodying the courageous resistance of the British after Dunkerque, nor Stalin, whose armies bore the brunt of the Nazi might and chief responsibility for the imminent victory—no, it was Roosevelt and America to whom the peoples of the world looked for the extirpation of barbarism and the inauguration of a new and more compassionate world. A heavy responsibility!

Suddenly a guttural shout erupted from the courtyard of the neighboring barracks and swelled into an eerie wolfpack yelp as black-garbed, bearded wraiths, Jewish DPs, stampeded to a central point, flailing their arms and screaming. Someone had recognized a nazi informer. In what seemed no more than seconds they shoved, punched to the ground, and trampled a man to death. Their task accomplished, the mob dispersed in a deliberate retreat, and silence settled again over the area.[4]

---

4. In previous visits to DP barracks, I had decided that these god-infatuated Jews with their medieval dress and rituals and I did not exist in the same world. But my anti-Semitism was exposed abruptly when in Gonsenheim a Russian approached me and after cautiously glancing about to confirm that we could not be overheard whispered, "Are you Jewish?" I nodded.

"So am I," he said in a scarcely audible voice, "but don't tell anyone." Anti-Semitism in the Soviet Union!

Not until I met his son in the Ukraine in 1990 did I learn that Semyon Lvovsky, the political commissar at the Luxembourg assembly center, was Jewish. His widow assured me that he was, moreover, a connoisseur of Yiddish literature and an accomplished Hebraist. Seenya's especial warmth for me? . . . Did he realize that I, too, was Jewish?

Responding both to my concern about their welfare and to the common grief at the death of the president, Russians more and more approached me with private confidences. Hearing so often expressions of fear that they would be harshly treated upon arriving home, I began to wonder at the dismissal by the Soviet chargé d'affaires in Paris of such apprehensions as an invention of Nazi propaganda. When I tried to reassure them, they replied, "You haven't lived in the USSR. We have, and we know what happens."

I presented a consolidated report of the intelligence I obtained from fifteen Russian interviews during 11–14 April, anecdotes demonstrating a breakdown in German society and military that would provide useful material for Radio Luxembourg broadcasts—suicides of Nazi Party leaders and industry executives, desertions of Wehrmacht soldiers, savage punishment of Germans overheard making defeatist remarks, and escapes of forced laborers from work gangs.

A Trial of Two German Looters

I welcomed an invitation from Major Adams, chief of the MG Legal Section, to sit in on trials of two looters, certainly among the first such trials conducted by an American officer in Germany. I was struck first of all by the Jesuit interpreter's exploitation of what he assumed to be his position of authority as well as the major's total ignorance of the German language. The interpreter set to managing the trial as he saw fit, providing loose and often inaccurate translations of the proceedings. When the major at last apprehended that the man was overstepping his authority, he called him sharply to order.

Ironically, as though he was appearing before a German court the lawyer pleaded for leniency—both defendants having admitted their guilt—on the basis that one defendant had lost his only son at the front (fighting Allied troops!) and that both men had been bombed out of their homes (by Allied aircraft in raids in support of Allied ground troops!).

The major sentenced the first man to thirty days in jail and a fine of 1,000 marks. Having already spent two weeks in prison awaiting trial, the man had only an additional two weeks to serve. Noting, however, that the second defendant had run off with goods without even being aware of what he was taking, the major imposed a fine of 3,000 marks as well as thirty days imprisonment, with time off for the two weeks already served.

Upon hearing his sentence, the first defendant, who had been sniveling and not daring even to look at the major, immediately entered into a lively tête-à-tête with his lawyer after which the lawyer announced that his client begged to be allowed to pay an additional fine in lieu of further imprisonment. The major rejected the plea.

At the pronouncement of his sentence, the second defendant also perked up. He pleaded that because he suffered from diabetes he would endure hardship with additional time in jail. Under prodding, however, he admitted that during his two weeks in prison he had received medical care. Having failed with this ploy, he then complained that he could not afford to pay the fine. The major offered to substitute a day in prison for each ten marks he owed. After a hasty, whispered consultation, the lawyer reported that the man would borrow money from the first defendant to meet his fine.

After the defendants had been led away, the major asked the lawyer what punishment his clients would have received in a Nazi court. "A death sentence," replied the lawyer, "from a summary court and without trial." From the reactions of the two defendants to the trial proceedings, I observed in my report of the trials, it was clear that the task of democratizing this nazified nation would require much patience and strict adherence to SHAEF directives.

Convinced that I would gain little significant intelligence from further interrogations of Russians, the third day after my arrival, I directed my attention to a study of conditions in Mainz,[5] and a week later I dispatched by courier to Toombs in Luxembourg seventeen reports, most of which represented interrogations of Mainzers of varied backgrounds. I also included a history of recent events in Mainz extrapolated from interrogations and from accounts composed at my request by three German informants along with "A Picture of the City as It Is Today."[6]

Interrogations of Mainzers

On 13 April, the day I announced Roosevelt's death at the Gonsenheim DP barracks, two Russians took me to visit a German tailor who had sheltered them during the chaotic days before the arrival of the Americans. Upon the Nazi seizure of power in 1933, Heinrich Sohl, a pre-1933 Communist city councilman in his late forties, along with his wife and daughter, now a young woman twenty-five years of age, retreated to a shack in an isolated clump of trees.

Recently elected a party functionary, Sohl was eager to talk to an American intelligence officer, whom he looked upon, so he assured me, not as an enemy but as a liberator. Under Hitler, he admitted, the Communists had

---

5. I was not alone in shifting my emphasis in psychological warfare intelligence gathering at this time, a shift subsequently described in the 12th Army Group PW history as follows:"After entry into Germany, the intelligence job became more concerned with a political type of reporting. This was initiated by a small group of civilians attached to Group from civilian agencies [OSS and OWI]. They began to give a picture of the political climate in Germany. Their reports on the political thinking of German civilians gave the first clear picture of the mental processes of the average German after years of Nazism."

6. Extracts of the history reports are in appendix 9, pp. 190–92.

been unable to accomplish more than mouth-to-mouth anti-Nazi propaganda and the dissemination of news from foreign radio broadcasts. Nevertheless, he asserted, Communists had earned a reputation as the most dedicated and persistent resisters to the Nazi regime. They expected to capture 30 percent of the votes in the first city election, a considerable increase over their 1933 vote.

"We anti-Nazis have faith in the United Nations," Sohl declared. Indeed, all Sohl's comments were supportive of Allied directives, and his expectations for a thoroughgoing democratic transformation of German society seemed to me very optimistic.

Encouraged by this encounter with Sohl, the first individual with whom I had ever conducted a lengthy discussion in the German language, I established myself within the MG headquarters and selected interviewees from among Germans waiting to present petitions to MG officers. I assembled so much material that I transcribed for transmission to Al Toombs reports only on those interrogations that provided significant insights into the morale and attitudes of the Mainzers. I summarize herewith some of those reports.

HERMANN BUTZ

Hermann Butz, a Byronically handsome twenty-three-year-old devout Roman Catholic, had served first on the Russian front and then in Greece. Wounded in 1942, he was discharged from the Wehrmacht. After two years at the University of Munich, he found employment as an actor at a Bavarian film studio. During the first minutes of our conversation, uncertain of my views, Butz hedged his remarks, repeatedly replying to questions, "We Germans have no way of knowing that." But eager to express thoughts long suppressed, he at length abandoned all caution. Since he mentioned that he had written two anti-nazi film scenarios, I suggested that he submit proposals for programs over Radio Luxembourg. Two days later Butz returned with the materials I requested along with two typewritten folders of anti-Nazi poems he had circulated among close friends.[7]

JAKOB STEFFAN, POLICE PRESIDENT OF MAINZ

A Social Democratic deputy both in the provincial legislature and in the Reichstag, Steffan had been sentenced to seven years, from 1933 until 1940,

---

7. Reading Butz's poems more than fifty years later, I was struck not only by his talent but also by his courage. The first folder, "Chansons," contained eight poems attacking the voluptuous lifestyle of Nazi bigshots, the "mad ideas" of "our Fuehrer," the vainglory of Goering, the incompetence of the head of the German film industry along with a satirical belittling of the V1 and V2 "wonder weapons" and a lament entitled "We, the Bombed Out." The second folder, "Poems of Battle for 1944–1945," I must not have examined at all, for in my report I scarcely alluded to his sympathy with, if not participation in, the Munich university underground movement, operating under the name "Edelweiss" during the very period Butz

in the Dachau concentration camp. Along with Wilhelm Leuschner, the Hessian provincial minister of interior, Steffan participated in the conspiracy responsible for the abortive 20 July 1944 attempt on Hitler's life. Leuschner was hanged. Steffan was arrested on 22 August but escaped execution through the intervention of friends in the Gestapo's Mainz office. During the days before the fall of the city, Steffan traveled about the surrounding villages to urge members of the Volkssturm to desert. He succeeded in dissuading some men from constructing tank traps and digging trenches and estimated that he had mobilized 10,000 men from "mouth to ear" to cooperate with us when we launched our final assault.

On Monday, 26 March, four days after the fall of the city, MG installed Steffan as municipal police president. On Tuesday he ordered the posting of warnings and the dispatch of patrols throughout the city to put an end to looting. Although unable to dismiss all Party members immediately from the police, he appointed new officers from among men who had been expelled from the force by the Nazis and from among other reliable anti-Nazis. Within five or six days, he declared, order was reestablished in the city.

Announcing that the Party membership list had been found (actually only incomplete files were discovered), MG ordered all Nazis to register under threat of severe punishment. Not one person who came forward, Steffan related, admitted to having joined the Party voluntarily. Steffan put Party members to work clearing rubble and repairing the public utilities. "They must rebuild in some small measure," he said, "what they destroyed."

As I was taking my leave, Steffan declared:"Now Germans can appreciate the famous words of [Giacomo] Matteoti [an Italian Social Democratic leader of the first quarter of the twentieth century]:"F reedom is like the air and the sun. One must lose them in order to appreciate them."

MICHEL OPPENHEIM

On 14 and again on 16 April, I interrogated Regierungsrat (government councillor) Michel Oppenheim at the office of the Oberbuergermeister. A slight, balding Jewish man, married to a gentile, Oppenheim had been appointed by the Nazis as their liaison with the Mainz Jewish community. According to Oppenheim, on 15 February (a mere two months earlier), a Nazi decree ordered all Jews remaining in Germany transported to Poland—presumably for extermination. Two officials of the local Gestapo, "men of good character"—the same men who had saved Steffan from execution—

---

was a student at the university. It was subsequently infiltrated by the Gestapo and exterminated. In "Remembrance of the Munich Students" Butz displayed unequivocal admiration for these martyrs. I reprint translations of selected poems in appendix 10, pp. 192–93.

sabotaged the order, and about seventy-five Jewish families of a once large and flourishing ancient community in the region survived. (These Gestapo agents had been arrested by MG, but appeals had been entered on their behalf.) After the fall of the city Oppenheim was reunited with his son, a soldier serving in the Counterintelligence Corps of the U.S. Army.

Confident in his status as a Jew and as the father of an American soldier, Oppenheim boldly expressed concern about various conditions in Mainz. Relief at liberation from the Nazi terror, he declared, was tempered by dismay at the indiscipline of the American troops (a problem then receiving little attention from SHAEF or the American media). In the suburbs, he reported, men stood guard at night and concealed their women whenever American detachments halted in their neighborhoods. Germans were shocked as well at wholesale looting and vandalism by the troops.

OBERBUERGERMEISTER DR. WALTHER

Although expressing himself with restraint, Oppenheim conveyed his profound dissatisfaction with MG's appointment (upon the recommendation of the local bishop) of Dr. Rudolph Walther as the Oberbuergermeister. Walther, he granted, was the only former city official who had not joined the Nazi Party. If he had done so and dropped out of the church, Oppenheim asserted, Walther would have advanced to a high post in the provincial government. (He implied that if it had not been for his difference regarding the Church Walther might not have found it difficult to adjust to Nazi rule.) Oppenheim wondered whether Walther possessed sufficient strength of conviction to weed Nazis out of influential positions. "If he is properly supported by MG," Oppenheim ventured in a tone of little conviction, "he will be sufficiently strong."

Arriving during my second conversation with Oppenheim, the mayor took over the conversation and immediately afforded justification for Oppenheim's doubts about him. He insisted, for example, that Germans participate in determining who were war criminals, "of whom there are thousands, and not millions." He looked forward to a prompt freeing of German prisoners of war to participate in rebuilding the devastated nation. When I suggested that the return of the prisoners of war before the reconstruction of other countries in Europe implied that Germans bore no war guilt, Walther responded, "Blame for the war rests with many, even with the Americans."

HERR AND FRAU STENZ

From 1942 Ferdinand Stenz, the owner of some of the largest business enterprises in the city (coal, construction, and shipping), served as a corporal (Gefreiter) in the Wehrmacht until his discharge in February 1945 after suffering a leg wound and being diagnosed with a heart condition. He never joined the Nazi Party and laughed in relating at how, with his savoir-faire, he rebuffed "stupid" Gestapo agents when they summoned him to explain his associating with Jews and his statements critical of the regime. He and his current, second wife, French and considerably younger than he, preferred to speak French ("the prewar language of Mainz society"), which he spoke fluently though ungrammatically.

"The Nazis were parvenus, pugilists and 'crapules,'" the couple assured me. "Even before the war many Germans said that a Nazi is not a German and vice versa. At most the Nazis represent 15 percent of the population. The other 85 percent suffered a collapse in morale under the terror of the war and the propaganda. . . . People now listen to the German radio only to laugh. At first they thought they would be forbidden to do so. . . . If I had the opportunity, I would make Mainz the first American city in Germany."[8]

I had set as my goal investigating how receptive the citizens of this recently captured city were to the war goals articulated by FDR and Dwight Eisenhower.

I summarized the views of the informants regarding critical issues.

War Crimes

Oberbuergermeister Walther was the only informant who questioned the necessity for extensive punishment of war criminals. "They must be put to forced labor," Sohl insisted. "The Americans needn't worry about the punishment of the criminals. The Germans themselves will allow none to escape punishment." Evacuees from formerly German territories in the East, he declared, should be returned to their homes "where they are known in order that no one who committed crimes escape punishment."

"I cannot understand," Hermann Butz exclaimed to me, "how our people could have committed the atrocities for which they must now be brought to account. Hanging is too good for the worst of them." Unlike Heinrich Sohl, Butz had no confidence that his countrymen would cleanse Germany of nazism. "It is up to the Americans to take care of the Nazi leadership," he insisted.

"I am ashamed to belong to a people who have committed such atrocities," exclaimed Jakob Steffan. "This would not have been possible if the Nazis had not brought their *Unkultur* to Germany." No punishment, he declared, could be too severe for the leading Nazis, who should be tried

---

8. When I made a return visit to Mainz two months later, Stenz offered to make available newsprint filling a warehouse formerly belonging to his deceased brother. His gift resolved a shortage threatening our continued publication of German newspapers.

before a world court. The small fry he hoped would be left to the German people.

Strangely, Oppenheim, the sole Jew among the interviewees, agreed with the Stenzes that the mass of Germans knew practically nothing about the atrocities committed outside the Reich and were consequently rejecting accounts of them as incredible. "When they are told," the Stenzes remarked, "they say, 'Is it possible?' They don't want to hear because they would then have to accept responsibility."

Reparations

"The Nazis themselves must return all they pillaged," Sohl insisted, "and the German people must pay reparations for what the Nazis carried off from other countries, and other nations must be rebuilt before Germany itself."

"Germany must pay for what she has done in other countries," concurred Butz. "That will not be difficult. Germans are industrious."

Germans, insisted Steffan, would have to be sent away to rebuild the devastation they had wrought or have to work at home to provide reparations. On the other hand, it was his opinion that prisoners of war who were not Nazis should be repatriated since they had been victimized like workers of other countries.

German Industry and Reconstruction

Regarding German industry, Ferdinand Stenz remarked, "It is necessary to separate the old industrialists from the trusts that sprang up under the Nazis and were built on the confiscation of Jewish wealth. In no case should you permit an armaments industry to continue. Heavy industry will have to be watched. Still it would be a shame to destroy the German industrial potential instead of using it for the benefit of the world. . . . There is despair at the enormous task of reconstruction. I am sure that if one asked, one would find thousands, even millions, who would volunteer to work in other lands. It is rumored that prisoners now in Canada have been offered the opportunity to swear allegiance to Canada and to remain there in order to open the virgin areas."

The Unity of Germany and Attitudes Toward the Occupation Powers

Centrists (members of a prewar Catholic political party) and some of the Roman Catholic clergy called for separating the Rhineland from the rest of Germany, a proposal that received an impetus from the imminent French takeover of part of the region. The Communist Heinrich Sohl and the Social Democrat Steffan both rejected separatism. "We Germans," Steffan insisted, "have done this together, and we will finish things together. When Prussian militarism is wiped out, Germans will be able to live together."

Sohl did not fear the forthcoming French occupation of Mainz. "Although the French may be vindictive," he declared, "it will make no difference whether there is a French or an American occupation. What is important is that we are free."

On this issue Oberbuergermeister Walther again expressed a unique point of view:"People fear a French occupation because they think that the French will bring communism with them."

As for the treatment of Germany he expected from the Soviet Union, the bogeyman with the threat of whose vengeance the Nazis sought to terrify Germans into last-ditch resistance, Butz declared, "I have seen German soldiers order Russians to take off their shoes and hand them over as booty. I think," he continued, "that the Russians will act in Germany just as the Germans did in the Soviet Union. I can understand that. I think that if someone had killed my parents, I would not be very compassionate with him. But all we know about Russia is what Goebbels has told us. On a farm near Mainz I met a well-educated Russian young woman with whom I had intellectual discussions. From what I learned from her and from what I have read, I think there isn't much difference between the Nazi and Russian forms of government."

"I have great admiration for the Russian people," Steffan admitted. "I do not believe they will be cruel to the Germans. In constructing a freedom-loving world, one cannot repay like with like."

"I don't know what the Russians are doing in the East," declared one of the Stenzes, cautious because unsure of my point of view, "from what we hear we are glad that we are under the Americans. The ordinary people here are saying that the Germans are allowing the Americans to reach Berlin first on purpose. I know the Russians too little to judge them."

The Jews

"We expect the Jews," said Sohl, "to come back to rebuild their businesses. They will have no difficulty starting again."

"We want the Jews to come back to their homeland to regain what they lost," concurred Steffan. "A settlement can be reached with them."

"The Jews will return because they love Germany," declared the Stenzes. "All that has not been destroyed by the war must be returned to them."

In contrast, Oberbuergermeister Walther was of the opinion that the population did not desire the return of the Jews, fearing to have to compensate them for stolen properties. I did not ask Walther whether he shared this attitude.

Oppenheim was convinced that the majority of the Jews who fled Germany would not return. "Even as the princes in old Germany," Oppenheim related, "always had one Jew whom they protected, so in the last years each 'Aryan' family befriended at least one Jewish family as a security measure. Individual Jews did not always realize that they were being used by people who may have hurt ninety-nine others."

Denazification

Steffan assured me that Mainzers turned against the Nazis long before the fall of the city. "Stalingrad," he asserted, "produced a great awakening."

"The people of Mainz," concurred Oppenheim, "have seen the brutality of Party members here. National Socialism is dead in Mainz. It is dead in all Germany." Oppenheim and Steffan agreed that if the Western Allies had not imposed restraints the German people would have conducted a massive denazification on their own. "The war between the Americans and the Germans," insisted Oppenheim, "is not nearly so bitter as the war between the Germans and the Nazis." "The Nazis are grateful," said Steffan, "to the Americans. If not for you, there would have been a frightful bloodbath. All the Nazis would have been killed." (The "we do not call upon the Germans to revolt" directive, of course, prevented that bloodbath!)

Oppenheim was dissatisfied with the pace of denazification in Mainz. He noted that houses of non-Nazis were commandeered for the use of troops, while Party members were left undisturbed. Mainzers, Oppenheim declared, were still terrified of the Nazis since they saw many Pgs (*Parteigenossen*—Party members) walking about free, some still holding important administrative posts. Once MG took cognizance of the problem and carried out wholesale arrests, Oppenheim opined, more in hope than conviction, such fear would disappear.

"If the Germans had won the war," declared Stenz, "85 percent of the population would have shouted hurrah and forgotten all the evil that the Nazis committed." He, too, was critical of MG's denazification effort. "We have in our building," he reported, "an old Nazi family whom everyone in the neighborhood fears. They still give the Hitler salute. When Goebbels speaks, they spread his propaganda." When, on a recent visit to the home of Jewish friends, he made a derogatory remark about the Nazis, the hostess shushed him.

Democratization and Party Politics

Steffan assured me that he was not unique among his countrymen in his eagerness to denazify and democratize Germany, and he was optimistic about the future of his country. "We will show the world," he proclaimed, "that the majority of Germans are upright and that our country will merit a place among the nations of the world."

Of the effectiveness of any Allied program to democratize Germany, Butz was dubious. "We know nothing about other forms of government," he declared. "Democracy to us is only a name—something floating about in the air."[9] On the other hand, in one segment of his countrymen, one in which he included himself, Butz found hope for the future. "The students are our best people," he declared. "Some of them have managed to remain humane, especially those from good home backgrounds. . . . German youth have been repressed so long that now there are hundreds of young men who want to express themselves somehow whether by writing or acting or building."

"Wherever you go," Stenz counseled, clearly thinking of himself and expressing a conception of democracy hardly conforming to his professed admiration for the United States, "you must seek out the good families and the men of affairs. They will be the ones with the courage to take action. You often make the mistake of beginning with the little crapules, just as the Nazis did. In any event, keep control over our officials with a secret police. You must not permit parties to emerge in Germany for at least ten years," Stenz warned, "since the Germans are too stupid. They must first be given the opportunity to speak freely and to discuss in order to learn how to act in a democracy."

Heinrich Sohl advocated total Allied military control in Germany for months after victory with free elections following thereafter. "The popular reaction against Nazism," he declared, "will make it easy for the reappearance of the Communist, Social Democratic and Center parties."

The Communist Issue

After a dozen years of unremitting Nazi anti-Communist propaganda, it was natural that the informants posed questions about the future of the German communist party. Despite the party's anti-Nazi history and popular support, the MG commandant, Sohl noted, had appointed Social Democrats and Centrists but no Communists to municipal posts. A week earlier, on 7 April, he reported, 150 local Communists had met to plan the reactivization of their party organization. Spokesmen were selected to submit to MG and to the Oberbuergermeister requests that the municipal administration and the

---

9. Butz himself exhibited what Heinrich Heine denominated "the German misery"—the political backwardness resulting from a failure to participate in democratic revolutions like Britain, France, and America. Butz considered Rudolph Hess to be an idealist, unlike other Nazi bigwigs, and a man who, he said, many Germans thought would be a desirable member of any postwar German government. Reportedly chosen by Hitler to be his successor until he flew to England in 1942 on a mysterious and never fully clarified mission, Hess was condemned to life imprisonment at the Nuremberg war crimes trials.

police force be cleansed of Nazis and that Communists receive representation in the administration. In support of the latter request, Sohl quoted FDR's declaration:"We must support the Germans who weren't fascists."

"During the Nazi dictatorship the Communists were the only ones who mounted any organized opposition," declared the devout Catholic Hermann Butz. "They were responsible for anti-Nazi activity among students at the University of Munich. I don't know," Butz added tentatively, awaiting some sign of my political orientation, "whether it is good or bad that the people will be turning to communism. I think there is a difference between bolshevism [the derogatory term employed by the Nazis] and true, idealistic communism."

The Stenz couple declared, "Germany is very communist," but declined any further comment.

The Communists, Sohl reported, intended to open negotiations with the Social Democrats for the establishment of a united socialist workers party. The Social Democrats, he declared, had moved considerably to the left as a result of their experiences under Hitler and might now be willing to unite with the Communists.

Still embittered at the pre-Hitler antagonism between the Social Democrats and the Communists, Steffan retorted:"I hate the Communists as much as I hate the Nazis since I think that any kind of dictatorship brings misery to the people. Germany has already lived through twelve years of dictatorship and cannot experience more."

Although Oppenheim did not see "much difference between Nazis and Communists" and asserted that "Communists became Nazis quickly, and now Nazis are becoming Communists," he, nevertheless, expected a unification of the two left-wing parties, and he opposed MG's exclusion of the Communists from municipal posts, urging proportional representation of all anti-nazi factions within the city administration.

Reeducation

"We must find new teachers to reeducate the youth," Sohl opined. "Reeducation must start with the youngest children." In regard to religion, he did not share the dogmatic attitude of the Soviets. "The Centrists may, of course, practice their religion freely," he declared, "but religion must be separated from government and from the schools."

Sohl's view was shared by Steffan. "The young people must learn humanity," Steffan asserted, "and unlearn their admiration for force and brutality."

Oberbuergermeister Walther, on the contrary, saw a special role for the Church in postwar education. "Before the schools are reopened, it will be necessary to weed out all the Nazis. The Church will be able to contribute much in this regard."

I discovered among all these interviewees, with the exception of Oberbuergermeister Walther, serious grappling with the major issues looking forward to a radical transformation of their country and expecting the Americans to promote such a transformation. It was a question whether MG would respond to this ferment and put into effect SHAEF directives promoting the war goals of a thorough denazification of German society and the inauguration of a vibrant democracy in the country, the "why we fight."

Interrogating Victims of Nazism and Nazis

The evening of 17 April I interrupted my interrogations of Mainzers upon the arrival of fifteen Frenchman from the Buchenwald concentration camp. Liberated only days earlier by American troops, they were undergoing emergency medical treatment at the Gonsenheim DP barracks infirmary pending arrangements to return them to France. They were eager to talk, especially to an American, and I was eager for an opportunity to learn firsthand of an experience which seemed to me decisive in refining American postwar policies toward the Germans. (Word of the horrors in the death camps was not yet general knowledge.)

On 18 September 1943, they reported, 1,150 Frenchmen were dispatched from Paris. At Metz they were forced to alight from the train and to undress. They were beaten and then herded back into the freight cars. Upon their arrival at Buchenwald, it was discovered that in one car 80 men out of 180 had died of asphyxiation.[1]

Bloc 46, a concrete building with opaque windows surrounded by a double fencing of barbed wire, housed an institute for experimental medicine directed by an SS colonel who was assisted by prisoners of various nationalities with scientific training. Bloc leaders, who were German prisoners, were required to furnish a certain number of men for experiments with serums and typhus. Anyone who displeased his bloc leader by even as petty an act as stepping on his toe, sneezing, or looking too solemn could be dispatched to Bloc 46. No one ever returned. Those employed in experiments with phosphorous burns suffered most painfully, scorched on various parts of their bodies.[2]

At the end of January, in face of the Soviet advance, the Germans evacuated the camps in Upper Silesia, transferring inmates to camps in central Germany, forcing them to march on foot or transporting them in freight cars in snow and wind with temperatures as low as minus 20 degrees centigrade. Inmates from Auschwitz traveled for eight days before reaching Buchenwald, given nothing to eat on the way. When the trains arrived, it was discovered that the majority of the men were dead. It was necessary to dig through the piles of corpses to find survivors. Although the railroad station was no more than a kilometer from the camp, it took a half day for the

---

1. See appendix 11, p. 193, for details of the daily routine in the concentration camp as related by these Frenchmen.
2. See appendix 12, pp. 193-94, for further details about Nazi criminality at the camp.

frozen and starving men to crawl the distance. Those who fell on the wayside were shot by the SS. About 5,000 arrived alive. Each of the two huge tents set up outside the campgrounds accommodated about 1,000 men. The other 3,000 huddled in the open air, awaiting delousing before being granted entrance to the camp. The hundreds who perished were placed in heaps. The living hid behind the piles of corpses to protect themselves from the wind. The sick were separated from the others. When they could no longer walk, they were thrown on the piles of the dead, still alive. A wagon carried the bodies to the crematorium. Hundreds cried out, "I am not yet dead." Only a few managed to crawl free. For ten or twelve days the crematorium lay idle for lack of fuel. Bodies accumulated in the courtyard in a pile that grew to more than forty meters in length and two meters in height.

During February and March, to make room for the thousands evacuated from camps further east, hundreds of men were sent out on heavy-duty work details. One thousand, mostly Polish and Hungarian Jews, were set to work digging an underground factory at Ohrdruf. Others, non-Jews who had displeased their bloc chiefs, were sent with them. One man in this commando lost twenty-eight kilos in three weeks.

To prevent an uprising at the approach of the Americans, the Buchenwald camp commandant announced to the bloc chiefs that he would not evacuate the camp but would hand over the inmates unharmed to the Americans. Nevertheless, on 8 April the Germans began to evacuate the inmates, sending 5,000 off on foot every day. In the forests between Buchenwald and Weimar, Volkssturm and Hitler Jugend (Hitler Youth) stood guard, ready to shoot escaping prisoners. According to an order discovered after the camp was liberated, prisoners still in the camp were to be killed by flamethrowers. On 13 April the Americans arrived two hours before the massacre deadline.

At Easter, the Frenchmen reported, the camp population numbered 48,529; at the liberation 21,000, some 27,000 having been either evacuated or liquidated.

An Artist in a Political Vacuum

My meeting with the Frenchmen provided an impetus to my confronting Germans who perpetrated atrocities or stood by and applauded as they occurred. Accordingly, I arranged with the local CIC unit to interrogate in the Mainz prison three Nazis awaiting trial.

While typing his name and other personal particulars, I asked Prof. Wilhelm Haertner, winner of international awards as one of Germany's leading architects and bridge designers, when he thought the war would be over. On 18 April, 300,000 German troops encircled in the Ruhr surrendered to the First and Ninth Armies. With this momentous German defeat and the arrival of the Red Army at the outskirts of Berlin, Allied victory was clearly imminent.

"I don't know why I'm here," Haertner responded, ignoring my question. "I am only an artist. I have done nothing." During the previous twelve years the professor had been so preoccupied with drawing plans for bridges and in traveling from one international conference to another that he had no time for political matters. He had, indeed, noted that Hitler brought order to Germany, putting an end to Communist-inspired strikes and troublemaking. Under the Nazis, too, children were kept busy, everyone was healthy. The professor had not noticed what had been done to the Jews. He knew about such issues only from what he read in the press. He had no reason to doubt what the newspapers reported.

The professor smiled when I suggested the word "vacuum." Yes, that was it. He had lived in an artist's vacuum.

Had the professor encountered any personal problems in working for the Nazi regime?

Quite the contrary! the Nazis entrusted him with important assignments. It had not been necessary for him to join the Party to gain preferment.

No, he had no idea who started the war. It had something to do with the way the Poles treated Germans living in Poland and with their refusal to accept the Fuehrer's proposals for a settlement. The professor did not live in such a vacuum that he had failed to notice the presence of Americans in Germany more than 6,000 kilometers from their homes. He had always thought that America's business was in America, and Europe's in Europe.

(From CIC documentation I discovered that the professor forgot to mention that for his services to the state and his devotion to the Party Hitler had personally awarded him the title of professor as well as the Kriegsverdienst Kreuz Erste Klasse, a prized Nazi decoration awarded for special service in the war. An investigation was in progress into charges that "the artist" had emerged out of his vacuum to maltreat foreign forced laborers.) To establish his credentials at the time of his arrest, Haertner noted proudly that he had been a good friend to Dr. Fritz Todt—Hitler's chief engineer, a Nazi of the highest rank in charge of the construction of the Atlantic Wall against Allied invaders.

As I rose to take my leave, I paused to ask, "What do you think is going to happen to you?"

Haertner replied with smug assurance, "You Americans will need people like me."

"Und Siberien?" said I, waiting just long enough to enjoy the sight of the artist blanching. ("Sieg oder Siberien"—victory or a captivity supposedly worse than death in Siberia was the warning circulated among the troops in the Siegfried Line to encourage them to fight to the death against the advancing Allied armies. Rumor held that leading Nazis were to be turned over to the Soviets for punishment. Mere wishful thinking! But I could think of no other ploy to provide this exemplar of the Master Race with some nightmarish moments.)

An Unrepentant Nazi Physician

I read the arrest warrant for my second interviewee at the prison, Dr. Richard Richter, translated by a German interpreter at police headquarters. It described him as a Nazi fanatic who treated Jews with especial cruelty.[3] "Dr. Richter looks like a butcher," I noted in the opening paragraph of my interrogation report. "One imagines that he often obtained his way simply by scowling. Ferdinand Stenz said that you can always pick out a Nazi since they all look like prizefighters. He would be right with Dr. Richter." Richter declared that he had joined the Party late(!), on 1 April 1933, a week after Hitler was granted dictatorial power under the Ermaechtigungsgesetz (Empowerment Act) by a coalition of parties in the German Reichstag. The local Kreisleiter appointed him Leiter of the Mainzer Aertzeschaft (Mainz Medical Association).

Richter was content with Hitler. The Fuehrer eliminated unemployment and prevented bolshevism from taking over in Germany. Otherwise, there was nothing to complain about. The entire German people believed that what Hitler promised was right, that Germany would flourish under the Nazis.

Richter was aware that Jews had been driven out of the country, their wealth confiscated. "It was harsh," he admitted, "but it was part of Hitler's program. I understood what Hitler was doing, but I did not agree. In my own life, I did not discriminate against Jews."

Richter claimed ignorance of German atrocities in other countries. He thought that many of the foreign workers had come to Germany voluntarily. "I have never seen any maltreatment of the foreign workers," he declared.

Whether German newspapers told the truth, he had no way of knowing. He never listened to foreign broadcasts because it was forbidden to do so. In an afterthought, however, he admitted that recently he had listened to Radio Luxembourg. Yes, listening to foreign broadcasts was forbidden, but during the last weeks as the chief physician for the Volkssturm he had realized that further fighting was pointless. "One couldn't fight with such people [children, the aged and cripples]."

---

3. See appendix 13, p. 194, for the arrest warrant, drafted by a German translator at the police department.

Was there any aspect of the Nazi regime that displeased the doctor?

Yes, he was not satisfied with the Hitler Jugend. In the organization his fifteen-year-old son had not received a proper education. The boy would have preferred not to attend the HJ meetings.

Did the doctor believe that some Germans deserved trial as war criminals? The doctor nodded agreement, but he was not sure what I meant by a war criminal. "But you admit there are some?" I urged.

"Suppose you tell me first whom you mean," he insisted.

"A war criminal," I replied, limiting myself to a definition that I was convinced he would not dare to reject, "is one who although knowing the war was lost even as long as two years ago continued to fight." The doctor sat silent.

What about the Nazi slogan promulgated only recently, "Better death than enslavement"? Suppose that knowing the war was lost, the Party leaders continued the war on this rationale?

That, replied Dr. Richter, was something he would have to think about.[4]

A Teacher Who Learned, If He Learned, Too Late

Studienrat (supervisor) of mathematics and elementary English in the Mainz school system since 1917, Georg Wittig joined the Party in May 1933. With only a few exceptions, he explained, all the teachers in the city were Party members (Pgs). Those who for religious reasons refused to join suffered discrimination.

"Hitler attempted," Wittig recounted, "to eliminate and correct class differences. There were aspects of National Socialism I did not support," he admitted. "I did not like the constant pressure of the little fuehrers, who sought constantly to squeeze money out of their subordinates. Compulsory attendance at Party meetings was also unpleasant. I do not believe that the anti-Jewish campaign was conducted according to the Fuehrer's intentions. In my profession I have had many opportunities to meet Jews, and I generally obtained a good impression of them.

"Only during the last weeks have we come to understand why the Americans have come here. Before it was not clear because of the Nazi propaganda. Once I saw the technological might of the Americans, I said, 'Against such a people it is impossible to win.'"

4. I sought the opinion of Dr. Betz, one of two "Aryan" Mainz physicians who had refused to join the local Nazi medical association. Betz reported that before joining the Party Richter had relied upon a Dr. Levinsky, a Jewish physician, to provide him with patients. After April 1933 he would have nothing more to do with Levinsky or any other Jewish physician. When Richter learned that Betz was temporarily taking over the practice of his former professor, a Dr. Moeller, a half Jew, while Moeller went off on vacation, he telephoned Betz and screamed that it was "intolerable that a German doctor should treat the patients of a half Jew." Richter had himself appointed director at the Neubuddenbad spa after forcing out Dr. Nathan, a Jew and an excellent physician. Richter, according to Betz, treated patients and colleagues brutally.

Reminded that with this statement he had not explained the participation of the Americans in the war, Wittig replied that the Americans had come to Europe because they saw an opportunity for victory. Sensing my dissatisfaction with his response, he added, "Against such an evil as was coming from Germany, the Americans had no choice."

Like Richter, Wittig sought exoneration on the plea of being deceived by Nazi propaganda. "We were tricked," he repeated several times. "Hitler should have halted after Munich. We were tricked by our press. That is why I did not see through the swindle until too late." No one, Wittig declared, had ever transmitted to him news heard on Allied radio broadcasts.

Why was it, I asked, that none of the many Mainzers who did listen to Allied broadcasts ever passed on to him information they heard on these broadcasts?

Wittig saw the trap I was setting for him. "Oh yes," he declared, "people did give me news but never named the source."

From what he had seen, foreign workers were well treated. The majority, in any case, had come to Germany voluntarily. One of Wittig's sons, an army physician formerly stationed in Lithuania and now an American POW, had informed him that the people of that occupied country were well treated. Wittig's other son, currently somewhere in the Balkans, had fought in Crete, where, according to his letters, the Cretans afforded the German troops a warm reception. (In fact, the Germans encountered fierce resistance on the island.)

War criminals?

"A war criminal is one who is to blame for starting the war or for committing crimes during the war. The top leadership is in the former category." Whether Hitler was a criminal Wittig found it hard to say. He considered the Fuehrer to be an idealist. For lying to the German people, Goebbels, however, deserved punishment. "Goebbels was under the orders of a small group about Hitler." Dismayed at my incredulity, Wittig wriggled again. "In my opinion, Hitler also lied. If I believe his words, he wanted to accomplish all his goals peacefully, but Goering is a Schlappmaul [a blabbermouth], a dandy who loves fancy uniforms. Hess sought only good for the German people. He wanted to unite the British and the Germans. That was natural since the English are of Germanic stock. The French, on the other hand, are a Latin, a Mediterranean people. I think that 'Volk' ties are important." Maintenance of racial purity in a country was, he was convinced, a desirable ideal. It would have been desirable to expel the Czechs, Poles, and Jews from Germany, but not humane.

Wittig was convinced that few Germans belonged to the second category of war criminals, those who committed crimes during the war. But in face of my continued silence, he felt compelled to modify this judgment. "There are certainly thousands who performed crimes against the Jews. Especially those who denounced Jews in order to enrich themselves."

Concentration camps? "They told us that enemies of the nation were sent to concentration camps. Whether they were really enemies depends on how you look at things. Today people are for, tomorrow they are against."

As for the Russians, Wittig declared that Germans in the East feared them, but not Germans in the Rhineland. "The Russian workers who were here were peaceful. I believe that anyone willing to work will be able to live under any regime."

Asked why he had been arrested, Wittig replied, "I have been arrested on suspicion of association with the Werewolves and of anti-Jewish activity. I am the victim of a vicious denunciation." (In fact, an investigation was under way of reports that Wittig had given the order to burn down the local synagogue, that he had harangued against Jews in the schools, and that he had excused students from class to participate in anti-Jewish demonstrations. In addition, he had served as the commander of a Volkssturm battalion.)

Asked who could provide a character witness for him, Wittig without hesitation named Professor Haertner and Dr. Richter, "both upright and well-respected citizens." (He was unaware that both men were his neighbors in the Mainz jail.)

During the ten days I spent in Mainz, staying up late typing in triplicate reports based on the transcripts of my daytime interrogations, I had no leisure to reflect on the intelligence I was gathering. It was clear that Mainz was not a second Aachen, where MG had installed an administration composed almost solely of Pgs. Nevertheless, I left Mainz less enthusiastic about MG's achievement than I had been a week earlier, with apprehensions about aspects of MG's actions and policies certain to affect the accomplishment of our war goals—the aims of "why we fight." Valuing Michel Oppenheim's judgment and frankness, I was disquieted by his doubts as to MG's selection of Dr. Walter for the highest office in the city,[5] at the slow pace of denazification, and at MG's failure to appoint Communists to posts in the city administration (a violation of a SHAEF directive mandating appointment of representatives of all anti-Nazi factions to such positions). The possibility, as indicated by the differences between Steffan and Sohl, of a struggle over unification of the two workers' parties, the Communists and the Social Democrats, posed a troubling prospect in a Germany where the collabora-

---

5. In September, two months after assuming control of Mainz, the French removed Walther from his post as Oberbuergermeister. It was likely that they did not do so simply because of his opposition to the French Communist Party.

tion of all elements of the population was essential for the resolution of critical problems.

Out of contact with headquarters, I was not aware while engaged in my investigations in Mainz that Military Government officials were effecting in Leipzig an even more dramatic crushing of an Antifa than occurred in Wuppertal. Advancing into the outskirts of the city, American troops encountered fierce resistance. Abruptly, however, the German commander agreed to surrender, for inside the city a Free Germany Committee had raised a rebellion and overwhelmed the SS garrison. The committee posted a ten-point program calling for cooperation with the Allies, punishment of Nazi criminals, curbs on blackmarketing, a popular mobilization for rubble clearance, and the establishment of an antifascist administration and police force. Recruitment booths were set up to enroll citizens into a committee composed of Catholic and Protestant churchmen, trade unionists, Social Democrats and Communists, Kzler (former concentration-camp prisoners) as well as participants in the 20 July putsch against Hitler.

When American troops entered this major industrial center on 18 April, they saw white flags on every street and encountered only minimal resistance. But the exhilaration within the city evaporated abruptly when an MG major declared to a committee deputation:"I wish we had fought for this city. We would have shot you people along with the SS. You bastards are no better than the Nazis."

The suppression of the Leipzig, Wuppertal, and other anti-Nazi committees that mounted courageous rebellions resulting in saving American lives followed inevitably upon the SHAEF directive, "We do not call upon the Germans to revolt." In place of these Germans who proved their anti-Nazism at least during the last weeks of the war, MG officials in Aachen and elsewhere installed the opponents to these proven anti-Nazis—Nazis along with war profiteers.

The goals propounded by FDR and Eisenhower were at risk.

7

Wuerzburg: Another Military Government Experience

On 21 April, accompanying Colonel Richman, the Third Army DP officer, and his multinational staff, I arrived in Wuerzburg, a city in Mainfranken (the northern section of the province of Bavaria), which had been captured two weeks earlier. As with my Mainz study, I provided a covering document for my interrogation reports—"Wuerzburg Before and After the Arrival of the Americans."[1]

Gustav Pinkenburg

With Oberbuergermeister Gustav Pinkenburg I experienced the exuberance and optimism I encountered with the Social Democratic police commissioner of Mainz, Jakob Steffan. A director of an insurance company until removed by the Nazis, Pinkenburg was introducing business enterprise into the running of the city and appeared always to be in a hurry. "The first problem is food," declared Pinkenburg. "I hope that the present difficulties will be alleviated with the coming of spring. My second problem is housing. I am rehabilitating houses with slight damage first. The rebuilding of the city will take years. For the reconstruction we will have to mobilize the labor potential of the region, both intellectual and manual.

"A prime task is to teach children to be respectful to their elders," he said. "We will mobilize them in the reconstruction of the city and set up democratic youth clubs. We must look for untainted teachers. Four physicians have been appointed to supervise the children's health care. The general health situation of the city is good.

"As soon as the city administration is running smoothly," said Pinkenburg, "I will begin to clean out the *Fahnungsstelle* [the flag wavers]."

Lambert Greck

Pinkenburg was assisted by an equally entrepreneurial deputy mayor. Because of his fluency in English, MG had brought Lambert Greck from a nearby town to serve as their liaison with the city administration. Several times during our conversation Greck called in his secretary and posed such questions as "What did I always have on my desk?"

"A large letter S," replied the young woman. (Clearly, she had been primed to answer this question.)

---

1. I reproduce this report in appendix 14, pp. 194–96.

"And what did that signify?"
"Swine."
"And who were the swine?"
"The Nazis."

Greck explained that whenever his secretary reported the arrival of a visitor, he would point to the "S," and if she nodded he knew with whom he was dealing. "I can understand how you as an American can wonder," declared Greck, "that eighty percent of the population was in the Party. In the last year, however, only about ten percent subscribed to the Nazis' ideas, but this ten percent possessed a power difficult to describe. Terror lasted right up to the arrival of your troops.

"One must differentiate between the pre-1933 Party members and those who entered after 1933," Greck advised. "I was forced to join the Party in 1937 in order to keep my job. If I had not entered the Party, my family would have suffered, and I would never have held any position of importance. I frequently spoke before business groups, always beginning my remarks with 'ladies and gentlemen,' never with 'fellow Party members.' Three times I was called before the Gestapo and challenged about politically questionable remarks in my speeches.

"Our relations with the Americans, *except* with *the Negroes*, have evoked the gratitude of our people." (I had rarely encountered Negro troops during all my months overseas. A black engineering unit had very likely constructed the pontoon bridge in Wuerzburg and then moved on.)

Hans Stammler

In Dr. Hans Stammler MG seemed to have found an irreproachable anti-Nazi to serve as Wuerzburg police president. Stammler had served as a police official until 1933, when he was dismissed because he was married to a Jewish woman. She had been sent to a concentration camp, and Stammler did not know whether she was still alive. In November 1944 he himself was sentenced to a labor camp near Breslau, a camp for half Jews and for men with Jewish wives. Escaping in January, he returned to Wuerzburg, where he remained in hiding until the arrival of the Americans.

"Wuerzburg is a Catholic city," Stammler said. "It never supported the war nor the Party. Nazism was imposed here. At the beginning of February, when I returned home, people were war weary. You heard people exclaim, 'If the Americans would only come!'

"My most pressing task," Police President Stammler said, "is to clean out the dangerous Nazis. I arrest them and turn them over to MG. I issued a call for volunteers for the police force, using leaflets and public address announcements. I received a limited response. I assigned the men to antilooting duty, but few in number and unarmed they are not effective. The Poles [DPs] are the worst as far as looting in concerned. There have been many cases of rape, particularly by Negro troops."

Separatism

In Bavaria as in the Rhineland, apparently, a separatist movement existed. "There is no doubt," Pinkenburg said, "that the Bavarians want to be Bavarians, separated from Prussia. A Danubian state comprising Austria, Bavaria, Wuerttemberg and Baden, but excluding the Rhineland, should be organized." Pinkenburg expressed satisfaction that East Prussia and part of Prussia proper were to be annexed by the Russians and the Poles.

"We Bavarians," Stammler stated, "have always hated the Prussians. Since Hitler, the antipathy has grown more intense. . . . Greater Germany ideas never had roots here. If Bavaria had been a nation, the Bavarians would never have started a war. Whatever happens to Koenigsberg, Breslau or Danzig [the first was to be incorporated into the Soviet Union and the two others into Poland] is of no concern to the Bavarians."

Greck had a unique comment about his nation. "I would be content," he declared, "with a Europe divided between the Anglo-Americans and the Russians with Germany disappearing so that there would be no threat of war."

War Criminals

A war criminal, according to Pinkenburg, was "anyone who used force as the means of obtaining his will." The top leaders, he insisted, must be hauled before an international court. Other criminals should be returned for judgment to the countries in which they committed their crimes. Even the hurrah shouters who now hasten to change their loyalties should do forced labor. "The one-hundred percenters are incurable." The Allies, he insisted, had a responsibility to publicize both in Germany and in other countries the atrocities in the concentration camps. German heavy industry, which had profiteered under the Nazis, especially during the war years, he believed, should be rebuilt but kept under careful supervision.

A war criminal Greck defined as "one who has done wrong to people, who has not carried out the precepts of Christianity. I include among them those who attacked the Jews. I had the opportunity to see what the Germans did in the Poznan and Litzmannstadt [Lodz] ghettos. Those who participated in such activities are war criminals." On the other hand, repeating a standard German rationale, Greck excused those who committed atrocities under orders. The military commandant in Litzmannstadt, for example, expressed to him his shame for the atrocities taking place in the ghetto. "The common soldier who shot Jews under orders," Greck insisted, "is no war criminal unless he went out of his way to be brutal." He estimated that at least ten percent of the German population shared in the Nazi guilt. The German people, Greck asserted, did not want the war criminals shot but to be set to hard labor for the rest of their lives under conditions similar to those the Jews and other peoples suffered.

"We must appear before the United Nations with an admission of our total impotence and petition for the reconstruction of a unified Germany capable of contributing productively to the rest of the world," proclaimed the deputy mayor. "The militarists must be deprived of pensions. If they are sentenced to productive labor, they will have no time to prepare for war." (Not wanting to be a "little man" under the Nazis, Greck joined the Party. Now by saying what he thought Americans wanted to hear he was seeking to guarantee that he would not be a little man.)

Stammler's definition of a war criminal was broader than Greck's. "They include," he said, "not only those who promoted the war, but also those who believed in and practiced a policy of force." Most of the population, he declared, was aware of atrocities committed in other lands since almost every able-bodied man served in the army. Generally, people held the Party, the SS, and the Gestapo responsible for acts of terror. "People await a reckoning with these people," exclaimed Stammler.

All the leaders, including the former Oberbuergermeister, must be tried as criminals since they forced the population to fight to the last in an obviously hopeless struggle. The bigwigs must be pursued and captured and then either executed or sent to forced labor in Russia. The Bonzen [big shots] should be shipped off to Siberia with no possibility of ever returning. The small fry must be kept under surveillance.

(In his uncompromising call for severe punishment of war criminals and denazification of German society, Stammler proved unique among not only the Germans I interviewed but among many Americans I encountered as well.)

The Russians

Pinkenburg harbored no anxiety regarding the Russians

as long as there is a treaty between the three great powers. . . . As a German, I put my faith in cooperation with England and America. I think that war may break out if the English and Americans give the Russians a free hand. But that will not occur immediately. There is always a danger from the Russians. They have shown that they can develop an industry capable of mounting a war against the Western powers.

Greck professed to having no fear of the Russians, but the longer he spoke the more he betrayed his assimilation of Nazi racism.

I admire the capabilities of the Russians, but our outlook is more like yours. You and the English will unite, and France will have to follow. We should align ourselves with you because the future conflict will be between the white and yellow races. [He considered the Russians to be Asiatics.] I favor unification of all the white races into a great Rotary Club in which all men will enjoy justice regardless of their status in society.

Abruptly realizing that he was mouthing Goebbels's propaganda, Greck hesitated and then added, "I know the Russians so little. I have read nothing to inform me about them."

"There is a general belief," Stammler admitted, "that the Russians will take revenge for what the SS did in their country." In Breslau, he reported, when the Russians reached the gates of the city, people were amazed that Russian planes flew over the city without bombing or strafing. Stammler heard people express regret that they had fled before the Russians instead of remaining in their homes. He believed that Germans had a greater fear than of the Russians:"a recurrence of the runaway inflation that wiped out savings after World War I and brought widespread suffering and unemployment."

Political Parties

"The government will have to limit the number of parties," remarked Pinkenburg. There should be a balance of parties on the left and the right." Greck was of the opinion that the occupation powers should authorize only parties which accepted responsibility for reparations and were prepared to promote a domestic economy in which everyone would find work suitable to his station. The Social Democratic Party, he said, would certainly fit such criteria. "The difficulty with the Communist Party," he declared, "is that every member has a different conception of communism. The party should include only those who are dedicated to an ideal. With such a criterion for membership, I would join the Communist Party immediately."

Ernst Seifert

My first Pg interviewee, recommended by a cooperative American counterintelligence officer, was Ernst Seifert, a stauncher Nazi than any I interviewed in Mainz. I questioned him in the Wuerzburg municipal prison, where he was awaiting trial.² "From 1921 I was a member of the Stahlhelm [a nationalistic paramilitary organization]," he recounted. "When the Stahlhelm merged with the SA, I went along. The reconstruction of Germany was our aim. National Socialism brought socialism and a sense of a folk community [*Volksgemeinschaft*]." Like Deputy Mayor Greck, Seifert was convinced of the validity of the Nazi racial theories. "Other countries," he asserted, "must investigate whether these theories are appropriate for their conditions."

The Jews? Had they not been in Germany for many centuries?

"Yes, but blood is stronger than other considerations." Seifert did not approve, or so he said, of the methods employed to rid Germany of its Jewish population. "I myself," he insisted, "did nothing but observe. I did not profiteer on Jewish property as I have been accused of doing." As far as Seifert knew, the only inmates of the concentration camps were *"Volksschaedlinge"* (antisocial elements). No, he did not apply that term to Jews.

Seifert had no conception of German actions in the East beyond what he read. His eighteen-year-old son left in November for military service somewhere on the Eastern Front. Seifert had not heard from him since January. Before then, his son wrote nothing about German relations with the civilian populations.

"We have known since 1920," Seifert declared, "that we would have to have it out with Russia. As a result, I have always advocated a powerful German army. Adolf Hitler tried to reach an understanding with England since he believed that the English were also a Germanic people. We had no such tie with the French." Seifert had no idea why the Americans had come to Europe. "In the papers we read that they have come to fight for freedom, but we do not feel oppressed in Germany. The war criminals are those who attacked Germany on the pretext of liberating it. Churchill is one of them." As for the current situation on the battle fronts, Seifert asserted, "It is not clear when the war will end. The Russians are advancing deep into Germany. The danger of bolshevism is great for America."

"You know very well," I countered, "that Hitler is our enemy and the Russians are our allies. I'm asking you when you think the war against Hitler will be over."

"That is not clear," he insisted. "When I heard the Fuehrer's speech on 1 March I said that he had always been right, and I believe he will be right about victory."

"But you are not answering the question!"

2. See appendix 15, p. 196, for a reprint of Seifert's arrest report.

"It's hard to say just when open conflict [between the Western Allies and the Soviet Union] will begin."

What was the reason for continuing the war now that all the German cities had been destroyed and further fighting would merely mean increased suffering?

"We don't know the reason for the continuation of the war. We have always trusted the Fuehrer. When Hitler says that we must fight for survival and freedom, we must obey. Even in America people do not understand the real plans of their leaders."

Seifert expressed surprise at learning that it was permissible for Germans to listen to German radio in Allied occupied territories. "I suppose," he commented, disconcerted, "that you feel that you have nothing to fear from the truth, and the German radio always tells the truth."

Asked what he anticipated would be his fate, Seifert replied that with the critical shortage of physicians, doctors would be freed sooner than other prisoners.

"And Siberia?" (I was repeating the scare tactic I had employed a week earlier in Mainz with the Nazi bridgebuilder.)

Seifert hesitated and wiped his brow. "The enemy has the power," he admitted, "to send us to Siberia, but I think that you will have to take into consideration the age of prisoners. If I were sent to Siberia, I would not last three weeks."

Heinrich Schramm

I interrogated my second Nazi, Heinrich Schramm, two days after he was picked up by the CIC. "In appearance," I wrote in my report, "this SS man looks harmless enough. He is skinny, small, bespectacled—a mouse." Forty-four years old, with a doctorate in economics, Schramm claimed that he had been forced to join the NSDAP on 1 January 1940. In October of that year he was inducted into the SS. In November 1944 he was released from his post at the Reichssicherheitshauptamt (the headquarters of the National Security Service) when a neurologist attested that he was indeed ailing and not malingering, as his superiors charged.

Schramm offered as evidence of his anti-nazism the fact that while he had been compelled to leave the Catholic Church, his wife remained and his child was secretly baptized. "As you can see in this devastated city, the Nazis have done nothing but lie and betray." He had read official reports about the critical national economic conditions and then heard the economics official Albert Speer announce on the radio that all necessary war materials were available in abundance. What was especially shocking during the last days, he insisted in an obvious attempt at ingratiating himself, was the Nazi propaganda accusing the Americans of atrocities. "I am happy that because of you Americans," he said, "I am able to express my thoughts without fear."

"A war criminal," Schramm declared, "is one who attacks other peoples and ruins and lies to his own." He was convinced that only a small percentage of the German population remained dedicated Party members, "perhaps five percent."

Schramm expressed ignorance of the Russians, but he had advised his wife to remain in Vienna though it was in the path of the Red Army. "I think they probably have a disciplined army," he declared hopefully.

Stefan Schaeffer, an Anti-Nazi Worker

In contrast to that Nazi weasel, Stefan Schaeffer, a burly blond, genial, inarticulate worker, inspired hope for benighted Germany. Schaeffer had not been invited to join the Party because as a devout Catholic he was considered politically unreliable. From 1939 through 1941 he was drafted three times into the Wehrmacht and discharged each time after brief service. (Presumably, with his limited intelligence he had difficulty in carrying out orders.) In September 1942 he was assigned to guard duty at an annex to the Wuerzburg prison holding forced laborers and POWs.

On Good Friday, shortly before the arrival of the Americans, Brigade Fuehrer Naumann, inspector-general of the Security Police of North Bavaria, came to Wuerzburg with another high SS officer, a Dr. Riess, to consolidate Wuerzburg police units under SS command. The next day Vulkel, the commandant of the prison and chief of the local Gestapo, informed Schaeffer that a decision had been taken to blow up the prison along with the prisoners upon the arrival of the Americans. Fifty kilos of dynamite were delivered to the prison, and holes for explosives thirty centimeters deep and fifteen centimeters wide were dug in four corners of the central corridor.

Schaeffer informed some French prisoners of Vulkel's plan and advised them to tell the other prisoners to flee. During the night with Schaeffer's connivance about thirty-five of the seventy-five prisoners escaped, including twenty-two Russian officers. Vulkel, Schaeffer related with glee, was furious. "How could this happen?" he shouted. He abandoned the plan to blow up the prison.

Schaeffer related to his wife what he had done, and they fled to a nearby village to hide until the arrival of the Americans.

In both Mainz and Wuersburg MG officers, ignorant of the German language and German history, focused their efforts on clearing the rubble and restoring the utilities. In Mainz they appointed an ultranationalist to serve as Oberbuergermeister; in Wuerzburg, in blatant defiance of a SHAEF directive, they selected as deputy mayor a Pg who had profiteered under the Nazi regime and mouthed Nazi racist teachings. Indeed, the Nazi physician Seifert, like the bridgebuilder Haertner in Mainz, appeared justified in his expectation that the Americans would employ specialists, regardless of their political histories, to "get things moving." A hopeful sign for the future was Oberbuergermeister Pinkenburg's declaration that for the reconstruction of his devastated city he would mobilize the labor potential of the region, both intellectual and manual. I had heard no similar statement from any other informant—or from any MG officer—although the thought was implicit in Michel Oppenheim's insistence that the Communists be invited to participate in the Mainz municipal administration.

An Experience with Soviet Repatriation

At Colonel Richman's request I accompanied Nikolai, a Soviet liaison lieutenant, to a small DP assembly center to persuade a group of Balts (Lithuanians, Estonians, and Latvians) to return home. An American lieutenant of Polish extraction assembled the DPs in a small auditorium. "These people," he declared to me, "are adamant in resisting transportation to their homelands. Almost all of them want to go to America, and I'll do what I can to help them get there."

"You speak to them," said Nikolai, who retired to a chair in the rear of the small stage. Bewildered by his request, I asked for a show of hands of those who did not want to return home. Every hand shot up. "After Nazi captivity, what could you desire more," I asked, taken aback by the unanimity of the response, "than to return to the villages where you grew up and went to school, where your parents are buried?"

"You know nothing of what we have suffered?" cried a man. Shouts erupted in the room:"Stalin killed my brother! . . . Stalin seized our farm and left us to starve. Where are my parents? Tell me, where are they? . . . Stalin will kill us if we go back!"[3]

I looked to Nikolai. He refused to meet my eyes.

"If you accompanied us back to our homes, that would be different," someone declared quietly. Others nodded.

"You are the Soviet repatriation officer, not I," I exclaimed as I left with Nikolai.

"Artoor," he replied, "how could I answer them? Members of my family have disappeared. I myself have been hounded by the secret police. I know that what they were saying is true, and they know that I know that it is true."

3. The group consisted only of old men, women, and children. It occurred to me after the meeting that I should have asked where the young men were. Were they serving in the Wehrmacht or in Balt SS units?

8

"What We Russians Like to Consider as a Typical American"

On 25 April units of the 69th Division of First Army linked up with the Russians at Torgau on the Elbe. With the end of hostilities imminent and a shake-up in assignments certain to follow at PW headquarters, I returned to Luxembourg only to be informed that the PW unit had recently moved to Bad Nauheim, an undamaged spa a few miles to the north of Frankfurt. Setting out from Luxembourg the next morning, I came upon some GIs setting up a barrier at a detour. During the night Germans had removed a barricade before a destroyed bridge, and an American vehicle had raced ahead and dropped to its destruction. The Werewolf sabotage Goebbels had threatened!

I found Colonel Powell haggard and broken, an old man. One of his sons had died at the front—only days before the imminent termination of hostilities. He nodded in silence at my expression of sympathy. "What are you going to do now that the war is coming to an end?" he asked at length.

I replied that I would like to be involved somehow with the Russians.

"What about intelligence work against the Japanese?" he asked.

"One war," I declared, "is enough for one lifetime." The colonel nodded in agreement.

OSS had sent word that I was to report to Paris for discussion of a postwar assignment. Colonel Powell, however, was loath to release me. Upon the German surrender, 12th Army Group Psychological Warfare, as the 12th Army Group PW history records, was to be

reconstituted internally in order to perform more efficiently new duties of control of German information services . . . press, news agencies, publications, radio broadcasting . . . films, musical performances . . . opera, theaters and other public entertainment. . . . The greatest single task of a nonmilitary nature to face the victorious Allied armies on their last thrust through German territory was the collection, processing, care and repatriation of about 4,000,000 liberated foreign workers . . . and it became the responsibility of Psychological Warfare Detachments in the field to assist . . . in an attempt to control the flow of these peoples.

In accordance with this latter responsibility, Colonel Powell insisted that I undertake further intelligence investigations among Russian DPs.

Learning that at a DP assembly center outside Darmstadt large-scale preparations were under way for a May Day celebration, I saw an opportunity for preparing a program for Radio Luxembourg and for investigating conditions at the assembly point.

"So you're Artoor!" exclaimed the Soviet commandant, Col. Stepan Danilovich Kompanyeyets, upon my arrival on 30 April at a vast caserne. (A visiting Red Army major, a representative of the Soviet Repatriation Mission, had urged him to be on the lookout for me.) The colonel put a young man named Lonya (Leonid) at my disposal to assist in drafting an account of the festive May Day events.[1]

Patrick Gordon Walker, a director of Radio Luxembourg (subsequently Minister of Colonies in the postwar Attlee Labor government), approved a broadcast of a description of the Darmstadt May Day celebration. From my notes I quickly completed an account. Lonya and I translated it into Russian, and Lonya recorded the report for broadcast the very next day.[2]

Before I departed from Luxembourg (I had to return Lonya to Darmstadt before nightfall), Gordon Walker and I enjoyed some minutes of conversation. That very day, 2 May, after a ferocious struggle in which some 300,000 Russians lost their lives, the last defenders of Berlin surrendered. Glancing at Lonya, Gordon Walker asked, "What does your friend think awaits him when he returns home?"

Lonya apparently caught the drift of the question. "What did he say?" he demanded.

Taken aback by Lonya's dismay, I did not translate Gordon Walker's question, replying instead with a spur-of-the-moment invention.

Lonya was not satisfied with my response, but he did not press me further.

Still insisting that I ignore the OSS order recalling me to Paris, Colonel Powell dispatched me to Regensburg, a city close to the Czech border, to investigate the situation of DPs in a region just captured by our forces. Sitting with other Americans in the lobby of a Regensburg hotel, I heard a radio report of the unconditional surrender of the Germans and a proclamation by General Eisenhower of the next day as VE Day. Driving back to Bad Nauheim, I was bewildered at the sight of Germans lining the road and waving and smiling. They had anticipated until the last minute that Hitler might use a terrible weapon that would not only wipe us out but destroy them, too. The Werewolf activity they had feared was ordered discontinued by Radio Flensberg, the last functioning Nazi radio station. Now they were thinking that all that had stood between us was forgotten.

---

1. In 1941, along with hundreds of other Moscow university students, Lonya had marched out to the front to defend the city. He was captured and spent four years in Germany as a forced laborer.
2. In appendix 16, p. 196, I present a precis of this broadcast.

At the PW unit I did not encounter unbounded exuberance. For us the war was not over; we had not yet achieved for "why we fight."

During my brief May Day visit to the Darmstadt DP assembly center, I recognized the usefulness of a report on the organization and life at the Darmstadt assembly center to provide posterity with a sense of an important aspect of events during the last months of the war and immediately after victory. On 14 May I returned to Darmstadt. The Russian DPs, I discovered, had heard the Radio Luxembourg broadcast of the description of their May Day celebration.

"Now Moscow knows about us," exclaimed one man to me.

"You can't imagine how much it means to us who were not even allowed to listen to the radio under the Germans," declared another, "to have our own activities described and praised over the air."[3]

Upon the capture of Darmstadt on 25 March, Colonel Kompanyeyets recounted, American Seventh Army units assembled into the Wehrmacht barracks liberated prisoners of war and forced laborers of many nationalities. On 3 April Major Peryegudov of the Soviet Repatriation Mission arrived and arranged that the barracks be assigned exclusively to Soviet citizens. He appointed Kompanyeyets commandant and selected officers to serve on Kompanyeyets's staff. Six weeks later, in mid-May, the population of the camp had swelled to about 6,000 men and 3,000 women over eighteen years of age along with 800 children, including 70 orphans.

With an officer assigned as my guide, I toured the main building of the caserne—storage areas, clubrooms, theaters, a large ballroom, and a workroom for the camp painting crew. A red flag hung outside the building, and on the walls of the other buildings were displayed enormous portraits of Stalin. Slogans painted on banners were repeated from building to building: "Death to the Fascist Invaders," "The Friendship of the Three Great Peoples of England, the United States and the Soviet Union Ensured the Total Defeat of Fascist Germany," "Honor and Glory to those who died for the freedom and independence of the Fatherland." On each floor lists were posted of the outstanding residents as well as of those delinquent in carrying out their responsibilities.

The population was enrolled into regiments and battalions, and in every barracks a detailed activities schedule established how the units were to be

---

3. I had persuaded Gordon Walker to transmit over Radio Luxembourg personal messages from one Russian assembly center to another. Now I watched as a crowd awaited the broadcast of such greetings. With a shiver of excitement, men and women hushed each other in order not to miss a word. A typical message ran as follows:"V era Semyonova Voronkova heard her brother Paul speak on the radio from Berlin. She wants to inform him that she is alive and is now at the Soviet assembly center in Darmstadt. Also she wants to thank the American Army and its command for her liberation from fascist slavery."

engaged from 6:00 A.M. until curfew at 23:30. I watched several companies drilling, marching swinging arms, stiff-legged, and chanting under the prompting of NCOs verses of the "Song of Voroshilov." At a far end of the grounds, a battalion of young women attended a lecture by a young sergeant on the Blitzkrieg, an explanation of the German success in France as against the German repulse in the Soviet Union. "All this time," I heard him say, "our British and American allies were preparing their armies to help us to deliver the final blow. On 6 June they struck. From the moment of their landing, it was clear that the combined might of the great allies would soon bring total defeat to Fascist Germany."

The principal of the camp school, Tov Klopov, had set up first-, second-, third-, and fourth-grade classes. Only six texts were available for the classes, a history book, a reader, a second-grade text, a geography book, a copy of Pushkin's poetry, and another of Tolstoy's short stories. Teachers served as surrogate parents to the seventy orphans, some of whom had seen their homes burned and their parents shot before their eyes. They related with no sense of their own heroism stories of extraordinary personal endurance. A thirteen-year-old as diminutive as an American eight-year-old had walked seventy-five miles until he met American soldiers. "Did you go all this way by yourself?" I asked. "No," he replied, "I was with my brother." He pointed to a nine-year-old, as puny as a five-year-old.

I was shown a composition entitled "My Recollections" in which Anatoly Epifanov, a stunted twelve-year-old, related daunting experiences he had endured during the previous four years.[4]

Colonel Kompanyeyets reported that people in the camp were complaining of the lack of variety and the poor quality of the food. "All Colonel Shorthouse [the doddering English United Nations Relief and Rehabilitation Agency (UNRRA) representative] talks about," he said, mimicking Shorthouse's prim English, "is 'sanitation, sanitation.' Let him get the Germans to remove the huge pile of garbage and manure from the courtyard, and our people will clean up the rest. Let him find us medicines, beds, plumbing materials, disinfectant, proper food for the children, dental care, then we'll have 'sanitation.'

As the colonel was delivering his litany of despair, an American sergeant appeared at the door. He reported that Brig. Gen. Doyle O. Hickey, the commander of the newly arrived Third Armored Division, desired to learn of conditions in this camp.[5] I consulted with Kompanyeyets and then asked

---

4. See in appendix 17, pp. 196–97.
5. Actually, the sergeant burst into the room, and seeing my uniform, snapped, "You speak Russian?" I nodded. "Is this guy the commander here?"

"Sergeant," I responded, "this *guy* is an allied officer, a colonel, and he is to be addressed according

the sergeant to convey to the general a request from the Soviet commandant for a meeting. The sergeant returned within minutes to announce that the general would send a jeep for the colonel early the next morning.

The next morning Colonel Kompanyeyets, Colonel Shorthouse, and I were ushered into the divisional command quarters. Colonel Kompanyeyets saluted, and I introduced him. The general reeled off a series of astute questions designed to obtain a quick insight into camp conditions. Upon being told that in order not to render more difficult the living conditions of the local Germans MG officials were withholding critically needed supplies from the Russians, the general exploded. "If I knew," he thundered, "that there were Russian DPs living in these conditions in other parts of Germany, I would march off with my division to liberate them." He saw no reason, either, why Russians should continue to live cooped up within the barracks grounds, granted only twenty passes daily for entering the city while German civilians moved about freely. Colonel Kompanyeyets, however, declined the offer of unlimited passes. Outside the camp, he declared, he had no control over his people. Germans complained of being beaten in their homes and of the disappearance of cattle and sheep.

Studying a large-scale wall map, the general declared, "I see that there's a large field outside the barracks, can you use it?" The colonel replied that it would be excellent for the military drills with which he kept a large percentage of the young men occupied every day. The general signed to his adjutant, who was seated at his side with pad and pencil.

The general said that he would appreciate receiving a list of the most critical supplies required by the colonel. I handed him five typewritten pages, for Kompanyeyets, his two adjutants, and I had prepared a comprehensive list the previous afternoon. The general skimmed through the pages and handed the sheaf to his adjutant.

The colonel asked me to call the general's attention to the problem of the moldy, inedible bread delivered by the German bakery. The general scowled. His adjutant was to inform the Oberbuergermeister of Darmstadt that henceforth edible bread was to be delivered in sufficient quantity and with regularity to the Soviets. Indeed, local food stocks, he instructed his adjutant, were to be assigned to the Russians ahead of the Germans. "And see to it that the mayor gets the kind of warning that Germans understand," the general added. He ordered an inventory of medical supplies in the city. The Russians were to enjoy priority in this instance, too.

---

to his rank. I suggest that you leave this room and upon returning display the kind of military courtesy that is to be expected from a sergeant in addressing an officer."

The sergeant saluted, turned about and left the room. He knocked on the door.

"Enter," I replied. He came in, saluted briskly, stood at attention and gave his report.

"What is the colonel's most pressing single problem?" the general asked.

Kompanyeyets replied without hesitation, "Morale." After being liberated from the Nazis, the Russian men, women, and children found themselves cooped up in a hated country in overcrowded conditions, uncertain about their future. The general made no reply. He rose, announced that he would make an inspection of the camp the next morning, saluted Kompanyeyets and Shorthouse, shook my hand and nodded to his adjutant to show us out.

Shorthouse had said not a word throughout the discussion. As we walked to our jeeps, he remarked, "Maybe at last we will be the beneficiaries of the renowned American efficiency."

Kompanyeyets made no report to his staff of the meeting with General Hickey. He wanted to see whether the morning's conference would actually bring results.

He had not long to wait.

Early that afternoon men from the Third Division signal corps arrived with captured German communications equipment. At my urging, Major Voinov sent Soviet technicians to join the Americans in installing the public address and intramural telephone systems. Walking among the teams of workers, I found the GIs and the Russians attempting to communicate, slapping each other on the back and laughing together. "These are good guys, and they know what they're doing," one GI assured me. When I translated his remark, the Russians were overjoyed.

Suddenly we heard from the distance the sound of martial music. The sound grew louder, and the colonel and I hurried out to the parade grounds. Through the main gate of the barracks marched General Hickey's divisional band. They were playing "The Stars and Stripes Forever," advertising their nationality with a march recognized throughout the world. Men and women, some dragging eager children behind them, raced to the parade grounds. Others climbed out of windows or seated themselves on the sloping roofs of the barracks. When the band finished the march, people signaled their delight in the synchronized applause common in the Soviet Union. Others whistled. A man explained that they had heard that Americans whistled at baseball games and assumed that that was the way Americans showed their appreciation. Some people began to cry. Even the colonel, always reticent about expressing emotion, bit his lip.

"Why are you sad?" I asked.

"We're not sad," he replied, "but after being tortured and humiliated for years by the Nazis, now for the first time we are serenaded by an American band. An event like this proves to us that we are really free."

The next morning, 16 May, Kompanyeyets and his aides and I hastened to the caserne gate upon notification that the general and his escort were approaching. We began a tour of the barracks immediately. The general expressed dissatisfaction with the overcrowded sleeping quarters and the inadequacy of toilets, showers, and kitchen facilities. At every building the Russian officer of the day begged him to inspect the quarters thoroughly, and the general delayed our progress in response. The colonel, too, was eager to provide detailed information at every stop, and General Hickey listened patiently to my often clumsy translations. He expressed interest in everything, asking me to translate headlines on wall newspapers and titles of political lectures.

Accustomed to the strict discipline in the Red Army and the equally strict discipline among their German captors, the Russians were astonished by the general's informality.

"He's a general?" an incredulous officer asked.

"Yes," I replied, "he's an American general."

The general expressed admiration for the efficient organization of the population into regiments, battalions, and companies, the establishment under the most primitive conditions of kindergartens, schools, and clinics, as well as the involvement of the camp inhabitants from morning to night in a variety of activities and responsibilities: concerts, athletic contests, and cleanup details. "I'm not surprised at what I'm seeing," he confided to me, "since I know that only a capable people could have accomplished what the Russians have done on the battlefield." When he was about to depart, he instructed me to express to Kompanyeyets his admiration for the efficiency with which he had organized the camp.

"We now know," declared Kompanyeyets, "that anything we do not receive from the Americans we will lack because it is not available, not because no attempt has been made to obtain it. This is a military man one can rely on. He is what we like to consider as a typical American."

That afternoon trucks arrived loaded with cot beds and mattresses, medical supplies and sports equipment along with a consignment of Army C-rations. This time the colonel did not need prompting to send out a detachment of his own men to help the GIs with the unloading. A few hours later the division signal corps arrived with a portable screen and showed a film outdoors to an enthusiastic crowd. They promised to return at the same hour every day.

The next morning the Oberbuergermeister of Darmstadt dispatched wagons to cart away a huge manure pile in the central courtyard. Immediately thereafter a work crew of some 2,000 Russians armed with shovels and rakes began a thorough cleaning of the grounds.

The colonel was hungry for news of the world, and he questioned me in detail on all kinds of subjects. An officer listening to our discussions declared that the people in the camp would be grateful if I would meet with groups to answer similar questions. It was agreed that he would assemble officers from different brigades for such discussions. Among my papers I preserved two official documents written in neat script, one dated 15 May and the other 19 May in which brigades thanked me for these discussions.[6]

Returning to the camp on 22 May, I saw a line of American Army trucks drawn up on the parade grounds. GI drivers with good-natured generosity were assisting Russians to board with their bundles. Embarking on a different journey from the one they had endured in German cattle cars years earlier, the Russians decorated the trucks with green branches, pictures of Stalin, red flags, and banners with slogans, one of which read, "We thank our American liberators."[7]

---

6. See appendix 18, pp. 197–98. During my trip to the Soviet Union in May 1990, I met a Ukrainian who at the age of eighteen had attended one of these Darmstadt discussions. He remembered that he and his colleagues had had one pressing question:when would they return home? I had answered, he said, that with the war just having ended and all kinds of problems to be resolved, they would have to wait a few weeks. "And you were right," he declared, "for within days contingents from the camp were on their way to Berlin."

7. In 1990 upon the publication of an article about my encounters with Soviets in a popular Russian magazine and subsequently my being interviewed on the television program *Panorama*—comparable to our *60 Minutes*—I was put in contact with Andrei, whom I had liberated from the POW camp; the son of Seenya, the political commissar in Luxembourg; Colonel Kompanyeyets's daughter, as well as other Russians and Ukrainians who remembered me from the events of almost a half century earlier. Andrei wrote: "I maintain a happy memory of you and thank you for your participation in my destiny. . . . Sometimes I have difficulty in believing that all that happened was real." I visited Seenya's son in Donetz in the Ukraine and learned that Seenya had been sent for several years to a gulag upon returning to the Soviet Union. He never spoke thereafter about his experiences in Germany.

Kompanyeyets's daughter wrote:"I regret that my father did not live to experience your visit to the Soviet Union." She reported that upon his return to the Soviet Union he had been sent to a gulag at the eastern extremity of Siberia. After his release he never spoke of his war experiences. I sent her a copy of the report I had drafted on the Darmstadt assembly point. One day in July 1995 I received a telephone call from Kompanyeyets's grandson, Alexander, who was leading an excursion of fellow factory workers to the United States! Alexander invited me to join his group at the Odessa nightclub in the Little Russia section of Brooklyn. He had told his companions about me, and I was given an affectionate welcome.

PART II: POLICY CLASH IN MILITARY GOVERNMENT

9
"Crack Patton's Military Government Wide Open!"
SUMMER 1945

At Bad Nauheim an OSS major was waiting to conduct me to headquarters. Arriving in Paris I discovered that no one knew of an assignment for me. I applied at other agencies, playing one against another until finally I was notified that within weeks I would be offered an OSS post that would keep me in contact with the Russians.

Awaiting word, I returned to my PW unit in Germany. Morale there was low because of uncertainty about future responsibilities. People expressed their frustration against the Germans, both in words and actions.[1] One evening, as we were relaxing on the verandah of our hotel watching wounded, convalescent German soldiers strolling past, Colonel Powell shoved back his chair and strode into the lobby, muttering, "Goddamn these bastards. I hate these people." He had spent a year of life in war against the Nazis and with the battlefield death of his son, he had, in addition, the most profound justification for hatred of Nazis and nazism.

Ordered after three weeks to report to OSS headquarters in Wiesbaden, a city about thirty miles from Bad Nauheim, I once again discovered that no specific assignment awaited me. I was uncomfortable among colleagues who never discussed German denazification or democratization but were obsessed with finding ways to thwart and weaken the Soviet Union.[2] At length I was offered a post in a group charged with organizing an espionage network in the Russian-occupied area of Germany. I had no desire to participate in a hostile operation against an ally through whose valor and sacrifices the might of Nazi Germany had been shattered. Above all, for me and my PW colleagues the war against Hitler had not ended at VE Day and would not end until the elimination of Nazism and Prussian militarism. In that struggle I saw my—our—continuing responsibility. I was confirmed in this convic-

---

1. A politically unsophisticated lieutenant, a hefty six-footer, boasted how he had pushed a German cripple, a veteran, flat on his back into the street—"Damn kraut, didn't know enough to get out of my way. Who the hell do they think won the war anyhow?"

2. With much free time, on 23 June I drove to Darmstadt to visit General Hickey, all the Russians having been repatriated. I related to him the astonishment of the Russians at his simplicity and quoted Kompanyeyets's praise. "I'd like to add a personal remark," I continued. "When I see that we have generals like you, I am even prouder to be an American." We discussed the "Polish problem." I described a recent visit to the PW unit of a group of some sixty-five Polish women soldiers captured by the Germans after the abortive Warsaw uprising. "I have never seen such hate," I declared, "as these women harbor for the Russians." They applauded when an American lieutenant of Polish extraction assured them that there would soon be a war with the USSR, certain to be a pushover. On a prior occasion I sharply rebuked a Polish liaison colonel when he expressed confidence that the United States would go to war to satisfy Polish territorial pretensions.

tion by the knowledge that my concerns were shared by General Hickey and by Colonel Powell.

Careful not to rouse suspicions regarding my sentiments, I made a pretense at naiveté, asking, "Why can't we simply approach the Russians directly if we have questions about developments in their occupation zone?"

I telephoned Al Toombs. "Well, old pal," Toombs replied, "if that's the way they treat you, you just come right back here."

Thus after little more than two weeks of renewed association with the OSS, I returned to my old outfit, which had just received new directives with which I felt at ease.[3]

Since the Sweet-Padover exposé in January 1945 of MG's appointment of Nazis to high positions in Aachen in violation of SHAEF directives, Psychological Warfare headquarters had been receiving reports not merely of MG officials throughout the American Zone appointing Nazis and militarists to posts of authority but also of their rejecting anti-Nazis for administrative positions.[4] In town after town frontline officers appointed Kzler (the abbreviation for former concentration-camp inmates) and other proven anti-Nazis to positions of authority only to see their appointees dismissed by MG officials arriving after the troops moved on.[5]

After visiting the newly liberated Dachau concentration camp, General Eisenhower ordered displayed in every military detachment posters with the caption "Whose Guilt?" and pictures of emaciated skeletons and piles of corpses. Nevertheless, few MG officers provided special help to liberated Kzlers or appointed them to official positions.[6]

With the collapse of German resistance in the spring of 1945, SHAEF faced a critical shortage of trained military government personnel, and MG detachments were overwhelmed by the catastrophic destruction and disrup-

---

3. See appendix 19, p. 198, for the directives.

4. See appendix 20, p. 199, for the description in *Betrayal* of how the radical changes demanded by Eisenhower after the Sweet-Padover exposé were ignored by MG officials in Aachen.

5. In Schaeftlarn, for example, the commanding officer of the unit that captured the Bavarian village appointed a Kzler as town commissioner. Two weeks later, when the Kzler announced that he was going to clear all Party members out of the local administration and hold them accountable for funds collected by the Party welfare agency, Nazis denounced him to the newly arrived MG lieutenant as a "Communist." The MG lieutenant dismissed the man from his post while allowing the mayor, a Party member since 1933, to remain in office. The Kzler unsuccessfully petitioned for reinstatement, noting, incidentally, that he had been imprisoned by the Nazis not as a Communist but as a Social Democrat.

"The combat troops in this instance as in many others captured the town," I commented in *Betrayal*, "and the MG officer lost it again, and the 'bolshevik bogey' once more was the cause of our retreat."

6. In appendix 21, pp. 198–99, I reprint a letter dated 5 June, one month after VE Day, from Captain Shrank, MG commandant in a rural county, to his wife describing his compassionate treatment of a returning Kzler.

tion of services in communities.[7] Of course, not all MG officers put "getting things moving" ahead of carrying out the Allied war aims. On 9 May, ten days after the U.S. Seventh Army captured Dachau, the site of the infamous concentration camp, Capt. Malcolm Vendig, the local military governor, granted permission for organizational activity to a group calling itself "the Anti-Fascists of Germany" and claiming a membership of 4,000. Explaining his action, Vendig declared that the group had proved helpful in restoring order and in weeding out Nazis. On 13 June Vendig licensed the group as the first political party in the American occupation zone.

Two days later Col. Charles Keegan, deputy military governor of Bavaria, ordered Vendig to dissolve the Anti-Fascist Party. "The Germans," the colonel declared, "are a conquered people and have no right to demand anything."

A general on Patton's staff boasted to Colonel Powell that as military governor of Bavaria Patton obtained all intelligence he needed from American expatriates who had remained in Germany during the Hitler years. He saw no reason to permit PW Intelligence men "to snoop about" in his province. "Go down to Munich," the colonel instructed me and Egon Fleck (an Austrian émigré and an OSS civilian with whom I had worked earlier on assignments in France), "and dig up as much dirt as you can. I want to crack Patton's military government wide open. Let's put this son-of-a-bitch in his place."

The PW Intelligence unit in Munich had been dispatching reports critical of Military Government operations in Bavaria and exposing the domination of government and industry by Nazis and pro-Nazi reactionaries. There was word, too, not only of Patton's pampering SS internees with rations of 2,000 calories a day—more than people in the Western European countries formerly occupied by the Germans were enjoying, not to mention the people of devastated Eastern Europe—but also of his insisting upon their engaging in military exercises to maintain combat readiness.

On 5 July, approaching Munich, Fleck and I saw everywhere on round advertising posts, telephone poles, walls of buildings, and rubble heaps large posters displaying an appeal from the Oberbuergermeister to members of the Nazi Party to make good for what they had done while in power by charitable donations of clothing to former concentration-camp inmates. Here and there, two months after the fall of the city, signs with swastikas still advertised the "Voelkischer Beobachter," the official Nazi newspaper, and a telephone booth outside a government building bore the warning,

---

7. In appendix 22, pp. 199–200, I reprint a segment from *Betrayal* describing the selection of MG personnel and the attitude of GIs to them.

"Jews are forbidden to use this apparatus." In the center of the city prisoners of war in unfamiliar brown uniforms were shoveling rubble out of the streets and sorting bricks into piles—Hungarian soldiers, Hitler's last faithful allies, assigned by Patton the task of cleaning up the city. Germans, undoubtedly including Pgs, stood by watching the foreign POWs at work.

During the last days of the war, as Seventh Army units approached Munich, an Antifa operating under the name Freedom Action Bavaria seized the radio station and broadcast appeals to the citizenry to cooperate with the Americans. Besieged by the SS, the anti-Nazi rebels escaped with their lives only upon the timely arrival of American troops. Military Government, however, immediately ordered Freedom Action Bavaria dissolved. Echoing the sentiments of colleagues in Wuppertal and Leipzig, an MG major announced, "I met these antifascists in the Ruhr. They're all bandits."

In the chaos following upon the capture of this city of almost 600,000 inhabitants, the municipal administration ceased to function; the police force vanished; food distribution broke down; and some 30,000 DPs, survivors of the Vlassov army of Russian deserters or Balts who had served in special SS divisions along with Polish DPs, terrorized the inhabitants, attacking civilians on the streets, raping and looting.

One day shortly after his arrival the MG commandant was startled by the appearance at his headquarters of a Baron von Kassel, an emissary from Cardinal Faulhaber. "And when may I have an audience with his eminence?" inquired the colonel. The baron, as he subsequently related to one of our informants, was taken aback, for he had come with a petition from the cardinal for an interview with the supreme secular power in Bavaria. All Military Government was talking about how for days the colonel was unable to attend to his duties, so excited was he at his forthcoming audience.

And thus it was that Michael Cardinal von Faulhaber, Prince-Archbishop of Bavaria, assumed dominion in the city of Munich and the province of Bavaria. "The cardinal is the greatest man in Germany today," whispered his aged secretary as one of our intelligence men was leaving after an interview with the prelate.

Munich had a stormy post–World War I history as a stronghold of an antimilitarist, antichauvinist, and militant trade union radicalism as well as of nazism. In 1919 the city became the capital of a revolutionary Bavarian Republic, which after a brief three-month existence was crushed by the Freikorps.[8] The Nazis dubbed Munich, the site of their abortive 1923 putsch, "Capital City of the Movement."

---

8. Guerrilla bands of officers under the clandestine leadership of members of the German General Staff organized after World War I to defend the nation against "bolshevism" and to resist the occupation powers. In an orgy of terrorism and assassinations, they stamped out the 1919 German revolutionary movement.

Cardinal Faulhaber's stance in regard to the two political streams of recent Bavarian history was unambiguous. He denounced the short-lived revolutionary regime as "perfidy and high treason [which] . . . will go down in history forever with the mark of Cain." He condemned the subsequent Weimar Republic, the only democratic government Germany had ever known, as founded on "perjury and treason." A pastoral letter he addressed to the Catholics of Bavaria before the March 1933 elections was, according to *The Sentinels of the Church*, a church history published under the cardinal's auspices, "responsible for the defeat of the Bavarian People's [Catholic] Party] and the victory [of the Nazi Party] in Bavaria." At a church conclave at Fulda on 30 May 1933, two months after Hitler assumed dictatorial power, Faulhaber joined with the other Roman Catholic bishops of Germany in issuing a statement of support of the Nazi regime, declaring:"The bishop in this [Nazi] state . . . established on authoritarian principles is the . . . spiritual Fuehrer alongside the political Fuehrer."[9]

With Patton's encouragement, the cardinal and his collaborators proclaimed the slogan *"Ordnungszelle Bayern"*—Bavaria, Cell of Order. "Order" connoted reestablishment of "the good old days" of the Bavarian monarchy with a restoration of the privileges of the landed nobility, renewed respect for the officer caste, and a reinvigoration of an established church—a Bavarian state on the model of Franco Spain or Vichy France. Ordnungszelle Bayern had no place for radical anti-Nazis, and several civil servants we interrogated begged us not to reveal that they were Communists.

Ignoring OMGUS[10] denazification directives, MG officials appointed to important posts men the cardinal recommended as individuals of "high moral standing and positions of business and intellectual leadership, people of experience and of conservative reliability, who understand the particular Bavarian problems." For minister-president, the highest office in the province, the cardinal nominated and MG appointed Fritz Schaeffer, even though the PW Intelligence team in Munich assembled sufficient negative data about his past to disqualify him from political life.[11] Under Schaeffer's

---

9. The statement is reprinted in appendix 23, p. 200. In the spirit of this pronouncement, Faulhaber appealed to the Roman Catholic cardinals of New York and Chicago to pressure the American press to abate their attacks on Hitler. Although he resisted a Nazi takeover of church schools and Party restrictions on the activities of Catholic priests, Faulhaber never protested against the persecution of the Jews or spoke out against other Nazi atrocities. Indeed, Pfarrer Emil Muhler, dean of the parish priests of Munich, who had spent several years in a concentration camp because of his anti-Nazi pronouncements, confided to Fleck that "Faulhaber's influence and activity against the Nazis during the past twelve years is largely overrated."

10. With the end of hostilities and the division of Germany into Allied controlled zones, SHAEF was dissolved and replaced in the American Zone by the Office of Military Government (US), abbreviated commonly as OMGUS.

11. In 1933 as leader of the Catholic Bavarian People's Party fraction in the Reichstag, Schaeffer maneuvered his party's support of the Empowering Act of March 1933, under which Hitler, not yet commanding a majority among the deputies, was granted dictatorial power.

leadership, the government fell under the control of pre-1933 Bavarian People's Party (BVP) officials, former Party members and collaborators with the Nazis.[12]

As police president of Munich, the Social Democratic leadership proposed to recall from exile in Switzerland Freiherr von Godin, who as a lieutenant in the provincial police had ordered the firing on Hitler's storm troopers during the Nazi 1923 putsch. The cardinal's men, however, preferred Oberst von Seisser, deputy chief of staff of Wehrmacht High Command South during World War I. The seventy-two-year-old colonel filled the reconstituted police force with his own kind of people, derided as "Seisser men" by the population. When Fleck entered von Seisser's office, the old man hobbled from behind his desk to greet him. "I'm the man who shot at Hitler," he announced gleefully. (Even if that were true, and it was not, von Seisser's notoriety rested rather on his signing along with Hitler and the ultranationalist army officers von Ludendorff, von Kahr, and von Lossow the proclamation of the "National Socialist Government" at the time of the 1923 Hitler putsch.)[13]

While Fleck interrogated provincial and municipal officials and other dignitaries, I sought assistance at the headquarters of the Kzler. Outside the Kzler cooperative welfare agency I saw a long line of people waiting for identification cards or with requests for jobs, clothing, shelter, information about missing relatives or complaints about people who had denounced them to the Nazis still living in comfort while they were barely able to provide for themselves. Appeals for medical care were common, too, since most Kzler suffered from years of deprivation and torture and were in need of lengthy rest cures in sanatoria. Such care was almost nonexistent. *Sueddeutsche Zeitung*, a Munich paper published by the Psychological Warfare Operations subbranch, printed a letter to the editor in which a Dr. Karl Ruedrich of Ehrengutsstrasse 5, a survivor of Dachau, described his disillusionment with the inhuman treatment he suffered upon returning home to Munich.[14]

12. Even committed anti-Nazi Catholics were excluded from positions of authority. Baron Freiherr von Kassel, a spokesman for the cardinal, admitted to his neighbor, a city commissioner, that the cardinal had persuaded Fritz Schaeffer not to appoint to a post in the provincial government a renowned Catholic philosopher named Steuermann, who had suffered imprisonment in a concentration camp. Steuermann opposed church interference in politics and advocated a program of social change. Schaeffer made him president of the Bavarian Red Cross, a position in which he could "do no harm."

13. The police force of the borough of Freising continued to be dominated by Party members. A police officer arrested by the Americans for crimes against Polish workers demanded and regained his post after a brief imprisonment. A police sergeant denounced in 1934 by a Nazi police lieutenant and imprisoned for anti-Nazi activity was rehired as a subordinate to this very lieutenant.

Knighted by King Ludwig II of Bavaria during World War I for his services as chaplain to the royal divisions, Faulhaber displayed his sympathies with the old military caste by further recommending the appointment of Generals Pirner and Ranner, Colonel Kopfmueller and Lieutenant Colonel Lorneck, all former General Staff officers, to high posts in the Bavarian Ministry of Interior.

14. In appendix 24, pp. 200–201, I reprint this letter to the editor of the *Sueddeutsche Zeitung*, a Munich paper published by Psychological Warfare operations subbranch.

I did not have to harangue the people at the Kzler office to win their collaboration. Solicitation of their advice by an American was a novel and welcome experience. The next day, indeed, at their headquarters I found assembled some dozen men eager to assist me. They expressed indignation at seeing "the blacks" (the Roman Catholic clergy) swarming in provincial and municipal offices defending Nazis in denazification procedures or recommending Party members or collaborators with the Party for appointment to high positions. Rare, they declared, was the clergyman who intervened in aid of Kzler or other victims of nazism, and Patton's subordinates ignored or enforced without enthusiasm directives for providing housing and employment to the thousands of liberated concentration-camp inmates who made their way back to destroyed homes.

Although I suspected that many of these men at the Kzler headquarters were either Communists or Social Democrats, I was gratified to discover that among the people they suggested for interviews were clergymen and members of the Catholic Bavarian People's Party (BVP) and even of the pre-1933 German Nationalist Party. In our discussion I noted that they frequently turned to the only man present who had not served time in a concentration camp, a young lawyer named Alfred Kroth, who, indeed, offered particularly astute proposals. He had been infiltrated by the Communist Party, I subsequently learned, into the very office of the Nazi mayor of Munich and had recently been appointed a Munich city councilman. He was to prove to be one of our most effective informants.

In our investigations, Fleck and I discovered that at every level of provincial and municipal government and industry, Nazis or military officers remained entrenched in high positions. The provincial economics minister, Dr. Carl Lange, for example, proposed as candidates for the provincial Chamber of Industry a former director of the BMW automobile firm who had been Hitler's district armaments production chief, along with another notorious Nazi. He also nominated the former chief of the German Economics Board for North Bavaria to serve as his deputy. Embarrassed at the flagrant challenge to denazification directives, MG rejected the first two men and even took them into custody under the mandate of automatic arrest for high-ranking Party members. The other Nazi, however, retained his post.

BVP and Pg officials appointed at the cardinal's behest did not dare to exclude anti-Nazi elements from government posts, and on 22 May Minister-President Schaeffer promised a delegation of Social Democrats that upon his return from exile in Switzerland Dr. Wilhelm Hoegner, the unofficial head of their party, would be able to choose a ministry in the Bavarian cabinet. Nevertheless, when Hoegner arrived two weeks later Schaeffer made no move. The week Fleck and I arrived in Munich, however, after three Social Democrats threatened to resign from his government, Schaeffer agreed to fulfill his promise.

"The Young Socialists, an underground resistance group which had committed acts of sabotage against the Nazis," Fleck and I noted in our final report, "have expressed their dissatisfaction with the fact that there are only old men representing their party in the government," pre-Hitler Social Democrats, tired old men who began conversations with Fleck and me with accounts of their bold political activism back in 1919. "It could be a lot worse," they declared, shrugging their shoulders, when questioned about the presence of Nazis in the provincial and municipal administrations.

Munich Deputy Mayor Fritz Stadelmayr had served as mayor of Wuerzburg for a year after Hitler came to power, resigning then after some technical disagreement with local Party officials. In 1939 and again in 1941, however, Nazi Party headquarters in Munich petitioned the Wuerzburg Party branch for permission to enroll Stadelmayr (the correspondence was extant), and in 1944, a mere year before the war ended, Stadelmayr was accepted into the Party with membership retroactive to 1939. (The MG officer in charge of denazification in Munich dismissed my query about Stadelmayr's Party membership with a "Well, after all, Stadelmayr is a family man.")

One of Stadelmayr's first acts as deputy mayor was to appoint as his deputy a Dr. Jobst, an adjutant to the former Nazi mayor of Munich and formerly Stadelmayr's assistant at a publishing firm. Jobst had also been a political propagandist in the Reichsleitung (national Nazi leadership). Such vehement protests were registered against Jobst's appointment that the Americans were forced to dismiss him.[15] Stadelmayr and the Oberbuergermeister, both old-time BVP members, appointed as heads of eight of the eleven city departments two members of the BVP, four former Nazis, a judge ousted by the Nazis who considered himself nonpartisan, and one Social Democrat, an elderly civil servant. The Nazi Party thus enjoyed the strongest representation in the city administration.

At the Friday meetings at which city officials reviewed records of public officials who had been members of the Nazi Party, "frequently," we recounted in our final report, "Party members bring vindicating recommenda-

---

15. Among other cronies Stadelmayr appointed to high posts was a Dr. Meister, a university fraternity brother of his and a close friend to the former Nazi Party boss in Munich. Although Stadelmayr protested that Meister was indispensable to the running of the city, MG officers prodded by complaints from anti-Nazis removed him from office.

tions from members of the clergy attesting to the fact that they were good members of the church, contributed to collections for rebuilding destroyed churches, and could not, therefore have been *real* Nazis." A city commissioner estimated that between 50 and 80 percent of his colleagues were former Party members. When Wilhelm Specht, head of Freedom Action Bavaria, complained to the mayor about the absence of a clear anti-Nazi policy in his administration, the mayor replied:"I do not take part in the fight against fascism. I leave that to the Americans."[16]

In business and industry, too, the cardinal's men protected and advanced the fortunes of Party members or Nazi collaborators,[17] but businessmen (some of them Jewish) who had been forced by the Nazis to sell their enterprises or surrender them without compensation were discovering that they had no legal right to demand the return of their properties from Nazis who had taken them over. In some cases the Chamber of Business and Industry refused to grant victims of nazism licenses for new enterprises.

The Food Crisis

Confronting a task of daunting breadth and complexity, Fleck and I resolved to focus our attention on the areas of food distribution and housing. At a meeting on 6 June, we were informed, the cardinal, Minister President Schaeffer, provincial Minister of Agriculture Rattenhuber, and a certain Dr. Weiss, a member of the cardinal's circle, decided which Nazis, several of whom were notorious war profiteers, should be permitted to continue their activity in the food industry. Rattenhuber expressed fear that food distribution would be disrupted if the 90 percent of his assistants and associates who were Party members were dismissed. "I don't know," he lamented, "where the city will find money to meet their pensions if I fire them."

At a subsequent meeting on the food crisis the cardinal offered to dispatch priests to the countryside to exhort farmers not to hoard their produce for profiteering on the black market but to release some of their harvest to the Church for charity and the remainder to the municipal authorities. Instead of requisitioning transport in the emergency, the city officials agreed to accept an offer of trucks from Prince von Arenberg, a venerable nobleman

---

16. On the other hand, MG officials apparently posed no objection to the pious rationalization for rejecting punitive action against Nazis and militarists expressed by Red Cross official Dr. Hihn at a 5 July meeting of the Bavarian minister-president's advisory council:"There is a Christian precept, 'Love thine enemy.'"

17. In the reopened BMW automobile works, one of the largest industrial enterprises in Bavaria, the personnel committee was controlled by Party members and former officials of the Nazi Workers Front, and only Nazis were being rehired. The head of the firm's Allach plant was a Goering appointee, and the managing director had been a Wehrmacht district production chief.

with extensive estates. The church food would be distributed to Catholic kindergartens and charity kitchens, to needy Catholic families selected by parish charity ladies and, in keeping with the precept "Love thine enemy," to Nazis and high-ranking military officers detained in an American internment camp. When Dr. Kroth, who was present as administrator of the municipal office of food supply *(Ernaehrungsamt)*, argued that any special food distribution should be directed to needy anti-Nazis and not to men who were the cause of the general misery, Buergermeister Stadelmayr retorted, "The Americans will certainly not be opposed if the prison chaplain requests that political internees benefit from the charity."[18]

The Housing Crisis

According to the municipal housing commissioner, nearly 400,000 of Munich's 560,000 inhabitants were inadequately housed, and the provincial labor minister announced on Radio Munich that no new apartments would be constructed during the rest of the year. The best he could promise was patching of partially damaged buildings. More than half the city's population would pass the winter in unheated apartments with leaking roofs, damaged walls, and cardboard windows. Nevertheless, Cardinal Faulhaber obtained MG authorization for the repair and reconstruction of four of the largest churches in Munich as well as of the Residenz, the palace of the former royal house of Bavaria.

For its own personnel and for American Army units, MG requisitioned buildings and apartments occupied by Nazi officials, but the majority of Nazi dwellings remained undisturbed. Among Party members who had not held official posts, only those who joined the Party before 1933 were subject to eviction. In addition, Nazis either ignored the order to register their apartments or appealed to the courts or other authorities to avoid eviction.[19] On the other hand, when a Kzler asked an MG officer why Nazis were allowed to remain in their homes while homeless anti-Nazis were left to shift for themselves, the officer replied, "We Americans do not want to be as tyrannical as the Nazis."

A consequence of Military Government's tolerance toward former Nazis was widespread social demoralization. At the Sendlingertorplatz, a huge square outside a medieval gate to the inner city, hundreds of "operators"

---

18. Under Kroth's direction, in the municipal office of food supply confirmed Nazis had been weeded out. Others who had joined the Party late or could not demonstrate mere nominal membership were about to be discharged.

19. Karl Oberhuber, for example, an SA Brigadefuehrer, Oberregierungsrat, former chief adjutant to Gauleiter Wagner and a recipient of the Gold Party decoration, was living undisturbed at Haus Groshesselche, Rosenstrasse 4. A German working for the U.S. Army Counterintelligence Corps informed Fleck that Oberhuber possessed a certificate of protection from Cardinal Faulhaber himself.

jammed within a small grassless park conducted transactions in whispered tones or by gestures, oblivious to the American MPs stationed nearby. Upon catching sight of my uniform, some blackmarketers attempted to hide their wares, but most continued their operations without fear, even offering me bolts of cloth, shoes, jewelry, cameras, etc. Bread was available at one hundred times the legal price. A bar of American army soap went for three dollars. I saw GIs selling cartons of cigarettes at two dollars a pack. Pfarrer Muhler told Fleck that he had been offered as many bicycles as he could use at two hundred dollars apiece and up to 3,000 cans of meat at the enormous black market price of twenty dollars each.[20]

Fleck and I accumulated an enormous quantity of data from conversations with groups of ordinary citizens as well as with a score of individuals representing all political parties except the Nazi Party—from the ultraconservative Deutschnational and the currently dominant conservative Roman Catholic Bavarian People's Party to the parties on the left, the Social Democrats and Communists—city councilmen, municipal commissioners, police officers, priests, labor organizers, businessmen and leaders of anti-Nazi resistance groups. Entitled "Munich, Lack of Democracy Brings Disillusionment," the document we drafted ran to seventeen single-spaced, legal-size pages along with nine pages of supporting documents. We noted:

Conversations with informants generally began with their recounting how they had eagerly awaited the arrival of the Americans, listened to the Allied radio, etc. When questioned on specific issues, however, interviewees expressed dissatisfaction with the failure to cleanse the city of Nazis and with the establishment of a new kind of German totalitarian or at least undemocratic regime. They were confused as to the true aims of the Americans.[21]

"Too bad you're not a Nazi, you'd get some place" jokes were circulating, and the Nazis were emboldened.[22]

Our Munich investigation demonstrated that despite repeated proclamations at the highest levels about denazification, demilitarization, decartellization, and a democratic rehabilitation of Germany, there was among senior American MG officials little resolve to carry out these goals or to undertake

20. Since the German mark had a purchasing power only about one-third its prewar dollar equivalent, these prices have to be at least tripled to be appreciated.
21. See appendix 25, p. 201.
22. The director of a mill, for example, jeered at his chief miller for not having had enough courage to join the Nazi Party. When the former official spokesman for the Gauleiter learned that neighbors were complaining about his still walking about free, he posted a sign on his front door reading:"The biggest sneak in the entire land is and remains a denouncer." A war of words ensued between the Nazi and his enraged but helpless neighbors.

a bold confrontation with the factors and elements that had led to Hitler's rise to power.

Although Colonel Powell expressed satisfaction with our exposure of Patton's violation of Allied goals and directives, Al Toombs, as a former Washington correspondent experienced in political maneuverings in the capital, was hesitant about launching a broadside attack on Patton, a military hero who enjoyed powerful support both at Military Government headquarters and in Washington. He feared, too, that with the intensifying anti-Soviet and anti-Communist atmosphere in Military Government and in influential circles at home, our unit might be accused of being soft on "Reds."

The colonel offered a compromise solution: about to return to the States on leave he would take the report with him and get it before the proper authorities in Washington, exploiting his influence as a former acting governor and majority leader of the New Jersey assembly and major general in command of Fort Dix.

On 13 July, upon our return to Bad Nauheim from Munich, I wrote to my mother:"Our job was to make an investigation of the city government, which we found as corrupt as can be . . . and then as Egon Fleck, my traveling companion said, 'We ought to make a quick dash home.' The Americans are doing about as bad a job in collaborating with the Nazis and in discriminating against the anti-Nazis as can be imagined. . . . I get less and less proud every day of being an American with what I see." My mother chided me for my "unpatriotic" outburst, for my "immature" indignation at my superiors. On 31 July I replied:

Here we are dealing with a sizable section of a large nation [the province of Bavaria] and employing vicious policies leading to the alienation of the very democratic forces that could do us most good. . . . [W]e had not prepared during these last three or four years to take care of problems that we should have foreseen. We had insufficient personnel available that was trained and capable. . . . On top of that, our whole policy toward the Nazis is heartbreaking. When we do eliminate the Nazis, we bring in the next most dangerous groups to assist us—the militarists, the churchmen, the industrialists. We absolutely disregard and leave to charity the thousands upon thousands of people who spent anywhere from several months to 12 years in concentration camps. We overlook them because they were too strongly opposed to the Nazis!

"If Only You Americans Weren't Here . . . !"

After the discouraging experience in Munich with flagrant violations of the war aims enunciated by FDR and Eisenhower, I was eager to engage in investigations of attitudes of various elements of the German population to see whether among the Germans there was a desire for denazification and democratization offering hope that democracy could be achieved despite the efforts of the Pattons and other Americans in high positions who were concerned either with "getting things moving" or with preparing for a new war against the Soviet Union.

While embarked upon these investigations I visited Jakob Steffan, the police commissioner whom I had interviewed three months earlier in Mainz.[1] I found him no longer so buoyant. "We are ready to begin all over again," he exclaimed. "If you people weren't here, we would have a real revolution and set up a truly democratic republic." Steffan did not elaborate on this statement, but I surmised that he was demoralized by word he had received of the failures to denazify government and industry in Bavaria and in other areas of the American Zone. In our earlier conversation, as I noted in *Betrayal*, he had assured me that the Americans "would find anti-Nazis with whom to work in every German city."[2] But, as I commented:

neither he nor MG was working with all the anti-Nazis in Mainz. To establish a firm democratic base in a city that had endured twelve years of Nazi rule, he and the MG officers would have had to mobilize all the democratic forces—the representatives of the churches, of the pre-anti-Nazi parties, of the various professions, of the trade unions, of the anti-Nazi business community—in planning the future of the city, discussing and clarifying fundamental ideological questions, rallying the youth to participation in reconstructing the city, rounding up Nazis, maintaining security and assuring a fair distribution of food and housing.

German Workers

"I discovered among the workers," I wrote in summing up my first set of interviews, "an openness and frankness and a generally positive outlook regarding democracy and denazification often lacking in others of their coun-

---

1. Recognizing Steffan's ability and dedication, the French, who had assumed military occupation of the Mainz region, promoted him to the office of Regierungspraesident of Rheinhessen, with responsibilities covering both Mainz and the surrounding area.
2. Kahn, *Betrayal*, 33.

trymen." "We will never be able to repay for what we have done in other countries in Europe, never," one worker exclaimed, covering his face with his hands and shaking his head in shame. Asked what advantages he had experienced from the Nazi regime, a middle-aged mechanic replied, "I lost my house, my wife, my two sons, and now I'm all alone. That's what I got from Hitler." "Some men," said a streetcar conductor, "were glad to get jobs in 1934 and 1935, but only the Nazis enjoyed *Kraft durch Freude* [Strength through Joy] excursions and vacations. Otherwise, we worked longer hours, ate less and couldn't speak up to protect our rights. We were locked into our jobs, but they could fire us arbitrarily. They spied on us and forced us to 'volunteer' for special labor details and later for the Volkssturm. By the end of the war, we had become slave labor."[3]

German Youth

A PW poll conducted late in July in the towns of Friedberg and Offenbach in the province of Hesse of 254 young people between the ages of fourteen and eighteen—139 boys and 115 girls—did not confirm the optimistic assessment by the Mainz young poet Hermann Butz of the democratic potential among German youth. The poll revealed that the girls had undergone more thorough nazi indoctrination than the boys (who confronted mobilization into the Volkssturm and eventually into the Wehrmacht), but all the young people exhibited effects of their Nazi education.[4] The poll demonstrated that the major problem we confronted with German youth was not a persistence of nazism among them, with attendant resistance to, and defiance of, the Allied authorities. German youth had lost their old leadership, and, "for the time being at least, Americans appear to be the substitutes for the Nazi leaders in the totalitarian-trained minds of these young people."

American Military Government, however, appeared to have no youth policy. Despite vigorous efforts by individual Americans reinforced with Coca-Cola and chewing gum, German youth continued to prefer soccer to the American national sport, and whatever benefits might have been anticipated from the introduction of baseball failed to materialize.

In Bad Homburg, a spa some fifteen miles from Bad Nauheim, with two of my colleagues I organized a discussion group of some twenty-five to thirty young people, nearly all of middle-class backgrounds. They were skeptical of any statements we made about denazification, democratization, and reeducation, but we were encouraged by their recognition of the necessity of

---

3. "We can probably accomplish something in Germany," I reported in a unique expression of approval in an official report of an entire class of Germans—"with these people on our side if they stick together and we give them support."

4. In appendix 26, p. 202, I reproduce the report I developed from the results of the poll.

their participating in the reconstruction of their country. They could, they admitted, join in collecting firewood, in assisting expellees from the East, in organizing programs for children, in helping to repair damaged dwellings. But when we asked when they would undertake such tasks, we met silence.

"We'd hesitate to gather wood," ventured one of the young people, "because we'd know that some would do all the work and others would do nothing."

"We need someone to lead us," protested another. "If you would take over, maybe we'd do it. Everyone is too involved with his own problems to bother about anyone else."

"You know, we have been told so many lies," declared a teenager in a tone of utter weariness, "we don't believe anything any more. It's all a swindle!"

We could not effectively respond to this despair. Despite the fanfare about denazification, young Germans saw Nazi bigshots escaping punishment and even retaining high positions. They heard rumors that Nazis in detention centers enjoyed larger rations than the rest of the population, including Kzler. Antimilitarism? A judge in Bremen had just sentenced a young man to two years in prison because he deserted from the Wehrmacht during the last months of the war. Ex-sergeants who exchanged Wehrmacht for police uniforms ordered civilians about with the arrogance of the Nazi police.

"All we know," I wrote, paraphrasing remarks I heard repeatedly from German young people, "is that we haven't enough to eat, we haven't a chance in the world to rebuild our homes, to clothe ourselves, to find decent jobs, and what's more, we're probably going to have another war that will destroy everything that's left. We've always been efficient and industrious, but with you here, we don't get anything done at all."

Local MG officials reported criminal activity by gangs of desperate adolescents and young adults under the leadership of former Hitler Youth leaders or of demobilized soldiers, often romantic paratroopers or charismatic SS men.

Confronting Winter Hardships

"The excitement over the British elections," I wrote home on 15 August, "died down very quickly here. . . . The news of the Japanese surrender was relayed here along with the prediction that some 5 million Americans will soon be unemployed." The mass of Germans, however, had other concerns than international developments, as I discovered in an informal poll I conducted on expectations regarding conditions during the coming winter among nine men and women applying for travel passes at MG headquarters in Frankfurt. A mechanic declared that having lived through six terrible years of war he was prepared to confront yet another hard winter. "One lives from day to day," he said, "and there will always be potatoes." A Kzler was discouraged by the abrupt discontinuance of double rations for former concentration-camp inmates, a privilege granted only two months earlier. A tailor earned extra rations by working for an American unit and also bartered his services with farmers for food. He feared widespread hunger, however, if people were prevented by bad weather from going out to farms to supplement their rations. A refugee from Breslau complained that as a newcomer from the East she could not obtain additional food supplies since she had no acquaintances in the countryside. A saleswoman hoped that the fat ration would be increased. Everyone with whom she spoke expressed fear of food shortages and of epidemics. A housewife declared that if MG did not increase the potato ration she would have difficulty surviving. Her monthly noodle-rice-macaroni allowance sufficed for only a week's meals. She was distressed at the shortage of sugar, without which she could not can fruits and vegetables. An employee in a municipal labor office noted that laborers were barely obtaining enough food to keep an inactive person alive. Conditions, he was certain, would deteriorate with the seasonal decline in the supply of fresh vegetables and fruit. He predicted an influenza epidemic with high mortality among the malnourished children. He warned of the possibility of food riots.

Although none of these informants blamed the Americans, it was clear that they were convinced that the occupation forces were not making adequate provisions against a winter crisis.[5] Indeed, inured to the misery, in my letters I never expressed distress at seeing five- and six-year-old children outside the Frankfurt PX crying, "Candy, candy, soldier," ceasing their appeals only upon catching some sweet tossed to them. Candy bars would supplement the meal at home or be sold on the black market. At railroad stations boys, some as young as ten years old, often wearing dirty Hitler Youth caps, many of them bombed-out runaways or orphans, fought for the privilege of carrying luggage for Americans or to shine the shoes of GIs or simply begged for cigarettes. Thousands of boys and girls were wandering throughout Germany, begging, stealing, and blackmarketing, or surviving through prostitution.

5. I wrote home:
Unless basic changes are made in our administration—which seems unlikely—there will be vast starvation, freezing, sickness next winter.... The food situation even today is critical. Workers are too weak to report to the factories. The absenteeism is unbelievable....

The German people ... have only enough to eat to keep them going, they must spend all their time grubbing for food and fuel, they are numb from the barbaric bombings that we brought against them—bombings in which we buried 50,000 in Darmstadt, 35,000 in Kassel, 10,000 in Wuerzburg, 25,000 in Pforzheim, 15,000 in Mainz—in a single air raid in each case.

The Wiesbaden School System: An Experiment in Democratization

In mid-August, ten days after classes had begun, I commenced a study of the school system of Wiesbaden, and for three days I observed teachers in two schools and interviewed the regional and local MG education officers, the Wiesbaden superintendent of schools Herr Prediger, an official of the German regional education office, and a principal of one of the schools.[6]

Because of the limited number of classrooms available,[7] the school year commenced with only the first four grades, conducted in separate morning and afternoon sessions. Herr Prediger established a longer school year to make up for days lost during the final chaotic war months. Because no fuel could be spared for schools in the approaching winter, plans were drawn to have children report merely one hour a day during the cold months to have their homework checked by their teachers.

In cooperation with the local MG public safety officer, the Army Counterintelligence Corps and committees of carefully screened teachers, Herr Prediger supervised the vetting of personnel. Approximately 125 teachers who had joined the NSDAP before 1937 or were known to have militaristic ideologies were dropped from the city payroll, and 215 teachers were rehired, of whom some 165 were immediately assigned classrooms. Herr Prediger was confident that parents would inform him of any unacceptable political tendencies among teachers.[8]

To prepare teachers for the radical change in educational philosophy, evening reorientation meetings were scheduled at which selected teachers, university professors, and other qualified individuals lectured and led discussions. At conferences with principals, Herr Prediger discussed the new educational aims and objectives. The principals, in turn, held similar meetings with their staffs. Under the supervision of the regional MG education officer, committees of teachers were engaged in revising Nazi textbooks and in rewriting courses of study. Major Bursch encountered the greatest difficulty in the cleansing of the history books since the Germans on the revision committee lacked information for correcting distortions. But other texts posed complications as well. Party and chauvinist slogans used as illustrative

---

6. In 1933 Herr Prediger was dismissed from his position as an elementary school principal, investigated by the Gestapo, and then reinstated as "a teacher under surveillance." Following his appointment as superintendent of schools, he immediately conducted a survey of school conditions under the guidelines of an MG document entitled "Education Situation Survey and Related Data for Application for Reopening of Schools."

7. Of the thirty-seven schools in Wiesbaden, one was totally destroyed, fifteen were 85 to 95 percent destroyed, and the remaining twenty-one from 40 to 65 percent damaged. Eleven could be readied for occupancy by 1 September; an additional six by 1 October; no date could be set for the remaining seven. Of twenty-five serviceable buildings, however, eleven had been requisitioned for the use of American troops.

8. Concerned at the shortage of young teachers, Major Bursch of the Regional MG detachment arranged to have students previously enrolled at teacher training institutions observe classes and serve as teachers' assistants. Plans were being drawn for the reopening of a normal school.

sentences in grammar books had to be eliminated. Even in arithmetic books the committee found subtle nazi and militaristic indoctrination. Pictures of airplanes and military equipment as well as problems involving the Hitler Jugend or the armed forces had to be removed. The old-fashioned "Hans" and "Fritz" replaced "Adolf" as well. A musicologist checked music books for militaristic and Nazi songs. Because of the paucity of texts, most classes for the 8,000 pupils in the four grades had to be conducted without books. Teachers based their preparations either on the newly drafted courses of study or on the rare copies of authorized schoolbooks. To compensate for the lack of paper, the superintendent ordered several thousand individual slates.[9]

Frauelein Doktor Stuebel, an official at the regional education office, and Herr Prediger accompanied me on a visit to the Bluecherplatz elementary school. Sections of each floor where extensive repairs were under way were roped off. Water dripped through the roof over the main stairway and collected in puddles on the steps. Hallways were partially blocked by scaffolding. The classrooms, however, were in acceptable condition, high ceilinged, light, and commodious, but not all the broken windows had been replaced.

In Herr Weiss's class of forty-two eight-year-olds, the boys and girls were segregated in different rows. (Generally, I was told, the sexes were assigned to different classes.) On the blackboard Herr Weiss had written:"Wir sagen nicht mehr Heil Hitler!" (We no longer say Heil Hitler!) and "Wir wollen Frieden!" (We want peace). As I had seen American principals do on visits to classrooms, Herr Prediger took over the class, leading a discussion of the sentences on the blackboard. The children explained that they no longer said Heil Hitler because Hitler was to blame for the war. He had attacked first and was as much to blame as a boy who picks a fight with his neighbor is responsible for the other boy's bloody nose. When asked the difference between war and peace, the children promptly recounted the wartime horrors they had experienced—air-raid alarms, hurrying home from school to take refuge in the cellar, food shortages because of disruptions from the bombardments, the destruction of their homes. Peace meant not only the discontinuance of these horrors but also the return of fathers and brothers from the army, the possibility of playing without fear and of creating works of peace.

Before we left the room, Herr Prediger instructed the children how to sit at ease, explaining that a free people that says "Good Morning" and

---

9. Under the new syllabi stories in the elementary readers and the games and other activities resembled those in American schools. On the other hand, some topics assigned for class discussion would have raised questions in the United States:"F reedom of the Rhine region," "Legends from the inner soul," "Everything depends upon the blessing of God," "Remember that you as a German have duties."

"Good Day" instead of "Heil Hitler" also sits and stands at ease, and not like soldiers. (Herr Prediger considered a primary objective in the post-Nazi elementary grades was permitting children to act like children again and teaching them how to laugh and play. He was confident of eliminating Nazi influences quickly. "Our philosophy," he declared, "is so much more profound and decent that the children will respond to it quickly." He feared more problems, however, with older children who had undergone Hitler Jugend and Bund der deutschen Maedchen indoctrination.)[10]

When I asked a teacher in another class how she explained to her ten-year-old girls why pages had been cut out of their reading book, she replied that the children had helped her to remove offensive material—whatever glorified war or those responsible for the war and whatever preached that German children belonged to a Master Race. The girls laughed when Herr Prediger declared how ridiculous it was to say that some children were better than others.

In another school, housed in a former gymnasium since its building was occupied by American troops, I attended a class of ten-year-old girls conducted by the principal, a Dr. Schaab. The children were at ease and cheerful. They snapped their fingers in their eagerness to answer questions and frequently burst into laughter. Dr. Stuebel took stenographic notes of the first minutes of the class:

Teacher: Today we have three visitors, a lady and two gentlemen. What do you think they want to hear from us?

Student: They want to hear what we know.

Teacher: We don't know very much. Why is that?

Student: Because we were so long out of school.

Teacher: How long was that?

Student: Half a year.

Teacher: Why?

Student: Because of the war.

Teacher: Is there still a war?

Student: No, now there is peace.

Teacher: Since when?

---

10. In my report I quoted from a statement on the goals of the newly reopened Wiesbaden schools Herr Prediger had submitted to the MG education officers:"A general agreement concerning the aim and task of the instruction:elimination of all National Socialist and militarist influences; instruction in, and cultivation of, a spirit of humanity and justice, development of a religious moral character, inculcation of solid learning and scholarship."

Student: Since March.

Teacher: Since March there has been no war here. But since when is the whole world at peace?

Student: Since two days ago.

Teacher: Who were the last to continue the war?

Student: The Japanese.

Teacher: Where does the gentleman come from, do you think, who, as you see, is dressed differently?

A general shout: He comes from America.

Teacher: And what does he want here?

(The students giggle, and the teacher prompts them.)

Teacher: He wants to see how things are going in our school, what we are thinking....

Student: He wants to see what we are learning. We don't study what we used to study.

Teacher: What did you used to study?

Student: National Socialism.

Teacher: What did you learn then, what did you used to say?

(An outburst of laughter among the students)

Students: We used to say Heil Hitler! (more laughter)

Teacher: Yes, every morning you said Heil Hitler. We don't say that any more, we don't think about that any more. We don't think about what lies behind us. As I recently said to you, we now think about what lies ahead.

Clearly, the children were happy at being back in school. The teachers were succeeding in associating the horrors the children had endured with National Socialism. The children expressed antipathy to anything nazi and were eager to assimilate another view of the world. The enthusiasm of the teachers was as contagious as the cheerful spirit among the pupils. The boys and girls praised and criticized each others' work in a friendly tone. They associated the reopening of the schools with the arrival of the Americans and the end of the bombing.

The reopened schools in Wiesbaden offered possibility for confidence in Germany's future. The question was whether the efforts of the MG education authorities and our efforts at Information Control Division (ICD)[11]

---

11. On 1 August, Twelfth Army Group Psychological Warfare was renamed the Information Control Division of the Office of Military Government, US (OMGUS).

In mid-July all OSS personnel assigned to the Twelfth Army Group PW subbranch received telegrams ordering them to report to London by 1 August to be shipped home. Al Toombs was able to arrange, however, that I be assigned to the Office of War Information (OWI).

would suffice to counter the policies, equally, if not more critical for Germany's future, promoted by MG agencies charged with denazification of German industry and political institutions.

Farmers

I spent three days, 22–25 August, interrogating twenty farmers and their wives along with farm workers in five hamlets in a thinly populated agricultural area in the province of Hesse where farms ranged in size from ten to fifty morgen (a morgen is approximately two-thirds an acre).[12] I found unanimity among the interviewees that the Nazis had promised farmers much and given little. Farmers had minimal control over their lives. They could not sell a strip of land without Party permission. On the other hand, they recalled the chaotic conditions in 1933, when farmers were in need of help, which the Nazis provided by regulating the market. None of the informants had been a Party member. In the hamlet of Pohlgoens, they reported, about 10 percent of the farmers had joined the Party, but few of these had been fanatics. The local Party leader had run off at the approach of the Americans. Several of the farmers volunteered the opinion that one of the worst crimes committed by Hitler was his mistreatment of the Jews. "Even Party members in Pohlgoens did business with Jews," recounted one of the farmers.

After years of Nazi repression, the farmers had lost interest in politics. One of three former Social Democrats, however, thought people in his village wanted parties reestablished so that they might express their opinions again. A fellow villager, however, insisted that farmers had no more faith in parties and feared persecution if they engaged in politics in the event of the appearance of another Hitler.

Almost all the informants expressed fear of communism except one, who declared that the people in his village had no idea what communism was in any case. Only in Pohlgoens had there been some pre-1933 Communists. Three farmers who expressed fear of the Russians nevertheless insisted that they themselves had seen through Goebbels's anti-bolshevik propaganda. "I believe the propaganda about the Russians was employed to rouse the soldiers' military spirit," declared the mayor of Glashuette. Soldiers returning from Russian captivity reported they were well treated and that the food ration in the Russian zone was more generous than in other zones. A Catholic farm worker who had served two years in Russia thought he would have been able to make a better living in Russia than in Hitler Germany because there were more opportunities there for little people. Kiev, he recounted,

---

12. One interviewee was a leader of the local farm association; two were village mayors. Two of the farm workers were recently discharged prisoners of war, one of whom had volunteered for farm work to escape the rigors of winter in Frankfurt.

was just like a Germany city, much like Munich before 1933. The people in Russian cities he thought highly civilized. The Russian peasants he considered backward.

The few informants who had had direct contact with Americans declared they were pleasantly surprised by the gentle and just treatment they encountered. They had had no idea what to expect after Goebbels's terror propaganda. The farmers now anticipated that their lives would go on much as before with perhaps some relaxation of controls over their production and property.

The farmers were aware that city people accused them of withholding food supplies. All insisted that with the system of controls instituted by the Nazis and continuing in effect it was impossible for the farmer to retain more than he needed for his own use. The mayor of Kroeftel declared that the adults in his village never drank milk, saving what there was for their children and for delivery to the city.

The farmers had no regrets at the overthrow of the Nazi regime, but they harbored no resentment at neighbors who had joined the Party. Caught up in immediate problems, they had little interest in engaging in politics. They were involved with a shortage of tools and problems in obtaining seed potatoes. Because they were forbidden to own guns, they were harassed by marauding foxes and deer. A twenty-three-year-old farmhand who had been in the army since 1939 complained that he had learned no trade. His hometown in Upper Silesia had been destroyed, and his family had been evacuated to Bavaria. In the spring he intended to set out to look for them.

The Darmstadt Clergy

In August 1945, three months after VE Day, Military Government headquarters awaited a policy statement from a conclave of Roman Catholic bishops in the city of Fulda. A pastoral letter translated into clumsy English submitted to the MG religious affairs officer in attendance offered grudging recognition of the Four Power Control Council as "the highest secular power in Germany" as a result of the "complete military overthrow of Germany." Emboldened by the influence they had assumed in the selection of officials on every level of government in the American Zone, the bishops called for an end to the expulsion of Germans from the eastern territories annexed under Big Power agreement by the Russians and the Poles and from the Sudetenland territory, now restored to Czechoslovakia. They demanded an immediate importation of foodstuffs to end German hunger, warning that continued distress would "bring the German people to desperation by which once more new troubles will be caused for the whole world." They condemned the denazification program, charging that the dismissal of "indispensable specialists" was hampering reconstruction. The bishops called for the arming of the German police and strong measures to put an end to rape and other lawlessness by American troops. They offered assistance in soliciting "their faithful parishioners to take a loyal attitude toward the present holders of the public power." They did not state their price for such cooperation.[13]

Exploiting a license not enjoyed by others of their countrymen, clergymen summoned their parishioners to a new anti-bolshevik crusade, this time under the cross instead of the Hackenkreuz (swastika). At a national conclave of Evangelical bishops at Treysa, for example, a Professor Ivant of Koenigsberg (an East Prussian city annexed by the Soviets under the Potsdam agreement) proclaimed:"W e must not let the borders of the Evangelical faith be pushed back. . . . We must not shun any means of fighting for our Church. . . . We must not let them take territories which are purely German and a homeland of our Evangelical faith." The Catholic Caritas joined the Evangelical Inner Mission in disseminating lurid tales to promote the collection of alms for "the suffering Germans" in the East.[14]

In the context of such ecclesiastical pronouncements, during the second week of September I embarked upon an investigation of the attitudes of the four Catholic priests, seven Evangelical and two Confessional ministers ministering to the people of Darmstadt.[15]

"Only one-third of the Evangelicals are good," asserted Father Christian Adam Danz. "The rest are spoiled by rationalism." Dr. Valentin Degen, one of two Darmstadt clergymen still in their thirties, a parish priest who also served on the staff of the Roman Catholic bishop of Mainz, described National Socialism as the inevitable outgrowth of the antihumanism pro-

---

13. Shortly after the publication of this declaration, an MG religious affairs officer reprimanded the bishop of Limburg for circulating a pastoral letter expressing opposition to the occupation power and praising Wehrmacht troops for "loyally performing their duty to their country." The bishop's adviser, a cosmopolite Jesuit who spoke idiomatic English without a trace of an accent, complained to me that the elderly prelate considered himself "a prince of the Church and above criticism."

14. The Inner Mission circulated a report of horrors purportedly suffered by expellees from the East written by an Evangelical pastor in the jargon employed by the Nazis in describing supposed Czech atrocities against the Sudeten Germans in 1938 and Polish atrocities against Silesian Germans in 1939. (The author of the pamphlet, it was subsequently revealed, had been a Nazi activist.) An October ICD poll of Germans expelled from the Eastern territories revealed that these people had experienced no picnic; expulsion of some 9 million people was certainly to be accompanied by tragic experiences; but close questioning exposed a tendency among the interviewees to color and exaggerate charges against the Russians and the Poles. One man who related a particularly chilling tale of horrors turned out to be a former SS man. He admitted that he had invented his story after a German official advised him "to make conditions in the Russian Zone sound as bad as possible."

15. Catholics represented approximately 17 percent of the city's population; members of the Confessional—*Bekenntnis*—church formed a tiny minority; the remainder of the population associated themselves with the Evangelical, that is, Lutheran, denomination.

Fifty percent of the church buildings in Darmstadt had been destroyed. Fragebogen had been distributed to all the clergy but none had as yet been returned. No churchman had been dismissed because of political unreliability.

pounded by Martin Luther. In turn, Dr. Wilhelm Berger, the Evangelical superintendent of the Starkenburg area of the province, a man in his fifties whose dueling scars proclaimed his former membership in a nationalistic university fraternity, responded with equal animosity. "The Catholic Church," he declared, "will always look to Rome rather than to Germany. Cooperation between the two churches is often difficult."[16]

On every topic wide-ranging differences existed not only between the two faiths but among the clergymen within each church. While Dr. Degen, for example, charged that Hitler's rise resulted from "the despicable stupidity of the German masses," two other Catholic priests, Wilhelm Michel and Philip Waldheim, along with five of the Protestant ministers attributed Hitler's success in seizing power to the severe economic conditions in the early 1930s. Waldheim insisted that Hitler received his main support from industrialists and the great landowners, but he concurred with Degen in citing the harsh terms of the Versailles treaty as a significant factor leading to the overthrow of the Weimar Republic.

Dr. Thomas Mueller, president of the Evangelical Church of Land (province) Hessen, a man in his fifties, a pre-1933 supporter of the nationalist Deutsche Volkspartei and admirer of Field Marshal von Hindenburg ("a strong leader who saved the Reich from the Marxists"), attributed the 1933 triumph of the Nazi Party to a twofold spiritual yearning in the German people:the desire to break the chains of Versailles and a sense of drift among traditional emperor-worshipers after the overthrow of the monarchy. In addition, he believed, the precipitate industrialization of Germany after 1870 evoked social tensions difficult to resolve. Germans, he asserted, always pursued ideas to the limit. Thus Hitler.

The clergymen did not agree at all regarding the roles of the churches under the Nazis. Father Waldheim pointed out that before 1933 the Catholic Church forbade membership in the Nazi Party and outlawed the wearing of Nazi insignia. Dr. Michel recalled, too, that the German bishops repeatedly warned against the dangers in National Socialism. He admitted, however, that the church shifted its position during the summer of 1933 after Hitler signed a concordat with the Vatican. Only one Catholic priest in the province of Hesse, he noted, joined the Party, and he had recently been transferred out of his parish.

Protestant ministers insisted that the reason why more Protestant than Catholic clergymen joined the Party was that the Catholics owed primary allegiance to Rome and opposed German governments of whatever stripe.

---

16. None of the clergymen questioned me as to my religious affiliation. I did not introduce myself by name, and I suspect that it did not occur to any of them that I was Jewish inasmuch as I did not resemble the Nazi stereotype that many Germans had come to accept during the previous twelve years.

Protestants, on the other hand, considered theirs a state church and were attracted by Hitler's promise to establish a positive Christianity. Nevertheless, according to Dr. Mueller, Hitler's attempt to impose the Fuehrerprinzip on the church organization evoked strong opposition. Such a policy, Mueller insisted, would have denied the Reformation and transformed the Evangelical Church into another Catholic Church. Hitler, Ley, and Goebbels, he noted, had all been born into the Catholic faith and National Socialism found its first base among the Catholics of Bavaria because the Fuehrerprinzip conformed with the doctrine of papal infallibility (as indeed a 1933 pronouncement of Roman Catholic bishops proclaimed). Pastor Robert Wolf, who numbered many intellectuals and rich Evangelicals within his congregation, recalled that many withdrew from his parish because of his outspoken opposition to National Socialism. Young people complained to their parents that he did not understand the times. Father Waldheim insisted that now even children of "godless" parents should be compelled to undergo religious instruction.

Pastor Friedrich Wiedmann alone declared that he had never anticipated anything other than the kind of denazification we were conducting. "Everything that smells of Hitler must be eradicated," he insisted. All the other clergymen regretted what they considered to be an American failure to distinguish between "muss" (coerced) and "real" Nazis. Father Waldheim quoted young people as saying that Hitler had predicted correctly that we Americans would treat all Germans alike, not discriminating between the real Nazis and nominal Party members. Though deploring our denazification program generally, Father Michel applauded our making political appointments first among those who had never been in the Party. Echoing, whether consciously or not, the sentiment of numerous MG officials, Dr. Mueller expressed regret that some of the people most capable of contributing to the reconstruction of the devastated nation were being discharged because of their Party membership. He hoped that when, "inevitably," we reappointed Nazis to positions of responsibility, we would seek the counsel of the clergy. Dr. Degen foresaw chaos resulting from the denazification program and was incensed at being required to fill out a *Fragebogen* (a Military Government questionnaire to test ideological reliability). He made no effort to conceal his contempt for Americans, particularly those in the local MG detachment.[17]

17. The Evangelical Church, Mueller reported, had distributed its own Fragebogen among its pastors. As a result, twenty ministers had been summoned before an investigating committee and temporarily relieved of their duties. They were to be pensioned, dismissed, transferred, or reinstated according to the findings of the committee. The only dedicated Party member among the Darmstadt pastors, he declared, had died in an air raid.

Most of the Darmstadt clergy were uncertain what stance to adopt in current politics. The thirty-three-year-old Evangelical pastor Reinhardt Grohrock eschewed all political involvement, declaring, "Our task is with the soul and not with politics." In regard to parties of the Left, opinions also varied. "I have always treated Catholic Communists as Catholics," insisted Father Michel, "but have fought Catholic Nazis." Among the Protestants, the two Confessional pastors exhibited the greatest tolerance toward the left parties. "One cannot judge a man's inner Christianity by his party membership," stated Pastor Weiss. Pastor Wilhelm Weinberger, a Christian socialist, asserted, "The Church stands toward communism as communism stands toward the Church. The Church has no expertise in economic matters."

Pastor Wiedmann, another Christian socialist, expressed himself more forcefully, declaring:"The Nazis made the name of Germany stink throughout the world. The church must merely see to it that all the parties protect the church and every form of religion, that they promote reconstruction and battle fascism and militarism." "I am a minister," insisted Pastor Wolf, "for members of all parties." Two Catholic priests, Father Waldheim and Father Danz, on the other hand, warned that former dedicated and "incurable" Nazis were now masquerading as Social Democrats and Communists. "He who is not with me is against me," proclaimed Danz. He favored an episcopal prohibition against joining left-wing parties. "There are two ideas in the minds of Germans today," concurred Evangelical provincial president Dr. Mueller, "Christianity and communism, and there is no compromise between them." He had believed that it was the Allies' intention to reconstruct a "Christian" Germany and was dismayed to discover that MG consulted leaders of the Social Democratic Party and the Communist Party in selecting candidates for political positions. Father Degen did not believe that the idealistic Communist leaders with whom he was acquainted would be capable of keeping the "stupid" masses in check.

But the clergymen with strong antipathy toward the Left did not agree on the action they should take in opposition. After twelve years of Hitler, they had lost the practice of democratic politics, and none of the Darmstadt clergymen thought of imitating the activism of the clergymen in the village of Hugenheim, who were arrested for calling an unauthorized public meeting to protest the MG's appointment of a Communist mayor.

Dr. Mueller rejected a request from the Roman Catholic bishop of Mainz to collaborate in organizing a "Christian" party. Pastor Waldheim, on the other hand, favored the establishment of a Christian Democratic Party backed by both churches in order to offer a Christian alternative to "politically unsophisticated voters." The Catholic clergy were split on the formation of a "Christian" party with Father Degen reporting that at a recent meeting the four Darmstadt Roman Catholic priests agreed to oppose the formation of such a party, while Father Danz quoted the bishop of Mainz as favoring an accommodation with the Social Democrats (to prevent their unification with the Communists) before seeking to organize a Christian party.

Although some of the Darmstadt clergy were disgruntled about the American denazification program, none of them expressed pro-Nazi sentiments or general dissatisfaction with the American occupation. Several displayed extraordinary toleration of the leftist parties, including the Communist Party. None yearned for American fostering of Church intervention in politics as was taking place in Bavaria. In almost every particular, there was every reason to expect collaboration of these churchmen in carrying out OMGUS mandates.

After six weeks of investigations of varied elements of the German population, it seemed to me that an overwhelming majority of Germans were receptive to a popular mobilization for the rehabilitation of their country. A minority, indeed, rendered suspicious and fearful of engaging in political activity after years of Nazi oppression or demoralized by the current slow rate of reconstruction and denazification, despaired of a significant change in their nation. What none saw emerging was the American vision of a new Germany that the industrialist Ferdinanz Stenz had expressed in declaring: "I'd like you to transform Mainz into the first American German city."

Mainz City Councillor Michel Oppenheim had asserted: "The war between the Americans and the Germans is not nearly so bitter as the war between the Germans and the Nazis." During the summer of 1945 a variation on Oppenheim's statement appeared ever more urgent:

The war between Americans and German Nazis and reactionaries was becoming not nearly so bitter as that between those Americans and Germans who were committed to the war aims proclaimed by FDR and Eisenhower and the Americans and Germans seeking to subvert these war aims.

11

Patton's Last Stand

A Magna Carta for Germany?

On 2 August, after a two-week meeting at Potsdam, Clement Attlee,¹ Harry Truman, and Josef Stalin issued a communiqué subsequently denominated the Potsdam (or Berlin) Declaration, in which they reconfirmed their collaboration and dedication to the war aims earlier agreed upon. They provided for Four Power (including France) rule of Germany with a goal of a unified nation after denazification and decartellization and punishment of war criminals.² Reaction to the Potsdam Declaration at Information Control Division headquarters was soberly enthusiastic. "Over here," I wrote home, "we consider the Potsdam Declaration to be the Magna Carta for the anti-Nazis of Germany." This sentiment was, however, not shared universally. "The Americans," I remarked, "are doing their best to delay the execution of its provisions and are not terribly happy about it in general."

Patton's Bavaria Again

On 1 August, seeking to strengthen Colonel Powell's presentation in Washington with an update of our July exposé of Patton's maladministration, I returned to Munich. Once again I benefited from the assistance of the people at the Kzler welfare office.³ Among documents they assembled for me was one describing how after Party activists and SS officers were served notice on 28 July to vacate apartments in a Nazi retirement village to provide housing for Kzler American Military Police arrested the director of the Munich Housing Office, charging him with failing to obtain an official MG stamp on the eviction order. When Kzler arrived to take over the apartments, women greeted them with shouts of "Heil Hitler!" Four Americans drew up in an automobile. When one of the Kzler sought their assistance, one of the Americans replied, "Shut your mouth, or you'll find yourself once again in Dachau!"⁴

---

1. On 26 July, defeated in British elections, Churchill yielded a place at the conference table to the new Labor prime minister Clement Attlee.

2. See appendix 27, p. 202, for major provisions of the Declaration.

3. "Although it is forbidden [under the nonfraternization regulation]," I wrote home, "I am bringing a huge box of cigarettes, candy, soap and canned goods for the Kzler." I also collected items of clothing from my colleagues. Arriving at the Kz welfare office in Munich, I asked whether some men would go downstairs to bring up some packages I had brought with me. With my gifts spread across the floor, the Kzler stood in amazement. "No one," one of them declared, "has paid any attention to us, much less provided us with such treasures."

4. To complaints from the Kzler agency, city and provincial MG officers retorted that transfer of dwellings was an issue for the German authorities to resolve.

On 24 August the *New York Times* reported that "large numbers of American troops are still living

In another document a Herr Huber, the head of the Security Police at the village of Penzberg, charged that at the Alpine resort of Bad Wiessee the daughter of Hans Frank, the former Nazi governor of Poland and a war criminal responsible for the deportation and murder of thousands upon thousands of Jews and Poles, was employed as a secretary at the local American counterintelligence unit. Miss Frank had established a liaison with an American officer and retained her father's house and all the treasures he had plundered as "King of Poland."

An SS Obersturmfuehrer named Gabl gloated to Huber that neither he nor twenty-six other SS officers nor several ministerial directors had ever been summoned for questioning by MG. All were anticipating appointments to positions in the Bavarian provincial administration. "Nothing can happen to them," Huber declared, "for they have a letter from Eisenhower's headquarters which protects them. The population has intervened at the Counterintelligence Corps but obtained no action."[5]

In Munich, responding to ever more insistent protests from the citizenry, MG officials dismissed one of the four Nazi officials in the Oberbuergermeister's office. New information regarding Deputy Mayor Stadelmayr's Nazi past threatened a major scandal, especially after Stadelmayr issued a statement asserting that at the time of his appointment MG officials were aware that he had joined the Party in 1944. When Stadelmayr's cousin revealed that the deputy mayor's membership actually dated back to 1937, Stadelmayr admitted membership from 1942.

Stadelmayr was not removed from his post.

During my previous visit to Munich, Thomas Wimmer and Gustav Schieffer, venerable SPD trade unionists, expressed indignation at the antidemocratic atmosphere in Bavaria. They were resolved, they assured me, to unite with the Communists and fight. "Communists like our friend City Councilman Hirsch are real democrats," Wimmer assured me. "We can work with such people." As I was leaving Wimmer's office, the doddering old socialists pounded the table and shouted in unison, "We are still revolutionaries!" Now, in fact, the leaders of the two workers' parties, emboldened by the publication of the Potsdam Declaration, had submitted to Military Government officials a joint program of radical reforms in the municipal

---

under canvas in Bavaria, while Germans, some of them nazis, luxuriously entertain American officers in fine houses.... No German can be kicked out of his house in Bavaria to make room for Americans without personal approval of Gen. Patton's chief of staff."

5. Refugees from Frankfurt, Huber further reported, recognized the American-appointed mayor of Bad Wiessee as a former Nazi bigshot in their home city. Among other Nazi criminals walking about freely in Bad Wiessee was a Dr. Schuhmann, a former prison warden and concentration-camp official. Another Nazi was safeguarding a large collection of fur coats belonging to former Foreign Minister von Ribbentrop, Hitler's mistress Eva Braun, Reichsleiter Borman, and many others.

and provincial administrations. "When and if the Social Democrats and the Communists come to the point," I noted in my report, "where they believe it impossible for them to carry out their common program because of the opposition of the German and American officials, they will submit memoranda about each department of government to show why they can no longer remain in the government. If MG does not meet the situation promptly and with understanding, a very unpleasant situation undermining MG's prestige is likely to arise."

On 11 August, only minutes before his departure for leave in the States, I handed Colonel Powell a report entitled "Munich, a Month Later—an Appendix to 'Munich, Lack of Democracy Brings Disillusionment,'" in which I confirmed the findings in the previous report of wholesale violations of SHAEF and Potsdam directives against the retention or appointment of Nazis and war criminals to positions of importance in government and industry. I concluded with the observation that "the basic problems described [in the July report] have not been corrected."

I drafted an additional memorandum to bolster the two Munich reports on a issue that I was confident would not rouse fears in Al Toombs to prevent their transmission on to OMGUS.[6] In mid-August, however, after General Eisenhower proclaimed his resolve to carry out to the letter the provisions of the Potsdam Agreement, Toombs at last authorized, with misgivings, the transmission of all the Munich reports.

The reports evoked a swift reaction at headquarters and impelled a spate of exposés of the situation in Bavaria by press correspondents.

On 22 August, the Internal Affairs Branch of OMGUS issued a denazification decree barring any "return to wealth, power or influence" of individuals with nazi associations. "These provisions," commented *New York Times* correspondent Drew Middleton hopefully, "will not only break the industrial families of Germany . . . but go a long way toward insuring that they will not rise again."

On 23 August, Eisenhower summoned to Frankfurt Lt. Gen. Wayne H. Haislip, commander of the Seventh Army (in occupation of the Western District of the American zone—Baden-Wuerttemberg and Hessen), and Gen. George S. Patton, commander of the Third Army in the Eastern District (Bavaria), along with members of their staffs as well as high military government officials to "seek to clarify American economic, political and

---

6. In appendix 28, p. 203, I present extracts from this memo, "Need for Propaganda on Atrocities Committed by Nazis in Occupied Countries."

military policy . . . and military government in the three months of control in this zone."⁷

Early in September, upon a complaint from American Jewish organizations that displaced persons in Bavaria, mostly Polish Jews (derided as "subhumans" by Patton), were living in desperate circumstances, Eisenhower made a tour of inspection of the assembly centers and, according to the *New York Times*, "read the riot act to [Patton] and astounded him by saying that he meant what he said when he said that Germans were to be ousted from their homes if necessary to make their victims comfortable."⁸

Within days thereafter an Internal Affairs unit under a Maj. Howard Ordway ordered Bavarian MG to discharge numerous German officials with Nazi associations, "including prominent persons sponsored by Minister-President Fritz Schaeffer."⁹

In a 19 September dispatch to the *New York Times*, Raymond Daniell reported:"Gen. George S. Patton, Jr. is reported to have asked a fiscal officer investigating the Nazi connections of certain bankers in Bavaria if he did not think it 'silly' to try to get rid of 'the most intelligent' people in Germany." Two days later Daniell reported that an officer cited a further remark by Patton as reflecting his own attitude. "Fragebogen?" the general was supposed to have bellowed when told that a certain businessman could not be employed because his questionnaire showed him to have been an elite guard (SS) member. "What the hell's a Fragebogen? If you need these men, keep them and don't worry about anything else."

On 22 September, *New York Times* correspondent Kathleen McLaughlin reported that further dismissals of high Bavarian officials "has precipitated an investigation and review of the whole military government in the eastern military district [Bavaria]." When, that very day, at a press conference a correspondent called Patton's attention to complaints by "liberal

---

7. In a 25 August dispatch to the *New York Times*, Drew Middleton noted an ideological divide within Military Government:"between those who want to 'get things done' using the nazis to do them if necessary and those who want to eliminate the nazis from all activity. In many cases Gen. Eisenhower or Gen. Clay have intervened to see that the denazification was carried out at the price of efficiency, and as one official remarked, 'after a week or so those officers who claimed that this or that nazi was indispensable have found that the thing ran pretty well as usual without him.'"

8. The American officer in charge of the Landsberg Jewish DP camp told me that MG officers, openly anti-Semitic, were hampering his efforts to provide his charges with supplies and proper housing facilities.

Although German provincial administrations drew up legislation for the compensation of German Jews, the laws were not implemented, because, so German officials reported to me, Military Government opposed "too hasty action."

9. Heading the list was a Dr. Gessler, German minister of war from 1920 to 1923 (when plans were first drafted for the rearmament of Germany) and a confidential adviser to Schaeffer. Gessler was charged with failure to submit the Fragebogen required of all appointees to governmental posts. Also on the list were the provincial ministers of interior and transportation (the latter to be prosecuted for falsification of his Fragebogen) as well as a previously dismissed minister of finance—a former deputy leader of the Nazi Party—whom Schaeffer had reappointed as his personal secretary.

elements" that reactionary nationalists and Nazis still dominated the life of the province, the general snapped, "Reactionaries! Do you want a lot of Communists? I don't know anything about parties. I'm here to see that they do what they're told." When a reporter pressed the general on his assertion that he had "never seen the necessity of the denazification program," Patton offered a startling response:"This nazi thing is just like a Democrat and Republican election fight. The thing is that these damned Nazis got people by the scruff of the neck, and other Germans just didn't have the guts to fight back." Summoning Patton to Frankfurt the next day, 23 September, to give an accounting of his "stewardship in Bavaria," General Eisenhower ordered him to report back in a week on "the state of the union in Bavaria."

On 25 September, at the insistence of Eisenhower's chief of staff Gen. Walter Bedell Smith, Patton called a press conference at which, at Bedell Smith's instruction, he read a letter dated 12 September addressed by Eisenhower to him and to Lt. Gen. Geoffrey Keyes, Patton's newly appointed counterpart in the Western District, in which Eisenhower reiterated his insistence upon a thorough denazification of the American Zone.[10] Patton followed with a statement in defense of his own policies, concluding with a patently disingenuous pronouncement:"It is my opinion, to the best of my knowledge and belief, there are no out-and-out Nazis in positions of importance whose removal has not already been carried out."

On 26 September, Bedell Smith admitted to the press corps that Eisenhower's summoning Patton to Frankfurt three days earlier followed upon "a flare-up over Patton's belittling the importance of ousting Nazis from high positions in industry." Bedell Smith went on, Raymond Daniell reported, to note that dubious reactionary elements predominated in the Bavaria administration. (His statement read like an epitome of the ICD Munich reports.)[11]

On 28 September, Eisenhower once again summoned Patton to Frankfurt. On 29 September, Fritz Schaeffer and his entire cabinet, with the exception of the Social Democratic Minister of Justice Wilhelm Hoegner, were dismissed from office.[12] (Appointed to his cabinet post three months earlier, Hoegner, it was now disclosed, had never been confirmed in his position.) Hoegner was installed as minister-president with authorization to form a new cabinet.

---

10. See appendix 29, p. 203, for the text of Eisenhower's letter.
11. See appendix 30, pp. 203–4.
12. MG barred Shaeffer from holding political office thereafter. Three years later, however, Chancellor Konrad Adenauer appointed Schaeffer to a cabinet post in the newly created Federal Republic of (West) Germany.

Patton's administration of Bavaria had been "cracked wide open." On 2 October, Eisenhower relieved Patton of his command.[13]

Eisenhower delivered a blow in defense of the FDR war aims and of the provisions of the Potsdam Declaration. It was yet to be seen, however, whether Patton's dismissal would inaugurate a turnabout in the trend of political events in the American Zone.

---

13. Patton died within weeks in an automobile accident.

12

Elections, the American Cure-All
FALL 1945

On 7 August, responding to a Potsdam directive, General Eisenhower authorized the licensing of local political parties. His action evoked an immediate response of applications for licenses by politicians whom Eisenhower characterized as "holdovers from the days before Hitler's advent to power."

On 29 August I commenced an investigation in Wiesbaden of German political attitudes. The twenty-eight interviewees confirmed Eisenhower's warning that the Germans were "ignorant of democratic processes and responsibilities." In fact, though expressing conviction that a political system like the American or the British would be desirable in Germany, several interviewees insisted that their country did not possess the political maturity to aspire to such a goal. The son of an East Prussian landed aristocrat and an American mother opined that "the masses" were incapable of ruling themselves. Another interviewee insisted that Germans enjoyed being ordered about. Half of the informants opposed women's suffrage. About a third of the informants were of the opinion that MG was doing a good job and should continue to rule Germany indefinitely.

Others remarked that the crisis in living conditions rendered political activity impossible. A majority believed that Germany was not ready for authorization of political parties, and on the basis of their recent experience with the Nazis most expressed fear of associating with any political party. On a recent visit to Berlin, however, a twenty-three-year-old social worker, who had never experienced democracy, had found a general enthusiasm for the party activity initiated by the Soviets two months earlier. Otherwise, it was the eight Social Democrats and two Communists who expressed gratification at the authorization of political parties. School superintendent Prediger and Buergermeister Maas, both Social Democrats, concurred that the Germans could best learn democracy by participating in political activity. Indeed, half of the interviewees believed that a large segment of the electorate looked to the SPD and KPD for radical solutions to the current misery. On the other hand, among the more prosperous of the twenty-eight interviewees (four of whom were former members of the Nazi Party), ten expressed fear of the Communists.

On 30 August, the day after I commenced my investigation, General Eisenhower announced plans to hold elections in the American Zone. On

15 September he ordered local MG officials to prepare mechanisms for "the first democratic elections in Germany since 1932." "The progress in eliminating the former party structure," he asserted, "has made it possible to set a time when the German people will be permitted to take a more active voice in their own government." Eisenhower's assertions that the achievement of denazification in the zone guaranteed readiness of Germans to participate in electoral campaigns were greeted with disbelief and apprehension at ICD and in the press corps. Raymond Daniell drafted a series of dispatches exposing the actual state of denazification in the three provinces of the zone.[1]

On 22 September, ignoring admonitions from the press and statements of disapproval from the other occupation powers, OMGUS published a schedule of four successive American Zone elections, the first to take place in rural communities in January 1946 and the last, province-wide, in October 1947. To the bewilderment of officials in Washington and at OMGUS HQ in Frankfurt who lauded elections as America's particular contribution to the promotion of democracy throughout the world, an ICD canvass of political leaders in Munich revealed that Germans of all political persuasions reacted with consternation to the elections announcement. When the American-appointed minister-presidents of the three American Zone provinces jointly protested that in a period of four months they would not be able to screen Nazis from the electoral rolls, Eisenhower rejected their request for a postponement of the elections.

Four days after the elections announcement, in an implicit admission that denazification was not the success he had claimed it to be, Eisenhower issued yet another, more stringent directive, this time mandating that German business and industry purge itself of Nazi managers and supervisors. Commented Raymond Daniell:"The issue now is whether the Berlin [Potsdam] declaration on denazification is to be implemented or by-passed by commanders in the field."[2]

---

1. On 19 September Daniell reported:"Although most of the territory in the United States zone . . . has been in Allied hands six months, the Nazis who actively helped Adolf Hitler mobilize the nation's resources for aggressive war still hold some of the best jobs in commerce and industry. . . . In many instances, various branches of the occupation authority are pursuing their own course for their own purposes without regard for the overall effect of what they are doing on Allied and American policy in Germany as a whole. It has become a fairly common thing for military government officers to remove an important executive of industry for Nazi activities, only to be ordered by Army officers to reinstate him, with a consequent loss of prestige to the military government."

2. At a press conference on 29 September, Eisenhower admitted, according to the *New York Times*, that "in the British and French as well as the American zones leaders of various [German] groups have not always been men interested in cooperating with military government officials." In the Soviet Zone, on the other hand, he conceded that "a different approach was evident in view of the authorization on 10 June of political activity. Communists, Social Democrats, Christian Democrats and Liberal Democrats have organized themselves into an anti-fascist coalition in the Soviet zone. Joint political meetings have been held, and all the parties have stressed the need for the German people to pay for the evil deeds of the Hitler government and to work out their own future." (Marshal Zhukov also permitted the parties to publish

The Affaire Blaum

Even before Eisenhower's announcement that elections would be held in the American Zone, events in Frankfurt demonstrated the unreadiness of the populace for participating in election campaigns.

Early in August, in an action without precedent since Hitler's assumption of dictatorial power, the *Frankfurter Rundschau*, licensed by the Information Control Division only a week earlier, attacked Kurt Blaum, the Oberbuergermeister of Frankfurt, for tolerating an inept and unresponsive municipal bureaucracy. (As a Wehrmacht major responsible for expediting production in a large munitions plant, Blaum fell under a denazification category of automatic disqualification for public office. When I called an MG officer's attention to Blaum's past, he replied, "Blaum is a good man, he's efficient, he has had organizational and administrative experience, he'll get things moving, he's the man we need.")

Two weeks later the *Rundschau* endorsed the demand of a group of leading citizens that Blaum follow the example of other American Zone mayors and appoint a council to assist him in administering the city.[3] When General Eisenhower proclaimed that Frankfurt could be considered completely denazified, the *Rundschau*, in an implicit confutation, complained of the failure of the city administration to provide relief to Kzler:"The victims of the Nazis in the concentration camps . . . have received publicity for months all over the world. . . . And in Frankfurt hundreds of these victims of fascism are going around without a decent suit of clothes, not to mention their more tragic needs."

Late in September, upon reports of a mounting partisan fracas evoked by the attacks on Blaum I undertook an investigation to determine whether political conditions in Frankfurt demonstrated a readiness to participate in the imminent electoral campaigns. I sought to gain insights into the positions of the leaders of the newly authorized local political parties as exposed in their stands on the attacks of the *Rundschau* on the mayor. On 2 October I issued a report entitled "The Attitudes of the Leaders of the Political Parties in Frankfurt toward the *Frankfurter Rundschau*."

Resentment of the newspaper's attacks on the mayor, I discovered, was centered in the "bourgeois" (the epithet they applied to themselves) parties, whose leaders considered the *Rundschau* leftist and not representing their interests. (The editorial board of the publication was, indeed, composed en-

---

their own newspapers and involved them in implementing Soviet denazification and demilitarization directives, judging war criminals, developing a new educational system, and reorganizing the German economy.)

3. The *Rundschau* further embarrassed the mayor by publishing his address to the first session of the newly constituted council in which he expressed chagrin at the fact that the denazification of the municipal administration was leaving him without properly qualified personnel.

tirely of Kzler—three SPD, two Communists, one representative of the pre-Hitler [Catholic] Zentrum party, and one nonparty man.)[4]

The Christian Democrats

The opinions of the Christian Democratic Union (CDU) interviewees exemplified the varied views within a party united only on the issue of government support of religious education. Prelate Herr, dean of the Catholic clergy in Frankfurt, protested the cooperation of Dr. Gerst, the Zentrum editor on the *Rundschau*, with Communists and Socialists. Herr advocated the establishment of a second, Christian Democratic newspaper. Knappstein, the editor-in-chief of the pre–VE Day *Frankfurter Zeitung*, considered an all-party editorial board an impossibility since he believed that leftists always win control in such circumstances by labeling their opponents Nazis. As evidence of the "Communist orientation" of the paper, Knappstein pointed to favorable descriptions of reconstruction efforts in Berlin (initially under sole Russian, now under Four Power administration). He shrugged when asked whether in defiance of Allied directives the paper should criticize the policies of the occupying powers.

In contrast, two other Christian Democrats, Postal Inspector Husch, who lost two sons in the war and suffered a demotion during the Hitler years because of suspected political unreliability, and Dr. Hilpert, the president of the Chamber of Commerce and a veteran of Buchenwald, denied that the *Rundschau* could be labeled "red" or "socialist" and praised the antifascist stand of the paper.

The Liberal Democrats

The Liberal leaders, all old men, hoped to restore the status quo of the post–World War I years, to reestablish trade relations quickly with the West, and to obtain from the Western powers a guarantee of protection against Russia. Leaders of the other parties, on the other hand, feared that nationalist, militarist, and Nazi elements might group themselves about the Liberals and use these old men as their tools.[5] Schwarzhaupt, a former Deutsche Volkspartei deputy in the Prussian Landtag (provincial legislature) and a retired school official, objected to the attacks on Germany's past voiced in the *Rundschau* as "bad taste before the Americans." Dr. Fertsch, a director

---

4. Cedric Belfrage, the press officer in charge of licensing newspapers in the Western District, gave preference to Kzler in choosing editorial boards. "We may not have the finest journalism," he declared to me, "but we will have an anti-Nazi press."

5. According to Christian Democrat Dombrowski, who represented his party in abortive coalition negotiations with them, the Liberals objected to the following plank in the Christian Democratic platform: "We desire above all that the idea of force that has been implanted in our people as a spiritual disease for some two hundred years of Prussian-German history be eradicated from our political outlook."

of a large cleaning and dyeing plant and head of the Liberal Party, complained that a letter he sent to the *Rundschau* had not been published. In it he had sharply criticized the Americans for not allowing him to use the one-quarter of his plant they had requisitioned. He was surprised to learn that criticism of the occupying powers was not permitted. Like some of the Christian Democratic informants, Herr Ellers, an official in the Sandoz Chemical Works, objected to the predominance of Kzler on the staff of the newspaper, complaining that "these people" now demanded special privileges for having opposed the Nazis despite the fact that people like him had suffered just as much. (Ellers had been bombed out of his home in an Allied air raid and had demonstrated his anti-Nazism by refusing to write "Heil Hitler!" at the end of his letters!)

The Social Democrats

The SPD leadership was divided between those favoring cooperation with the Communists and those desiring no cooperation with any party. In Frankfurt the second faction seemed to be winning the upper hand; a Communist proposal for a public announcement of a coalition of the two parties had been rejected. The major issue dividing the two parties lay in their attitudes regarding the issue of German collective guilt. The Social Democrats held the Western democracies and Russia as well as non-SPD Germans to blame for the rise of Hitler, a contention that had grave ramifications in regard to the issues of reparations, denazification, and decartellization as well as the tenure of the Allied occupation and administration of Germany.[6]

The Communists

The Communists did not consider the difference over collective guilt an insurmountable obstacle to a coalition of the two workers parties. Furthermore, since one of the cardinal goals of Communist policy was to unite all democratic elements against nazism and for reconstruction, the Communists were in favor of adding a bourgeois representative to the paper. They insisted, however, that bourgeois political leaders in turn grant equitable leftist representation in the city administration.

All the newspaper's editors, non-Communist as well as Communist, opposed the hiring of any of the old *Frankfurter Zeitung* editors, charging that they had reached accommodations with Goebbels. In addition, they accused the

---

6. Ulrich, a pre-1933 SPD leader, expressed dissatisfaction with the Americans for announcing through a statement by Thomas Mann that they were coming as liberators and then coming actually as conquerors. He declared that as "the sole irreconcilable enemies of Hitler" Social Democrats did not share in any collective guilt and deserved to be treated as liberated people.

bourgeois elements of opposing privileges for Kzler because of bad consciences and accusing them of coming to the defense of "muss" Nazis in order to win their support for the Christian Democratic and Liberal parties.

Blaum

A "nonparty technician," Blaum dismissed the attacks on him as an example of the kind of "leftist" and "Nazi" maneuvers to be expected from a paper like the *Rundschau*. He echoed Knappstein in asserting that the population wanted to know more news than "what MG permitted them to have"; they wanted to know the "actual" conditions in other parts of Germany. According to Blaum, too, the letters to the editor in the *Rundschau* were selected for their criticism of Germany's past—a Communist tactic. The people, he declared, were not eager to have the past thrown up to them.

This investigation revealed traditional German nationalism among the bourgeois parties, latent opposition to the Occupation forces as well as a continuing impact of the years of intensive Nazi anti-"bolshevik" (anti-Communist and anti-Soviet) propaganda with a resultant eagerness to split the Western Powers from Russia, resentment at the Americans' granting preference to confirmed anti-nazis for posts of authority, and an unwillingness to cooperate with people of different political orientations in the solution of general problems. It was clear, on the other hand, that the *Rundschau* did not exhibit any of the anti-Potsdam attitudes of its opponents.[7]

The discord emerging among the political leaders provoked in this instance by the *Rundschau*-Blaum conflict was certain to be exacerbated in the heat of the forthcoming electoral campaigns. The warning of Munich Oberbuergermeister Karl Scharnagl upon Eisenhower's announcement of elections seemed justified:"Elections always bring political disunity, and that is not desirable at present."

---

7. A week after the completion of this report, an ICD poll of public reactions to the *Frankfurter Rundschau* revealed that "the overwhelming majority of the Frankfurt population were pleased with the paper" and that "the particular criticisms voiced by conservative leaders in the previous study found little agreement among the general population."

13

Rehearsal for McCarthyism

Threats to the Wartime Alliance

After VE Day in the highest circles in Washington, according to Willard C. Matthias, editor of the daily Diplomatic Summary in the Military Division of the War Department General Staff during World War II and the subsequent years:

there were those who quickly concluded that the Soviets were bound and determined to move aggressively toward a world dominated by the USSR and to do it by force if necessary. . . . It was their position that we had the bomb and the Soviets did not. We needed to force them by military action to change their leaders and their policies—before they could recover from the war, build up their military establishment, and develop their own atomic weapons capabilities.[1]

Although at ICD no one was aware of the extent of such division among top officials in Washington, the growing anti-Soviet atmosphere that I encountered at OSS headquarters in Wiesbaden impelled caution in regard to various issues as in Al Toombs's holding up transmission to higher echelons of the Munich reports. Members of the American press corps, however, displayed little restraint in exposing a shift in occupation goals.[2]

The Soviets were fully aware of a shift in attitudes of the Western Allies. "After Franklin Roosevelt's death," alleges Marshal Zhukov, "the United States policy took quite a different course."[3] On 5 June 1945, at a meeting in Berlin of the commanders of the four victorious armies, Zhukov accused the British of failing to withdraw their troops to borders agreed upon at the Yalta Conference. At a subsequent meeting he presented evidence that during the last days of the war "Churchill had telegraphed instructions to Montgomery to stockpile captured German arms for rapid reissue to German troops in the event of a Soviet advance toward the west." He charged that

---

1. Matthias, *America's Strategic Blunders*, 44.
2. On 24 August *Times* correspondent Drew Middleton warned:"Growing regard for the docile Germans—'they're hard workers' as a typical comment—and *the negative attitude toward the Russians* that has been adopted by many senior officers within a group that does not include Gen. Eisenhower or Gen. Clay are . . . attitudes rather than definite problems and hence more difficult to deal with."
3. Zhukov, *Reminiscences and Reflections*, 429–73. On 22 April 1945, a week after the death of Franklin Roosevelt, recounts Soviet ambassador Andrei Gromyko, the newly installed president Harry S. Truman, "untutored in foreign policy . . . spoke harshly to Soviet Foreign Minister Molotov in their first conversation. . . .' His tough words left a lasting impression" (Gromyko, *Memoirs* [New York, 1988], 96).

"German armed forces and German land, naval and air forces still exist in the British zone of occupation in Germany."

At the Potsdam Big Three conference in July, as recently released Soviet archives attest, Stalin and Molotov made major concessions in an attempt to preserve the wartime collaboration with the Western Allies, yielding to demands by Clement Attlee and Harry Truman that agreements reached at Teheran and Yalta with Churchill and Roosevelt be abandoned.[4]

General Eisenhower, indeed, insisted upon meticulous implementation of the provisions of the Yalta and Teheran conferences,[5] and he had no doubts about the Soviet commitment to postwar American-Soviet collaboration.[6] During his post-Potsdam visit to Moscow, Eisenhower reported, Stalin turned the conversation to the Berlin (Allied Control) Council "and remarked that it was important not only because of its specific task but because it provided a testing ground to determine whether great nations victors in a war could continue to cooperate effectively in the problems of peace."[7]

Other Americans in Germany, of course, took seriously the commitments undertaken at Potsdam. Mere days after the publication of the Potsdam agreement, Col. Charles S. Reid, chief property control officer at OMGUS, declared to the press:"If we leave the economic power of both big and little business in their [Nazi] hands, a potential and actual totalitarian control will remain from which Nazism . . . will be resurrected." In a 29 September dispatch, Raymond Daniell warned that strains in the relationship between the Western Allies and the Soviet Union threatened implementation of Potsdam provisions.[8] Simultaneously, Sen. Harley M. Kilgore, chairman of the Senate War Mobilization Subcommittee, issued a warning of "the disquieting impression that thus far some of our Military Government representa-

---

4. See appendix 31, p. 204.
5. See appendix 32, p. 204.
6. See appendix 33, p. 205.
7. Ibid., 458. Eisenhower quotes this additional statement by Stalin:

There are many ways in which we need American help in our great task to raise the standards of living of the Russian people, which have been seriously damaged by the war. We must learn all about your scientific achievements in agriculture. Likewise, we must get your technicians to help us in our engineering and construction problems. We want to know more about mass production methods in factories. We know that we are behind in these things, and we know that you can help us. (435)

On 6 September, a mere month after the conclusion of the Potsdam Conference, in a hardly disguised gesture of ill-will the three Western commanders informed Zhukov of their decision not to participate in a victory parade previously scheduled to take place in Berlin, where the Soviet suffered 300,000 casualties in the final major battle of the war.

8. Daniell wrote:"the fundamental split that is developing in the [Four Power] Group Control Council and within the American delegation itself . . . a schism between those who really mean to carry out the Berlin [Potsdam] declaration for the disarmament and demilitarization of Germany and those who, for one reason or another, seek to vitiate the Berlin agreement. Behind the whole thing lies the basic cleavage between one faction that would place its hope for future peace on the continuation of the Anglo-Russian-American alliance, and the other wing that wants to preserve a vestige of German industrial and military strength to defend western civilization at the Elbe."

tives . . . have not been carrying out either the spirit or the letter of the Allied agreement on the treatment of Germany. . . . reluctant to order the dismantling of war factories; they have retained Nazis in civil and industrial posts."[9]

Interrogating POWs Liberated by the Soviets
During my August visit to Munich I interrogated three German soldiers who had been released from Soviet captivity. One man, forty-two years of age, had been captured on 9 May in a village near Magdeburg and brought to an enclosure at Belzig, outside Berlin, where, the Russians, after interrogating a sampling of the 20,000 prisoners, announced that all soldiers over forty-five and under fifteen years of age were free to return home. He himself was released along with other POWs who had suffered punishment by the Nazis.

The second man, a thirty-one-year-old former construction worker, was taken prisoner by the Czech underground on 8 May 1945, turned over to the Russians and transported to a large POW enclosure near Dresden, where after ten days he and all the others in the camp were released. The third man, a forty-six-year-old policeman, had been captured in April in Austria. Upon presenting evidence that he had suffered punishment for political unreliability, he was provided with a pass to return home.

The three men reported that in captivity they were well fed; their guards were businesslike; and they suffered no maltreatment. All three, however, expressed a preference for American occupation because the Americans, unlike the Russians, did not requisition German industrial and agricultural machinery. The two who had fought on the Eastern Front did admit that they had seen the wanton destruction wrought by the Germans in Russia, and one of them insisted that any other nation—France, for example—would have torn Germany apart out of vengeance.

On the other hand, the three men considered Soviet denazification more thorough than the Americans' and not merely in regard to discrimination among German POWs. They pointed to the large numbers of important Nazis in Munich still living undisturbed in their villas, while returning anti-Nazi prisoners of war and former concentration-camp inmates were huddling in cellars. One of the men had heard that in Dresden Nazis were being forced out of their homes for the benefit of homeless anti-Nazis. Another had been told that in Vienna the Russians had mobilized all Party members into work commandos to clear the rubble and rebuild dwellings.

---

9. Quotations from Kilgore and his committee are extracted, except when otherwise noted, from the report of hearings before the Senate Subcommittee on War Mobilizations under the heading *Elimination of German Resources for War*, 79th Congress, Washington, D.C., 1946.

One of the men had been impressed by the fact that unlike the Nazis the Soviets did not propagandize for war, and (unlike Nazis and militarists I had interrogated as well as some Americans I had met) "no one of the three men expected a war between the Soviet Union and the United States."[10]

At a request from a conscientious MG officer, I investigated a committee headed by a Czarist admiral and composed of what I described as "some other fishy White Russians." In violation of an Allied Control Council directive, they were disseminating anti-Soviet propaganda among DPs from Eastern Europe. I battled with another MG officer until I got him to close the offices of the committee. Then with the Soviet liaison officer in Munich I drafted a report about the group and its activities.

How this émigré committee had obtained MG authorization to carry on its activities I was unable to ascertain.

Anticommunism

During the last months of the war, mindful of the revolutionary upsurge in Germany after World War I, policymakers in Washington and at SHAEF banned calls to revolt and ordered the disbandment of Antifas. After VE Day local MG officials in their weekly or biweekly intelligence reports listed two categories of "subversive" activities:"Nazi" and "Anti-fascist," equating the two. Many MG officers excluded Communists or those they denominated Communists from offices and failed to provide welfare to Kzler.[11]

During the last months of the war and after VE Day, SPD and KPD rank-and-filers collaborated in rebuilding devastated towns and cities. By late summer in numerous localities, joint councils of the two parties were being established, and there was increasing talk of unification of the two workers parties as resentment intensified at the failure to remove Nazis and

---

10. In my report I cautioned against drawing general conclusions from a mere three interrogations. It would subsequently become known that tens of thousands of German POWs, especially those captured on Soviet territory, died in captivity.

11. In the interwar years Americans underwent anti-Communist as well anti-Soviet indoctrination almost as intense as, if not as intense as, that the Germans suffered under the Nazis, and numerous Army and MG officials displayed the impact of this indoctrination. See appendix 34, pp. 205–6, for extracts from the *New York Times Index* for 1939 and 1940, for a sense of the feverish anticommunist atmosphere of the years preceding American entrance into the war.

Other Americans in Germany, men like Lieutenant Torland, the political affairs officer in Wiesbaden, praised the Communists as "hard workers" and insisted that "when you give them a job, you can be sure it'll be carried out." An MG officer in Stuttgart assured me that if he were a German he would vote for the Communists because they alone, he declared, offered a clear and realistic program for denazification and reconstruction and possessed the discipline to carry it out. Indeed, at a press conference early in September, Dr. Walter L. Dorn, deputy to the chief of Military Government, lauded the Communists as "the most reliable anti-Nazis," and Communists were disproportionately represented on the denazification boards pursuant to an MG directive mandating the appointment of proven antifascists as judges and prosecutors.

war profiteers from high posts in the American Zone.[12] A seesaw development ensued in which antidemocratic governmental actions impelled further moves toward workers party unification followed by repressive anticoalition maneuvers by military government.

Early in September, in response to the *Rundschau*'s publishing an open letter signed by leading citizens of one of the Frankfurt boroughs demanding an investigation of corruption and inefficiency in the local housing office, Oberbuergermeister Blaum issued an order forbidding city officials to speak to the press. A week later, on 16 September, the workers parties in Frankfurt staged the first postwar political rallies in the American Zone with representatives of each party attending the other's gathering, and, according to a *New York Times* report, "the leaders of the two parties . . . pledged that the parties would work together in bringing about the rebirth of the German 'political conscience.'"

A week after these meetings, carbon copies of a four-page mimeographed document entitled "Strategy and Tactics after the VII World Congress" were circulated in Frankfurt. After analysis I characterized the document, primitive and clumsy in composition, as "an example of the black anti-Communist propaganda that may become more and more common as political differences sharpen with the approach of elections." The statement, I reported, "seeks to split the Social Democrats from the Communists, to develop a suspicion of the Communist Party among MG officials, and to intensify the fears of anti-Communist Germans."[13]

A month later a certain Otto Kipp, a veteran of the Spanish Civil War international brigades and a Kzler, was arrested, charged with serving as an informer in the Buchenwald concentration camp. According to former Buchenwald inmate and current editor of the *Frankfurter Rundschau* Emil Carlebach, however, Kipp as a clerk in the Buchenwald headquarters saved fellow prisoners at great risk to himself. Denounced to camp authorities by informers, Kipp was sentenced to a punitive labor company and was rescued from certain death only by maneuvers of the camp resistance movement. Now, denounced once again, this time by Polish former Buchenwald prisoners, he had been imprisoned by the American War Crimes Commission in the former Nazi concentration camp at Dachau, where he was at risk of

---

12. On 27 September, Raymond Daniell reported to the *New York Times*: "Moves by the Social Democrats and Communists to merge their forces have been discouraged by the military government people on the ground that it is undesirable at this date to permit the formation of political blocs." Daniell noted "the constant German propaganda to the effect that unless something is done to help Germany on her feet again communism will become a real danger in Western Europe." Fear of the platforms of the leftist parties, he declared, was a fundamental factor in "the breakdown of the denazification program."

13. Although I had had experience with "black" propaganda, it did not occur to me at the time that the document had very likely been drafted by the OSS.

being murdered by fanatical Nazi internees. I retain no record of the outcome of Kipp's case, but by his arrest and incarceration at Dachau MG sent a warning to both the Communists and the Socialists.

On 13 November, in an editorial entitled "Fuehrer Prinzip oder Democratie?" the *Rundschau* reprinted an article by Blaum published in the 1940 *Reichsverwaltungsblatt* (German Administration Yearbook) in which Blaum proclaimed that "the accomplishments of the Strasbourg administration were due to the healthy Fuehrer principle." (Blaum had served in the Strasbourg administration).[14] Early in December the *Frankfurter Rundschau* once again sounded the alarm. The police president, the paper reported, was giving preference in hiring to former "twelve-year men," a corps of professional soldiers. Forbidden to join the Nazi Party, these fanatical Nazis were not excluded from police service under denazification regulations.[15]

Reacting to such developments, on 22 December SPD Buergermeister Maas of Wiesbaden, Hessian SPD Minister of Interior Hans Venedey, and Oskar Mueller, the KPD Hessian minister of labor, called a meeting of leaders of the two parties in the Wiesbaden area. The delegates issued an appeal for unification.[16]

A week later at a conference in Frankfurt the provincial SPD leadership issued an equivocal response to the unity resolution adopted at Wiesbaden: "Every attempt must be made to develop a positive unified belief in democracy among the working class . . . but the question of unification of the two workers parties can only be decided after Germany is unified, the peace treaty has been ratified, a national party meeting has been held, and the Socialist International has taken a position on the question."

With the rural elections only a month away, the antiunification SPD leaders were signaling their decision to go it alone, hopeful that by breaking off with the Communists they would win support of the British Labor Party and the French Socialists as well as the favor of high officials at OMGUS to gain numerous posts in the elections soon to be held in the anti-Communist rural areas.

14. Blaum also urged the Germanization of Alsace-Lorraine with the replacement of the French by "good German stock"—evidence that MG's appointee sympathized with other Nazi doctrines than the Fuehrer principle.
15. Three months earlier Komissar Fries of the Frankfurt criminal police was suddenly handed over to the French for trial for wartime crimes in Alsace.
16. When I interviewed him in August, the septuagenarian Maas professed his weariness with the repeated instances of internecine strife among German workers he had lived through since before World War I. If the Socialists had accepted the Communist call to general strikes in 1932 and again in 1933, Maas insisted, Hitler would not have succeeded in usurping dictatorial power. Subsequently, his sons had been sent off to war and his city destroyed. "I don't want my grandchildren to go through a period like the one we've endured," he said. "There's no reason why the two parties shouldn't unite. That's the only way we can assure our future."

Munich: The Persecution of Alfred Kroth

"In Catholic reactionary Bavaria any liberal movement starts off with two strikes on it," observed Raymond Daniell in a 27 September dispatch. Nevertheless, early in October, by which time it had become clear that Minister President Schaeffer's replacement by Dr. Wilhelm Hoegner (a proponent of SPD-KPD unity) did not signal a new direction in MG policy, SPD and KPD leaders issued a joint statement calling for thorough denazification and democratic renewal in Bavaria and for nationalization of industries which profiteered under the Nazi regime. MG reacted swiftly, targeting a city councilman who enjoyed the respect of colleagues of every party with an announcement that Alfred Kroth's membership in the Hitler Youth and the Nazi Party rendered him ineligible for the post in the Bavarian provincial cabinet to which with Hoegner's agreement he had been nominated by the KPD.

Over the next weeks the Bavarian Communist leadership submitted three separate appeals to this ruling, maintaining that Kroth joined the Nazi Party at the instructions of the Communist underground and rendered extraordinary service subsequently as an official in the Oberbuergermeister's office. They submitted affidavits in Kroth's support from numerous non-Communists—former classmates, neighbors, teachers, colleagues at work, and Jews whom he aided and protected. Former Army comrades attested that in the presence of their entire unit Kroth openly attacked the Nazi regime. Kroth, one reported, guided an American Army unit into a Munich suburb and participated in the Freedom Action Bavaria revolt against SS troops.[17] I submitted a memorandum in Kroth's defense, noting particularly the assistance he provided with the ICD Munich reports. Learning of my action, Kroth sent a letter of thanks to which he added an ironic postscript:

Deputy Mayor Stadelmayr has had to resign.

They have, however, arranged a very good departure for him. In a letter to the Sueddeutsche Zeitung published on 16 November, Oberbuergermeister Scharnagl accepted Stadelmayr's resignation as of 1 December with an expression of warmest thanks for his services. [Nazi] Party member Stadelmayr thus will be relieved of his post with thanks. Anti-fascists, who have had the bad luck still to be alive, are "discharged." You can imagine my reaction.

---

17. See appendix 35, pp. 206–7, for three of the numerous documents, two by Party officials; in the third a woman in her seventies who had spent years in a concentration camp quotes the judgment of Kroth of her son, who had been executed by the Nazis. These documents express implicit criticisms of MG's motivations.

MG subjected Kroth to two years of unrelieved hounding, dismissing him from his post as city councilman, blocking his bank account, summoning him repeatedly before judicial bodies, and even imprisoning him. After his belated acquittal of all charges in a series of hearings, Kroth was, nevertheless, barred from further political activity.

Anti-Fascists in the Soviet Zone

Paradoxically, while the Americans were maneuvering to block unification of the workers parties in their zone, the Soviets were following a similar policy. In his study of political developments in the Soviet Zone, Norman M. Naimark reports that after VE Day newly appointed commandants were given "no more guidance than . . . to seek out well-known anti-fascists and opponents of Hitler and name them, regardless of party affiliation, as the mayors, Landrats [county commissioners], and police chiefs." Members of the National Committee for Free Germany formed in Russia after Stalingrad "were gradually integrated into the state and political apparatus." To the dismay of German Communists, however, as Naimark demonstrates with impressive evidence, "the Soviet authorities *rejected . . . efforts at establishing socialist institutions and forbade the unification of the two workers' parties in the Zone* [my emphasis—ADK]. In the spirit of the resolutions of the VII Congress of the Comintern in 1935 regarding the Popular Front," Naimark explains, "the Soviets sought to support those political forces of the left and of the progressive bourgeoisie, which would complete the 'anti-fascist democratic revolution' in Germany."[18]

On 2 September, 80,000 to 90,000 Berliners, the largest gathering yet assembled in postwar Germany, marched through the Soviet sector of the city in a tribute "to the victims of fascism." "Two columns of former victims of the Gestapo headed by men in striped prison uniforms," an Associated Press dispatch recounted, "filed into the Neukoelln Stadium . . . more than 1,000 wreaths were laid beside a memorial 'to our dead heroes.'" Oberbuergermeister Arthur Werner proclaimed that Hitler had cost the world "hundreds of thousands of martyrs" and that the German people "must never again return to militarism and nazism."[19]

---

18. Naimark, *Russians in Germany*, 13, 253–55.
    After studying recently released minutes of three commissions established after Stalingrad to formulate postwar policies in Germany, Russian historian Alexei Filitov reported that the commission chaired by M. M. Litvinov recommended dismemberment and deindustrialization of Germany, a proposal comparable to one promoted by Secretary of the Treasury Henry Morgenthau in 1943; the I. M. Maisky commission urged bolshevization of the portion of Germany under Soviet control and eventually of the entire country; the K. V. Voroshilov commission recommended continuing the prewar Popular Front strategy of uniting all democratic elements in resistance to fascism and called for minimum intervention in German social and economic conditions as well as collaboration with the Western Allies in establishing a unified German bourgeois democratic state. Filitov ("Stalins Deutschlandplanung," 43–54) concluded:
    One can say: among the three contesting strategy proposals—"socialist" part or total Germany; "harsh peace"; or bourgeois-democratic German state—the last was chosen by Soviet officials with decisive authority. . . . Initiatives for sovietizing of Germany were either rejected or ignored by top leadership of the Communist Party and occupation officials.
    Melvin P. Leffler states in *Specter of Communism*, "New evidence from the archives in Moscow and the former German Democratic Republic . . . suggests that the Kremlin was thinking about permitting more pluralist policies inside their zone in Germany and of dismissing some of the hard-line administrators who were seeking to sovietize" (42).

19. Seated on the dais was the sister of New York's mayor Fiorello La Guardia, who, married to a German, had spent eleven months in a Nazi prison.

Ten days later, on 12 September, charging that because of the refusal of the Western Allies to implement the Potsdam decision for the establishment of central administrative departments for "the peaceful, democratic unification of Germany," Marshal Zhukov announced the formation of a central administration for the Soviet Zone.[20] Within a directorate composed of eleven representatives of the four "anti-fascist" parties, only three were Communists.

Two days later, on 14 September, 2,500 SPD leaders from all parts of Germany assembled for a conference in Berlin. Otto Grotewohl, head of the party in the Soviet Zone and the keynote speaker, drew applause when he declared that the German working class could "hold its head as high as those of Austria, Czechoslovakia, Italy and France" inasmuch as "large sections of the working class . . . never bowed to Hitler." He drew a standing ovation, however, when he called for collaboration between the Social Democratic and Communist parties in a "united working class front" and revealed that fusion of the central committees of the two parties in the Soviet Zone had already begun.

The contradictory positions of the Western Allies and the Soviets toward German unification and toward German anti-nazis exemplified their growing alienation from each other and their divergent policies in regard to the provisions of the Potsdam Agreement:the first intimations of Cold War.

20. With the repeated failure of the Western Allies to honor the provisions of Potsdam, the Soviets reversed themselves and (with the French) began to oppose German unification, and it was delayed for more than four decades.

PART III: TRIUMPH OF THE COLD WARRIORS

14
A Military Government in Crisis
WINTER 1945-1946

On 29 September, seeking to blunt press protests regarding developments in the American zone, General Eisenhower issued a statement in which he claimed "some initial progress . . . in the reeducation program" and noted that the circulation of licensed German newspapers had reached more than three million since the issuing of the first license to the *Frankfurter Rundschau* two months earlier. By 1 October, he reported, a million elementary textbooks would be ready for distribution to schools.

In praising two of the most effective MG divisions, Education and Information Control, Eisenhower could not dismiss the dismay arising from his ordering—simultaneous with his elections decree—a rapid transfer of authority to German officials. Under this directive ICD, which had barely initiated the licensing and staffing of newspapers, radio stations, publishing houses, and theaters, was to transfer to the Germans supervision of the media and the entertainment industry by June 1946.[1]

At a 12 October press conference, feeling compelled to defend both directives, elections and transfer of authority, General Eisenhower insisted, according to *Times* correspondent Drew Middleton, "that Nazis would be deprived of the vote in Germany, that the Army would 'uproot Nazism in every shape and form' and any officer who did not put his heart into the denazification program would receive another job." General Eisenhower admitted that "we expect to have a lowering of efficiency as a result of the denazification and are prepared for that," but, he declared, the American policy would in the long run "give the Germans a chance to lift themselves out of the gutter. I would not stay here," he proclaimed, "for five minutes if I thought that for expediency it would be up to me to modify the Potsdam Agreement. We got our orders from Potsdam and they are right down my alley."[2]

---

1. Of the transfer of authority to German officials Raymond Daniell noted in an 8 October dispatch: *The announcement . . . was couched in language designed to indicate that the denazification and reeducation programs had progressed to such a point that it was safe to turn over the administration of lower echelons of government to Germans acting under American direction. . . . The fact is we . . . cannot continue to manage German affairs and still send men home at the rate at which we insist upon sending them, without replacements, and so we are getting out of the business of occupation on the operational level and asserting that nevertheless we are directing affairs by remote control—a very difficult business with Germans.*
See also appendix 36, p. 207.
2. Drew Middleton, *New York Times*, 12 December 1945.

A month later, about to depart for Washington to assume a new post as Army chief of staff, Eisenhower issued a valedictory review of his policies in Germany, presenting an optimistic view of the future of the American Zone. He avoided mention, however, of one crucial issue, the cleansing of German industry of Nazi and militarist influence. Witnesses before the Kilgore Senate Subcommittee on War Mobilization were meanwhile offering alarming testimony, particularly in regard to Military Government's failure to break up I.G. Farben, "a world-embracing cartel and Germany's biggest single war industry . . . indivisible from the Nazi government and its General Staff."[3]

Proceedings in regard to Richard Freudenberg, the largest shoe manufacturer in Germany and one of the richest members of the Nazi Party, provided a striking example of sabotage of OMGUS and Potsdam denazification directives. Although Freudenberg had held government posts which placed him in a mandatory arrest category, the HQ denazification appeals board in a four-to-one decision abrogated a sentence imposed on Freudenberg by a German denazification court and restored his civil rights, wealth, and position. Colonel Babcock of the Public Safety division, who cast the dissenting vote, protested:"I voted against this man because if he is reinstated . . . it will be ridiculous for us to remove smaller Nazis and leave the big one."

Countering Babcock's objection, one of Ambassador Robert D. Murphy's aides, a man named Reinhardt, bluntly exposed the rationale for the Freudenberg ruling and for weakening the program for the denazification of German industry generally:"What we are doing here through denazification is nothing less than a social revolution. If the Russians want to bolshevize their side of the Elbe, that is their business, but it is not in conformity with American standards to cut away the basis of private property."

The American failure to persuade the American Zone populace of the justice of the denazification program was exposed in a December ICD poll

---

3. In mid-December, according to the *New York Times*, Maj. Gen. John A. Hilldring, director of the War Department's Civil Affairs Division, and Col. Bernard Bernstein, General Eisenhower's wartime fiscal adviser and until recently director of the OMGUS Division of Investigation of Cartels and External Assets, testified before the Kilgore Committee, charging that before the war I.G. Farben had been "able to gain support of the German war machine from American corporations with which it was linked." The corporation's "influence and war potential was so great," they and other witnesses asserted, "that it often guided the Nazi government's plans for world conquest." Colonel Bernstein declared that as a result of a cartel relationship with Standard Oil Co. of New Jersey, I.G. Farben was able to deny wartime synthetic rubber production to the United States. Bernstein further testified that orders for Germany's denazification and deindustrialization were "watered down" by officials "more concerned with getting things going." I.G. Farben, for example, still had 80 percent of its 1943 production capacity intact and its war potential was "much larger than at the outbreak of World War II."

In February, Russell A. Nixon, recently dismissed as acting American representative on the Allied Control Council External Property Commission, testified:"[The] directive to arrest key industrial and financial figures has not been applied. As a result of [the] lack of a specified operational policy and of clearly assigned personnel to handle the problem, shockingly few industrial and financial leaders . . . were in our custody at the end of 1945."

of German reactions to the trial of the major German war criminals then in progress in Nuremberg. Most Germans, the poll disclosed, were convinced of the guilt of the defendants, but about a third of the informants objected to the indictments of the Elite Guard (SS), the storm troopers (SA), and the Gestapo.[4]

ICD on the Defensive

Quixotically ignoring the trend evolving in OMGUS policy at an ever more rapid tempo, ICD Intelligence continued to maintain the Daily Digest and Weekly Intelligence Summary (ICIS) as organs of defense of the Potsdam Agreement.[5] From the mass of intelligence reports from ICD investigators and from Army and MG units throughout the Zone as well as from out-of-channels sources, the editorial staff extracted for publication examples of both violations and implementation of Allied directives.[6] I also drafted memoranda particularly but not solely on issues of immediate import to the Information Control Division, responding on 16 November, for example, to a sharp criticism in a MG HQ bulletin of the political orientation of the ICD-licensed newspapers. I pointed out that sample ICD surveys disproved the charge that Germans thought that the occupation power was preaching to them in the German newspapers. "The editors of all the newspapers," I declared, "have presented propaganda similar to our own because they have been chosen as anti-fascists who would present such a philosophy and approach."[7]

4. Commented the *New York Times* on 2 January in an editorial under the heading "Guilt of a Nation": *Our reporter did not think the trials had changed "the basic German attitude, which is one of self-pity, rationalization and shifting responsibility for the country's disaster to such leaders of nazism as the men now on trial." Perhaps the most appalling aspect of nazism is not its crimes but the manner in which millions of Germans were led to accept or condone those crimes. . . . Their punishment when it comes will be the gnawing of an awakened conscience. Only so can there be a reawakened and recivilized Germany.*

5. Expanded and produced in a new glossy format, the Weekly Intelligence Summary was praised by General Joseph T. McNarney, Eisenhower's successor as Supreme Commander in the American Zone, and called the most important intelligence document in the theater. It had a circulation of 200 among U.S. generals and ambassadors in Europe, top officials in the United States, and the British and French foreign offices.

6. The ICD publications reported MG appointments to posts of responsibility of such high-ranking Party members as Dorpmueller, formerly Hitler's minister of transport, entrusted with the rehabilitation of the railway system in the American zone; and Seeger, formerly an adjutant to Fritz Todt (who supervised the construction of the Atlantic Wall from which German shells mowed down Allied troops on D-Day), charged with the distribution of construction and building materials in the province of Baden-Wuerttemberg. (The memorandum providing this information came from a Mr. Baker of the Building Materials Section of the Industrial Division of Military Government of Baden-Wuerttemberg.)

7. On the other hand, Oskar Mueller, the Communist Minister of Labor of Greater Hesse, complained that a German émigré serving in Bavaria as the ICD District Chief of Press and Publications was refusing to appoint Communists to the staffs of licensed newspapers in the province. I confirmed that Mueller was correct in his allegation. In response to my memorandum Colonel Powell demanded an inquiry into Mueller's charge, which represented a violation of an ICD directive for representation of all anti-Nazi elements on editorial staffs.

One of the leading officials in the Bavarian Information Control Branch was violently anti-"red," declaring on one occasion:"When we go home we'll know how to deal with organizations like the Ameri-

Land Reform

On 5 December the Soviet Zone Liberal Democratic newspaper *Der Morgen* announced the completion of a large-scale zonal land reform conducted by a commission composed of the "four anti-fascist parties."[8] Colonel Powell asked for an investigation of the reactions of local KPD and SPD leaders to the measure, and on 14 December I submitted a report in which I noted that the Communists in the province of Hesse had established a committee to prepare a study of the issue in the province. Questionnaires had been circulated to each of the thirty-five Kreis branches of the provincial KPD to obtain relevant data. "We are merely trying to catch up with history," asserted the KPD chairman of the Land Reform Committee, "and remove feudal conditions which were abolished 150 years ago in France, twenty-five years ago in Russia and never even existed in the United States." He considered land reform necessary not only to further the democratization of the country but also to help relieve Germany's desperate food situation and to provide a livelihood to refugees. Anticipating MG hesitancy in regard to what would be, if enacted, the most radical democratic reform as yet introduced into the American Zone, KPD leaders expressed confidence that land reform would be carried out with American support inasmuch as the measure fell, they believed, within the political and economic aims of the occupation.

The Social Democratic leaders had not formulated any program on land reform. One of the party leaders declared that the SPD was not in favor of a land reform since the party held that all land belonged to the State and the People and thus could not be given to one individual after being taken away from another. He thought that the SPD would favor *socialization*, that is, dispossession of large estates with compensation and lending of confiscated lands to individuals. He contended, however, that land reform at present would probably curtail food production in the confusion during the implementation of the measure.

OMGUS did not acknowledge receipt of the report and took no stand or action on land reform.

With major policy decisions formulated at OMGUS headquarters, ICD Intelligence in Bad Homburg could exert influence, if at all, only on peripheral issues. I did occasionally achieve a coup as when I reprinted a letter in which

---

can Labor Party [a left-wing party in New York State] and the trade unions. We've had experience with those Communists over here."

8. The news story declared that 4 million acres were confiscated from the estates of some 7,000 Junkers and other individuals as well as organizations with dubious political backgrounds and distributed among some 280,000 farmers, including 59,000 land-poor peasants as well as 242,000 landless farmworkers and 64,000 expellees from eastern territories.

Cardinal Faulhaber of Bavaria (heading the list of personalities whose correspondence I placed under surveillance) exhorted Rudolph of Wittelsbach, the exiled heir presumptive to the Bavarian throne, to lay claim to the crown of a Roman Catholic kingdom encompassing Bavaria, Austria, and a segment of the Rhineland. Even a cardinal with pretensions to being a latter-day Richelieu would not have hazarded such a grandiose maneuver without encouragement from the highest circles in the American Military Government.[9]

In *Betrayal* I summarized the state of the American occupation at the end of 1945:

The history of our occupation during the first year is the story of the conflict between the two opposing philosophies which emerged in our Zone:the "be good to the Germans" philosophy, which in practice often proved more opportunistic than idealistic or humanitarian and led to the substitution of new objectives for our original war aims; and the "discriminate carefully among the Germans" philosophy, directed toward the accomplishment of our original purposes. The struggle began as soon as we entered Germany, in Aachen, in October 1944. By the end of 1945, it was clear that the former philosophy had won out.[10]

Forewarning of Collapse

At a press conference on 12 October Lt. Gen. Lucian K. Truscott, Patton's successor as commandant in Bavaria, declared, "Because of the demobilization program and the policy of releasing high-point officers and men, the troops now stationed in the Eastern Military District lack the point of view of the combat veterans toward the German population." To overcome "the widespread attitude of laxness and cordiality toward all Germans," General Truscott was instituting an extensive orientation program on the question of the guilt of the German nation for the war.[11]

---

9. The ICD Weekly Summary was classified "secret," and MG never released to the press the exposé of the cardinal's newest and most daring stratagem.

10. Kahn, *Betrayal*, 8.

11. An Army Education and Information Division study of troop attitudes (withheld from the press until late January 1946) revealed that 19 percent of the respondents believed that the Germans had some justification for starting the war; another 21 percent were uncertain; 59 percent were convinced that Hitler had done a lot of good for Germany; 24 percent said the Germans had a "good" argument when they said that as Europe's most efficient country Germany had a right to dominance in the continent. Of the men, 12 percent believed that some races were superior to others; 16 percent were undecided. Of the GIs 18 percent believed that Hitler's persecution of the Jews had been justified. A larger percentage absolved the mass of Germans of responsibility for concentration-camp atrocities. Paradoxically, 71 percent believed that the U.S. MG was not stringent enough with the Nazis. In sum, the poll revealed widespread ignorance of the causes and goals of the war and indicated that many of the troops had fallen for Goebbels's propaganda.

General Truscott made no mention of a recent report by the U.S. Surgeon General of a serious rise in sexually transmitted diseases among the troops. *New York Times* correspondent Tania Long suggested a relationship between the troops' sense of lack of purpose in their continued deployment in Germany and the sexual promiscuity generating the epidemic.[12] "The average GI and officer," Long wrote, "is primarily preoccupied with one thought only—when he can go home. He has forgotten, if he ever knew, why he came here at all, and he is not being told why he must stay to help demilitarize, occupy and denazify Germany."

Although the situation was clearly deteriorating within the occupation army, the New Year brought an encouraging development in inter-Allied relations. Under a Big Power exchange agreement five Soviet correspondents were invited to investigate conditions in Bavaria, while British and American journalists conducted a similar study in Saxony. A 3 January dispatch to the *New York Times* summarized the Americans' observations in Saxony, where they were welcomed by a provincial regime headed by a Social Democrat president (a pre-1933 mayor of Dresden) and five vice presidents selected from the four antifascist parties. The authorities of the German "self-government" (the newspaper's quotation marks) were compensating for scanty tax collections by developing wood-pulp production for the paper and synthetic textile industries in forests confiscated from the "big Junker estate owners" and by imposing heavy luxury taxes, particularly on liquor. The Soviet authorities had instituted a fundamental reform of the judicial system and were resolving the shortage in judicial personnel through "condensed eight-month courses for 'antifascists' with higher education but no training as lawyers or judges." A special court composed of judges especially "appointed by the state government and representing the civil administration, the four parties and the labor unions tried five Gestapo men and Elite Guards [SS] who murdered dozens of inmates of the Roterburg labor camp." Another trial was in the offing of the Dresden Gestapo chief on the charge of "guillotining three hundred to four hundred jailed prisoners and personally shooting seven to eight hundred others."

On 6 January, in an editorial entitled "The Three Occupation Reports," the *New York Times* compared recent investigations of the American occupations in Japan and Germany with that conducted by American correspondents in the Soviet Zone. Of the latter experience the newspaper reported that the journalists were impressed by "a record achievement—achievement

---

12. According to the Surgeon General's report, increases in mental cases among the troops occurred mainly at redeployment areas, where soldiers returning home were developing intense feelings of "shame and fear."

toward Communist control, which was to be expected, but also achievement toward restoration, reconstruction and even self-government which is winning German respect." Of the evaluation of the American Zone, however, the *Times* declared, "like the reports of General Eisenhower and like virtually every newspaper dispatch coming from that zone it is a further recital of what must be considered thus far as a failure." The *Times* attributed the failure to "confusion on the highest level of policy making, [and] . . . also in administration." After noting problems posed by the prescriptions of the Potsdam Declaration (especially the influx of millions of refugees from the East) and by the "precipitous American redeployment which robs the occupation army of its best personnel," the *Times* observed:"But the Russians also work under the Potsdam Declaration; and despite fewer resources they are reported to be further ahead in everything than the Americans, especially in the industrial field with the non-war plants in their zone working around eighty-three percent of capacity as against only 18 percent for the American zone."[13]

On 5 January, in spite of the intensifying confusion within the American Zone, I expressed optimism about the future of the intelligence editorial staff, writing home:"It appears that the Information Control Division is going to fold in June with only the Intelligence Section remaining. The publication I put out will become the Intelligence Weekly for all Military Government; my staff, now of eight people, will be greatly increased."

Four days later, however, the American Zone underwent an upheaval that threatened total loss of what the *Times* called "the fruits of victory."

For months ICD intelligence had been receiving reports from all over the zone of mounting indiscipline among the American occupation troops. In sermons German clergymen denounced GI rowdy behavior, and the press published letters from readers expressing fear of violence from the troops. The ICD Daily Digest of Intelligence reprinted a letter signed by a group of University of Marburg professors in which they protested that it was unsafe to walk the streets of their town at night. Only by a timely display of his Army identification did an ICD staffer traveling in civilian clothes escape being beaten and having his car and watch seized by a GI gang.

In an attempt to mitigate the rancor among the troops at the slow tempo

---

13. The *Times* sought to explain the disparity between the two zones: *we attempted to do too much much too quickly and with a most unsuitable instrument—a combat army never trained for such a job and determined to get home after the battle is over. . . . It is also more than a month since a recommendation was made for a complete revision and simplification of the "high level" instructions on policy, and a dispatch to this newspaper last November frankly told of the fear among informed Washington officials that we stand to lose the fruits of victory in Germany . . . . Washington itself has done little to correct the situation and the time is getting short.* ("The Three Occupation Reports," 6 January 1946).

of repatriation, Gen. Joseph T. McNarney, Eisenhower's replacement as commander-in-chief of American forces in Europe, announced a revised redeployment point system. His attempt at mollifying troop discontent evoked, however, an unexpected reaction. Leaflets distributed at unit messes throughout the Frankfurt area summoned troops to a protest demonstration. On 9 January General McNarney posted armed guards around MG HQ and that day a major demonstration and riot occurred in Frankfurt.[14] The leaders of the demonstration distributed among the soldiers copies of a protest cable sent to President Truman, Army Chief of Staff Dwight D. Eisenhower, the House Military Affairs Committee, and various American newspapers. "Are the brass hats to be permitted to build empires?" *Times* correspondent Kathleen McLaughlin reported as "the pivotal point" in the cable. Twenty soldiers were arrested.

The next day, 10 January, demonstrators assembled in Frankfurt in even greater numbers, and other protests were reported in Berlin and elsewhere in Germany as well as in Vienna, among airforce personnel in England and among occupation troops in Japan. When on 12 January thousands demonstrated in Frankfurt for a third time, Sgt. Anthony Tiano, one of the organizers, assured Kathleen McLaughlin that the men he represented realized "that our country made commitments over here that have got to be observed. But it looks as though . . . the people at home . . . have let us down after we went through plenty of tough days to win this war, and now it is the turn of somebody else to come and see things through. . . . We lost the best man we ever had," Tiano insisted, "when we lost Franklin Roosevelt. He wouldn't have taken any of that stuff about not being able to get enough replacements." Sgt. Hollis H. Connell concurred. "Long months ago," he declared, "it should have been obvious that plenty of replacements would be needed and they should have been scheduled." As a result of high-level diffidence, he declared, morale had plummeted. "Replacements are stepping off the gangplank now at Le Havre," he said, "asking the same question as we are asking:'How soon can we go home?'"

General McNarney ordered a halt to demonstrations but all but admitted his helplessness before the troops' fury.[15]

Times correspondent Drew Middleton offered an astute analysis of the breakdown in morale among the American troops, a breakdown not matched within the other occupation armies:

---

14. See appendix 37, pp. 207–8, for Kathleen McLaughlin's dispatch to the *New York Times* under the caption "Bayonets Disperse GIs in Frankfurt."

15. "We will get you home as quickly as we possibly can but if your Congressman gets the impression from his mailbag that what the public wants is 'to get the boys home and to hell with international commitments' then you'll go home regardless of what happens to surplus war property, displaced persons, German prisoners of war, Germans under mandatory arrest and all the other chores in Europe that the nation accepted."

the Army after a brilliant beginning in the summer of 1945 has neglected to impress upon the soldiers the reasons why it is necessary to maintain occupation forces in Germany. Nine out of ten soldiers do not understand why their presence is necessary or how a long-term occupation may prevent future wars. The average enlisted man . . . sees only a listless, subservient population and meets only accommodating women.

The general attitude among senior officers is that the disintegration in morale . . . can be checked only by appealing to the American people to consider whether they want troops home now at the cost of losing the peace.[16]

The German Reaction

Germans were astonished at the massive display of military indiscipline, a phenomenon they could hardly have imagined in the Wehrmacht. German officials boldly took to open criticism of Military Government, and on 8 January General Clay had to warn the minister-presidents of the three American Zone provinces that criticism of Four Power Control Council policies would not be tolerated. Headlines in the German newspapers on the protest demonstrations displaced those on the Nuremberg trials. On 12 January in a dispatch to the *New York Times*, Drew Middleton quoted a high-ranking American officer in Berlin as declaring that the demonstrations had "done more than anything else to lower the prestige of the United States in the eyes of the German population and weakened the authority of the Military Government." The officer regarded the demonstrations as encouragement to "nascent German resistance movements, which in recent weeks have begun to remind the Germans through pamphlets that national socialism is not dead, even though it is underground."

While General McNarney expressed frustration and helplessness at the disintegration of discipline among the troops, his subordinates pressed on with the devolution of authority to German officials. On 14 January, Drew Middleton reported "the most revolutionary step yet taken in Germany:the transfer of the responsibility for denazification from American to German hands." Middleton noted that in Nuremberg, where the trial of leading Nazis was being held, there were "still more than one thousand party members holding jobs in the . . . city administration." In addition to the failure of denazification, Middleton called attention to the parlous state of the Army of Occupation and to "the political tendencies of the German people toward

---

16. In the fall of 1945, claiming that the Army was not prepared for such a responsibility, Eisenhower urged President Truman to transfer the administration of the American Zone from the Army to the State Department. Secretary of State James F. Byrnes rejected Eisenhower's recommendation, insisting that his department was not equipped for such a task either.

fascism. . . . According to a senior American officer, German political leaders admit that an election held in Germany today would bring a modified nazi government into power."

Such developments demoralized the "old hands" at ICD, and on 20 January, little more than two weeks after my optimistic letter home, I wrote: "The changes that are taking place here are not at all pleasant. Konnie [my colleague Konrad Kellen, formerly Thomas Mann's secretary] says that there will not be much place for the old 'liberal' gang anymore, and I'm inclined to agree with him. . . . Toombs will be back [from two months' leave in the States] next week but only for a few months. After that, I can foresee all kinds of difficulty. . . . Things may fold up for us in June in any event."

Alarm Throughout the World

Nations throughout the world took alarm at what seemed to be a collapse in morale among the American troops, as a 13 January *New York Times* editorial titled "Power and Peace" warned:

Discussing the one subject that is not on the agenda of the first meeting of the United Nations assembly in London but must be on the minds of all the delegates there . . . is what dependence can be placed upon the United States to carry out its international duties . . . as the world's strongest, most dynamic power. They . . . can be pardoned for wondering how efficient a police force we can muster to help keep the peace. . . . When discipline breaks down the army becomes a mob and disintegrates as a fighting force.

Especially disquieting, the editorial noted, was the reaction of the other occupation powers, all of whom, unlike the United States, had suffered massive devastation and loss of life in the war. For them as well as for Germany's other neighbors, the *Times* reported, the collapse of the American occupation force evoked dismay:"France, Great Britain and Russia are already contemplating the possibility that they may have to take over our occupation zone in Germany, and the smaller nations are afraid to speak until they know whether the United States will carry out its commitments or whether the tragic years after the last war are to repeat themselves."

15

Elections: The American Panacea II

If in scheduling elections in September 1945 OMGUS policymakers had seriously sought to promote German involvement in democratic processes, as Eisenhower insisted, they would have set the first elections in urban centers, where embryonic political parties were establishing precinct organizations, instead of in the countryside, where party nuclei were nonexistent and, as reports from rural MG detachments attested, brutal intimidation of anti-nazis by Party fanatics continued unabated. Early in October Eisenhower's deputy, Lt. Gen. Lucius B. Clay, ordered the withdrawal by 15 November of rural MG detachments, already denuded of much of their personnel, effectively eliminating American supervision of the imminent rural elections and depriving voters of protection against Nazi intimidation.

In a November 1945 report to his provincial superior (intercepted by American military censorship and reprinted in the ICD Weekly Intelligence Summary), Dr. Hans Thiemo, the Christian Social Union (the Bavarian counterpart to the Christian Democratic Party) Landrat of Wolfratshausen (a rural county where 8,000 of the 40,000 inhabitants had been members of the NSDAP), exulted:"No one here feels any sympathy for the Americans except for a couple of parasites." On 2 December, in a campaign speech in the village of Bauerberg, Thiemo admonished his audience, "We've got to realize that the enemy stands in our land and will suck our last drop of blood." He roused alarm by predicting that "in a short time our money will be completely worthless. . . . All unpleasant happenings in the administration," he proclaimed, "are to be blamed on the Americans alone." On 13 January, *New York Times* reporter Drew Middleton cited "an official Army report" admitting that in Bavaria MG had no plan for enforcement of the denazification law. He opined that political parties could win support by seeking absolution of "nominal Nazis" and thus "provide the basis for a resurgence of nazism."[1]

In the countryside, more than the other parties, the KPD lacked cadres and popular support, and MG officials could anticipate that in the initial, rural January elections the Communists would suffer a calamitous defeat. Their supporters, already intimidated by the hostility of MG officials, would lose heart, and Social Democrats opposing workers' party unification would argue more persuasively against entering into a coalition with the KPD.

1. Drew Middleton, *New York Times*, 13 January 1946.

The Election Campaign

In Frankfurt a similar situation prevailed. On 20 January, two days before the rural elections, the *Frankfurter Rundschau* exposed the existence of a secret clique of Nazis within the Frankfurt police department, a "justice committee" which was forewarning and otherwise protecting local Nazis. In contradiction to the policy of transferring authority to the Germans, MG was compelled to assume control of the force. Such a threat from German reactionaries, however, no longer impelled the SPD leadership to renew unification discussions with the KPD. On the contrary, during the last weeks of the rural election campaign the Social Democrats joined with the Christian Democrats and Liberals in a common assault on the Communists. When Social Democrats charged publicly that the KPD could not be considered a truly German political party because of its support of the Potsdam Declaration, General Clay felt compelled to rebuke them for this blatant challenge to Four Power authority.

Assailing the Communists as "agents of Moscow" and overzealous champions of the Potsdam Big Power Accord, the Liberals, Christian Democrats, and Social Democrats appealed to antidemocratic sentiments among the rural voters—nationalism and militarism, opposition to denazification and reparations, anti-Sovietism and racial bigotry. In contrast to the party with the most justification for complaints about the military government, the three parties engaged in brazen anti-American demagogy, repeating their accusation that all the victorious powers, the Western democracies as well as the Soviet Union, bore guilt for the horrors of nazism. In a last-minute campaign statement the Hessian LPD assailed the Potsdam provisions that called for dismantling German plants to supply reparations to the Soviets and the French and for ceding territory to Poland and the Soviet Union. "As the President of the United States explained in his twelve points," the statement announced, "America would never consent to the cession of portions of *friendly* nations without consent of the population, we ask that this policy also be applied to the purely German regions in the East." The statement continued with an undisguised threat:"A transfer of these purely German regions in the East can never be recognized by Germans as a just solution."

Cynical about politics and impatient with interparty squabbling at a time of general misery, rural voters looked to the clergy for political guidance and leadership. The Roman Catholic Church, in particular, intervened vigorously in the electoral campaign. The bishop of Regensburg admonished his flock that "socialism is an antithesis to Christianity and much more dangerous now than nazism." Two weeks before the elections, in a pastoral letter entitled "An Admonition from the Bishops of Bavaria Concerning the Rural Community Elections," the Catholic hierarchy proclaimed:"F or the first time since the total collapse, [for the churchmen the Allied victory signified not liberation but debacle] the people of Bavaria are being called to the polls." They exhorted their flock to

Vote Christian! Elect men of proven character and Christian ideals who will strive for peaceful and friendly relations between Church and State; for the education of Catholic children in Catholic schools, for social justice, for the protection of the poor and weak, for peace and reconciliation among nations and within our own people. . . . Beware of agitators and parties unworthy of the trust of the German people!

With characteristic German discipline, 80 percent of the registered voters in the rural communities turned out to vote, a percentage never paralleled in the United States. Colonel Newman, the military governor of Greater Hesse, exulted:"I think this should prove to the world that democracy had not been completely smothered by years of Nazi oppression."

The numbers were indeed impressive, but other aspects of the "triumph" were not reassuring. An ICD poll scarcely bore out General Eisenhower's expectation that elections would promote German democracy. While 38 percent of the informants rejected National Socialism as "a bad idea," 48 percent considered it "a good idea badly carried out"; 19 percent had no opinion.

In an atmosphere of antileft violence, the KPD, as anticipated, suffered an electoral rout. Returning to a rural county where he had previously served as MG commandant, an officer of my acquaintance recounted how upon asking a woman how she had voted, she burst into tears. She would have liked, she declared, to vote for SPD and KPD candidates, whom she considered good and capable men, but the parish priest warned that such a vote would be a mortal sin. The local MG public safety officer was about to send the ex-mayor of the village of Rimbach, a Kzler and Communist and an irreproachable anti-nazi, to MG HQ for trial on an allegation that as an undercover SS agent he had murdered a Jewish resident of the hamlet. The plot, the officer discovered, had been instigated by two SS men recently released from an internment camp in collusion with a former local Nazi official. Under the officer's interrogation, one of the four accusers admitted that he had been intimidated into signing a deposition against the Communist.

"How could you expect to get away with such a conspiracy?" the officer asked.

"Oh, we've just had back luck," the Nazis replied. "You showed up."

A week after the elections ICD Intelligence invited Oberbuergermeister Kurt Blaum and representatives of the four Frankfurt political parties to a preview of the ICD Film-Theater-Music branch documentary exposing the horrors of the Nazi concentration camps, a film which the entire German adult population of the zone was to be compelled to view on pain of losing their ration coupons. At a discussion following the showing, Blaum praised the film as a valuable contribution to the reeducation of the German public. In the middle of a sentence, however, he was cut off by *Frankfurter Rundschau* editor and Buchenwald veteran Emil Carlebach. "Who was responsible for these horrors?" Carlebach shouted, pounding the table. "Did you utter a word of protest while they were taking place? No, you were living in comfort as an expediter in an armaments plant, prolonging the war and the suffering! Now you think you will win pardon by praising an exposé of atrocities for which you share the blame!" Carlebach's outburst, as everyone present realized, reflected the partisan antagonisms roused in the recent election campaign.

Rearguard Resistance

The 2 February issue of the ICD Operations weekly bulletin presented an appraisal of the activities of the Publications, Film-Theater-Music, Radio, Library, and Intelligence sections during the six months since the establishment of the Information Control Division. The comprehensive evaluation opened with a telegraphed report from Bavaria claiming success in regard to the public reaction to the newly released concentration-camp film.[2]

The success of the concentration-camp film evidenced the positive contribution of ICD to the reeducation of the German population. But the ICD Operations bulletin's evaluation of the ICD Intelligence section exceeded in length those of all the other sections taken together and was the most laudatory.[3] Appearing only two days after Toombs's return from two months leave in the States, the praise of the Intelligence editorial staff boosted spirits and reassured Toombs as to the staff's performance during his absence. But the exhilaration evaporated almost overnight. After reviewing developments of the previous weeks affecting the Intelligence section, Toombs expressed

---

2. See appendix 38, p. 208. On 9 March an ICD German informant reported that while mingling with a Bad Nauheim audience emerging from a viewing of the concentration-camp documentary he heard a woman declare to her husband, "It is intolerable that we should be compelled to watch a film like that for which there is no evidence that the claims are not exaggerated. Can you call it democratic that we are forced to see such a film under threat of being deprived of our ration coupons?" Her husband replied, "They can exercise their will by withdrawing ration coupons, but under democracy we have none of the compulsion we had before. The Nazis accomplished everything by force. We must adjust to present circumstances, for everything has an end."

3. See appendix 39, pp. 208–9.

doubt as to his decision to return to Germany. The editorial unit, in particular, newly assigned responsibility for summarizing all political intelligence in the zone, required additional personnel, but MG rejected any expansion in staff. I, who early in January had expressed exuberance at the future of the editorial unit, on 7 February reported home:

All over there is a breakdown in morale. . . . All services are cut below the minimum level. . . . Every day we turn more and more responsibility over to the Germans. The original error of not putting anti-fascists into positions of authority is wreaking its damage. Individuals in administrative positions . . . never know when they will be told to cut their staffs or to cease operations. . . . Our troops are the most ill-disciplined of all the occupation forces. There is drunkenness, assault, robbery, wanton destruction.

Contributing to the deterioration of morale was an ever more pervasive atmosphere of conformity threatening to stifle free expression of opinion. Responding to complaints that the publication was colored politically, Gen. Robert A. McClure, director of the Information Control Division, expressed interest in the background of people who worked on the Weekly Intelligence Summary. To such charges I retorted that the publication was biased as anti-fascist and did not allow fascist opinion equal weight with democratic.[4]

Reminded daily that in the new stage in occupation policy we at ICD were fighting a rearguard action, I transformed the ICIS and the Daily Digest of Intelligence into organs that not merely exposed violations of Allied directives but also promoted democratic countermeasures. In addition, I produced action memoranda based on data in the publications. In the first of these, dated 5 February, I called attention to ICD polls conducted in Berlin, Marburg (a Hessian university town), and Munich, which disclosed that women who had been members of the Nazi Party had "no understanding of the present discrimination against former Party members and [were] in need of complete reeducation." I observed:"The Nazi policy of reducing women to an inferior position seems to have had considerable success in making them feel incompetent and uninterested in dealing with problems of importance to the nation. Since German women considerably outnumber men, it is essential that they assume responsibility for the reconstruction of

---

4. Toombs, who displayed pusillanimity in delaying transmission to OMGUS of the Munich reports in July and August, now reacted with resolution, as I noted in a letter home:"My boss says he will protect me since he realizes that after they fire me for my political stand, he will be next in line. He assured me that he thought I was an invaluable member of the staff since I give the viewpoint of the extreme left—rarely to be found in any of the other agencies here."

Despite Toombs's reassurance, I reported:"I must be more and more cautious. I weigh every sentence I print—I measure the number of lines given to different opinions."

their country." I noted the availability of "public-spirited" women "enthusiastic about organizing a non-political and non-confessional organization" to promote the reeducation of German women. This enthusiasm, I suggested, should be encouraged through licensing of magazines and newspapers directed to women and through broadcasts of women's programs over the licensed radio stations. (ICD policymakers, exclusively male, had given no thought to targeting German women.)

The next day, 6 February, I submitted a memorandum on a substantially different topic: "Polish atrocity stories reprinted in *Die Neue Zeitung* [ICD's zonal German-language newspaper]." Under the headline "What Will They Find?" Captain Wallenberg, the editor, devoted three-quarters of a column in the paper's "World Political Roundup" to a reprint of a Swiss newspaper account of a trip by eight British parliamentarians to the Polish-occupied territories of East Germany. The reprinting of the article by the editor of the official American German-language newspaper—a violation of the Four Power directive forbidding criticism of Allied nations—was the more reprehensible in that a month earlier editors of a licensed German newspaper had been "strongly censured for reprinting that very Swiss article . . . and threatened with the revocation of the paper's license in the event of a repetition of such a violation of directives."

Colonel Powell returned the memorandum to Toombs with a covering routing slip on which he jotted in longhand, "I discussed the attitude of *Die Neue Zeitung* toward friendly and allied nations with [Hans] Habe [who as head of ICD Operations was Wallenberg's superior] over the weekend and raised hell with him."

The Weekly Intelligence Summary of 16 February reported the results of a poll of editors of the licensed press on their reactions to the ICD's *Die Neue Zeitung*. "The major criticism of the editors," the investigation revealed, "was that the newspaper did not sufficiently represent American policy, points of view or American life."[5] I drafted a memorandum on the poll, which I concluded with a proposal certain to evoke a stormy reaction in the ICD press section:

The absence in many issues of the *Neue Zeitung* of articles directly concerned with American policy might indicate that a reconsideration of the paper's directives is advisable. The scrutiny . . . would seem to indicate that many

---

5. An ICD public opinion survey revealed that a large percentage of the readers of the *Neue Zeitung* were not certain whether this American-published paper was expressing an American or a German point of view. "Indeed," I observed, "one of the reasons why many Germans are enthusiastic about the *Neue Zeitung*, according to some of the editors of the German-licensed newspapers and according to our spot intelligence, is that it avoids reminding its readership of things they do not like to hear, in contrast to some of the more forceful licensed papers, which risk their popularity in doing so."

items appearing in the newspaper might evoke unfortunate reactions among its German readership, always on the lookout for indications of inter-Allied disunity and of a complaisant attitude among Americans in regard to some of the basic issues in the occupation.

Meanwhile, the licensed press was undergoing new attacks. Once again the *Frankfurter Rundschau*, the zone's most vigorously anti-nazi newspaper, was singled out as a target, criticized in Army and MG publications for its "leftist slant." At a request from Arthur Eggleston, recently appointed as press chief in the Western District, I drafted a response to these attacks, calling attention to summaries appearing in consecutive October issues of the ICIS of a study conducted among Frankfurt political leaders and of a public opinion poll following immediately thereafter. "The particular criticisms," I noted, "voiced by conservative leaders in the study referred to above found little agreement among the general population." I went on to set the attacks on the paper in the context of attacks on other outspoken, antinationalist, anti-nazi licensed newspapers. "Intelligence investigations and press analyses have in each case," I noted, "shown that there is very little basis for the accusations of leftist bias. It appears that conservative leaders who resent the 'desecration of German honor' and blunt criticism of German militarism and ultra-nationalism, consider such stands on the part of licensed editors as indications of 'communist bias.'"[6]

In the darkening atmosphere of conformity and repression in the American Zone, Eggleston could hardly be confident that any documentation, no matter how unimpeachable, would put an end to the sniping against the *Rundschau* and other licensed newspapers.

Goebbels's Triumph

Early in March I submitted to Al Toombs a proposal for the establishment of a scrutiny board to check on the newspapers and publications and radio in the zone. (The Soviets were constantly calling attention to violations of the Potsdam Agreement in the American Zone media.)[7] When General McClure rejected the proposal, I persisted with the project, explaining in a 9 March memorandum to Toombs:"As a result of the broad, inexplicit directive covering the licensing and printing of publications and periodicals, it appears possible for publishers to bring out works of dubious value and even of a subversive nature." I adduced as examples three publications recently

---

6. "It appears probable," my memorandum continued, "as one informant stated in the investigation of the *Rhein-Neckar Zeitung*, that conservative leaders would not criticize a newspaper for being leftist if they did not know of the presence of a KPD licensee on the editorial board. Attacks may often be considered as attacks on the KPD licensee rather than on the political orientation of the paper."

7. See appendix 40, p. 209, for a United Press report of 16 September 1945 on Soviet press policies.

produced by ICD-licensed publishing houses which, if they did not flout OMGUS and Potsdam directives, clearly undermined our reeducation efforts with the German people. In *Only Fourteen Days, a Factual Report*, a Walter Schumann recounted that in fourteen days of interrogation by the Gestapo he found that the agents were really "good chaps." He concluded that "among all peoples—including the English, French, Americans and Russians—there are good and bad." Charging the German nation with collective guilt was therefore unjustifiable.

In *War Madness*, Wilhelm Greiner, after citing opinions of philosophers and theologians, concluded, "What is decisive in war is not righteousness, not readiness to self-sacrifice, and not contempt for death and bravery on the battlefield [as presumably exhibited by the German troops!], but superior manpower, resources and weaponry." Accordingly, no question could be posed as to whether the recent war was a just war!

In *Die Konzentrationslager: Eine Gewissensfrage fuer das Deutsche Volk und die Welt* (Concentration Camps:A Question of Conscience for the German People and the World), a Jesuit priest named Kueble after many on the one hand and then again on the other hand protestations determined that guilt for the atrocities of the last decade lay with Satan:leaders of the Nazi Party were his tools, and the German people could with good conscience reject any charge of collective guilt.[8]

The memorandum exposing the dubious propositions in these publications evoked no reaction either from General McClure or from officials at OMGUS, and I made no attempt at conducting further investigations in this area of ICD responsibility.

---

8. I commented:"The author admits atrocities were committed against millions in the concentration camps but then proclaims:'Such gigantic numbers are, of course, only estimates. . . . One can see how easy it is in spite of the greatest caution to overestimate the numbers.'"

16

Democracy, American Zone Style!

With their 20 January victory in the American Zone rural elections, German reactionaries grew bolder. In Frankfurt, Blaum's appointee as deputy police commissioner, a former high-ranking SS officer, was caught distributing counterfeit Austrian identification documents to ex-Nazis. (The Allies had denominated Austria a German-occupied country and conducted no denazification program there.) "This high ranking Nazi thus conceals wolves in sheeps' clothing," remarked an ICD German informant sarcastically, "and out of gratitude the lambs carry out their effective work [of sabotaging the denazification program]."

From Bavaria, the ICD publication *Die Neue Zeitung* reported that Dr. Hans Thiemo, the Christian Social Union (CSU) Landrat in Wolfratshausen who brazenly attacked the occupation power during the recent election campaign, had set up a Nazi fiefdom ruled by a council of thirty former Party members. He also replaced a village mayor with a Nazi crony and appointed former officers to civil service positions "befitting their station." He and his gang of Nazis hobbled the operations of the local denazification court by stamping "nothing prejudicial known" on Fragebogen of notorious Pgs. In the village of Viechtach the CSU nominated for the county council (Kreistag) a former member of the SA and SS. In Wuerzburg the local CSU unanimously reelected as their chairman a man whom MG had barred from political activity because of an attitude "at variance with the denazification and demilitarization policies of Military Government."

On 11 February, General McClure received a request from Lieutenant General Clay for additional information on a Weekly Summary report exposing the dubious platform of the recently organized National Democratic Party (its "NDP" initials reminiscent of the "NSDAP"). In response I drafted a "Recommendation on the National Democratic Party," assembling data exposing the pro-Nazi histories of the party's leaders and providing a list of their violations of Allied directives in printed material and speeches of party leaders, including vigorous opposition to denazification, advocacy of a reestablishment of a German army, and military training as part of the education of German youth.[1]

---

1. A month earlier, on 20 January [1946], Dr. Buchenau, the deputy leader of the party was removed by the Greater Hesse government as a teacher in a school in Bad Nauheim on account of inflammatory sentiments he expressed in election campaign speeches.
   The party published a proclamation redolent of Nazi phraseology:"Working people in city and

"Deutschland ueber Alles," proclaimed a party leader, "to us refers to a superior civilization."[2]

"It is not to be anticipated," I observed in summation,

> that the large percentage of Germans holding dangerous philosophies will continue to be unrepresented by a political party. . . . [T]hey will either exert their influence in one or more of the four [licensed] political parties or form their own organizations. It is probable that the present policy of licensing any party that submits a democratically worded platform signed by a small number of politicians does not provide an adequate safeguard against the formation of nationalist-militarist political groups.

This memorandum elicited no reaction from MG Headquarters. (Some months later the party united with the Liberal Democrats.)

Maria Sevenich and Other Omens

I first heard about Maria Sevenich in September 1945 during my interrogation of the Darmstadt clergy. Suspecting that she was being groomed for a significant political role, I investigated her background. Before 1933 Sevenich, I discovered, moved from the SPD to the KPD and then to a Trotskyite splinter party. After Hitler came to power, she fled first to Switzerland and then to France, where in 1940 she was arrested and imprisoned in a concentration camp. Now she was seeking, so she said, to organize Catholics and Protestants into an anticommunist "Movement for German Reconstruction." She informed MG that she used papal encyclicals as the guide for her activity and anticipated backing from former Centrists, from German soldiers who had lost everything and had only religion to rely upon, from youths tainted by National Socialism looking to the Church for reeducation, and from disillusioned Pgs (party members) who were, in her judgment, not dangerous.

But Sevenich told Darmstadt Catholic priest Dr. Wilhelm Michel another story. Perhaps advised that unlike many other clergymen Michel did not respond sympathetically to red-baiting, she pretended that her main goal was to induce Communists to give up their antireligious program and return to the Church. Dr. Michel assured me that he did not trust her. Captain Louis, the Regional MG political affairs officer, noted that no one knew what Maria Sevenich's real goals were or how she was able to live without any visible means of support.

---

country, Germans from all provinces of our Fatherland unite. . . . Close ranks. . . . On our flags . . . we write in blazing letters the principles of our DEBAP [Democratic Peasants and Workers Party].

2. In a public meeting one of the leaders revived the Hitler concept of "Greater Germany" and urged the establishment of a western bloc in opposition to the Soviet Union with military and economic headquarters in England.

In November 1945 I learned that Sevenich had entered politics when I noticed her name among the signatories of the Christian Democratic Union's petition for provincial authorization and read in a German newspaper that she had delivered a stirring speech at a national conference of the party.

On Sunday, 10 March 1946, I attended a CDU meeting in the Helipa cinema in Bad Homburg at which Sevenich was the featured speaker. Emerging on the stage, a motherly woman in her mid-forties of moderate height, she gazed at the audience with a look of benign resolution. After an appeal for a Christian approach to current critical problems, she delivered a challenge:"What is the greatest danger to Germany today?" She had a ready response:"The greatest danger to Germany today is the wave of heathenism from the East. The terror now taking place against Germans in the East is the most frightful misery our people has ever known. Germany's mission today is to lead the Western world in a crusade against Eastern heathenism." But horrors, Sevenich warned, were occurring not merely in the East. "When I read the denazification law," she announced, "as a Christian I shuddered. No good can come of this campaign of hate." The audience—middle-aged women in furs, men sporting homburgs (upscale hats which originated in Bad Homburg), and several nuns with their pupils along with youths in Hitler Youth uniforms and men in Wehrmacht uniforms—murmured approval.

The German people, Sevenich admitted, had committed atrocities. The concentration camps and persecution of conquered peoples could not easily be forgiven. Her audience fell silent. "But," she asked, "where must we look for the guilt?" She had a reassuring reply to this painful question:"W e must look to the political parties now opposing the Christian Democratic Union." The audience was reassured. The leftists were responsible!

But, remarked Sevenich, the left-wing parties were not alone in bearing guilt. What about the victorious powers? "With their democratic freedom they knew what was happening. Many people in those countries praised Hitler and his policies. Under the Nazi terror, it was impossible for Germans to know or to do anything!"

Enthusiastic applause—interrupted, however, by an outcry from a woman sitting directly in front of the stage, "That's not true! we all knew!"

The audience jeered.

"And if you knew," sneered a triumphant Sevenich, "what did you do about it?"

Enthusiastic applause!

Maria had an answer for the concentration-camp horrors. A former guard at Auschwitz, where four million human beings had been destroyed, she reported, had told her that he had no idea what was happening inside the camp. How then could the well-dressed citizens of Bad Homburg have known? In any event, Maria continued, "Where must we look for the guilt?" To the political parties now opposing the Christian Democratic Union! According to Sevenich, the very people who were the first to be thrown into concentration camps were responsible, having failed to provide sufficient opposition to Hitler in 1933. She did not mention, of course, that the centrist and right-wing parties, which many in her audience had supported back then, were the ones that voted to grant Hitler dictatorial powers.

Someone in the audience shouted, "What is happening in the Russian Zone is worse a thousand times than anything we Germans ever did in Russia or in the concentration camps."

A roar of agreement from the audience.

Sevenich had yet another problem of conscience to resolve—the accusations from German émigrés. "Only those who remained in Germany," she trumpeted, "showed the courage to fight against heathenism." (Sevenich herself had spent most of the Hitler years in exile.) "I have no respect for Thomas Mann," she continued, "for the louder a man spoke against Hitler in foreign countries, the more he won applause. He risked nothing."

Sevenich next addressed the veterans in the balcony of the theater. "If the soldiers returning home to find their cities destroyed and their futures uncertain," she announced, "are not provided with Christian leadership, they will turn to nihilism, for they thought they were fighting for a good cause and as soldiers they had only done their duty."

"That's right!" came shouts from the balcony. "She's right!"

(It did not occur to her audience that Sevenich did not offer a single proposal for rebuilding the devastated cities and towns, for providing work to the unemployed, for resettling the expellees from the East, for conducting a just denazification, or for preparing a democratic regeneration of the nation.)

I rose from my seat and advanced slowly toward the stage, searching along the audience as though fixing faces in my memory. Silence descended upon the hall. Sevenich's speech became halting and a tic appeared on her face. She lowered her voice so that her words became almost inaudible and spoke quickly as though eager to finish her remarks. Ending her speech, she hurried off toward the wings. The audience scurried out of the theater.

"Frauelein Sevenich," I shouted as I mounted the steps to the stage. She turned. "Are you not aware," I demanded, "of the Allied directive prohibiting Germans from attacking any of the Allied powers?"

"But I submitted my text to Supreme Headquarters," Sevenich replied, clearly frightened, "and they offered no criticism of my remarks."

"If you are telling me," said I, "that some subaltern at the headquarters is unaware of this directive, I will investigate your allegation. Meanwhile, I urge you not to forget that you Germans are a conquered people."

As I stalked off, I heard Sevenich exclaim, "It is all these German émigrés who cause the trouble."

I had given the woman a momentary scare, but her mentors at OMGUS, I was sure, would dismiss any protest of her remarks with the same indifference with which they received the report on the National Democratic Party.[3]

German Youth

In the atmosphere of administrative disintegration and resurgence of reaction in the American Zone, the German youth suffered deepening demoralization. Conditions in the universities, strongholds of tradition in Germany, for example, offered little promise for the democratization of the country. "Our university gives the impression of a reserve officers' barracks," wrote a student to the *Sueddeutsche Zeitung* in March 1946, "—military boots, clicking heels, military jackets, affected military posture and a general lieutenant's atmosphere." "Whether in the university or not, German youth in our zone is a rubble heap," a youth leader in Frankfurt assured me:

Their old ideals are in disrepute, their futures are uncertain. They have no training except for war. The enthusiasm among them at VE Day has been dissipated. They have lost their will to assist in the rebuilding of their country. Only unskilled jobs are available. There are few apprenticeships open. In the employment offices, the officials treat them with typical German bureaucratic arrogance.

In the spring of 1946, one-third of the young people in Greater Hesse were unemployed.

"What future is there? This tormenting thought accompanies study and strengthens the tendency to despair and nihilism," reported a professor from Marburg University in a letter to the *Frankfurter Zeitung* in March 1946. "The students," he warned, "are the immediate victims of an educational

---

3. On 21 October 1946 the Polish mission delivered a protest to the Allied Control Council against "pan-Germanic and militaristic statements in a certain segment of the [western zone] German press," offering as an example a declaration by Maria Sevenich appearing in a British Zone newspaper:"We must organize the Black Reichswehr [an underground post–World War I German army] once again in order to solve the problem in the East by force." The British ignored the Polish protest. In November, the latter-day Joan of Arc went on a hunger strike to protest the meager British Zone food rations. Thereafter I had no further word of the adventuress.

policy which is supposed to prepare them for a useful life but fails to do so. The secondary victim may be the nation."[4]

In the summer of 1946 the Swabian People's Youth, the most effective youth organization in the American Zone, was dissolved by Military Government after its leaders attempted to establish contact with the Free German Youth in the Soviet Zone.[5] On the other hand, in September, recalling in an impassioned speech at a Hessian Christian Democratic youth meeting how in 1919 revolutionaries ripped off epaulets of German officers, a Wehrmacht officer warned that such a disgrace would not be tolerated again. The last two wars, he proclaimed, were political and economic conflicts, the next one would be religious, a crusade against the heathens of the East.

---

4. On 30 March 1946 the *New York Times* reported that Brig. Gen. Edward Sibert, the U.S. Army chief of intelligence, announced the arrest in the American and British zones of some 800 Germans, the result of a ten-month combined British-American operation to crush what he described as "the first major attempt to revive nazi ideologies." According to General Sibert, the long-term goal of the movement, which was led by Artur Axmann, former Fuehrer of the Hitler Youth, was to provide cover and financial backing for reviving the Fuehrer principle in German politics. Gun battles had taken place between Nazi fanatics and the 7,000 British and American troops deployed in raids on the Nazi cells.

5. A year earlier the Soviets had established a zone-wide youth organization and begun the publication of a magazine directed toward the youth.

17

Summing Up and the Collective Guilt Issue
SPRING 1946

Early in March, while on a three-week tour of the American Zone, Cyrus L. Sulzberger, the *New York Times* chief for global affairs, visited ICD headquarters in Bad Homburg. In a report of a conversation he held with me, Sulzberger noted my criticism of "the absence of a definite policy and political support from Washington," which I associated with "the disaster" of "the stampede home—few high type officers are willing to make personal sacrifices to do this job. The replacements are inexperienced people."[1] Asserting that I had "every right to speak bluntly on the issues involved since [I] could have gone home long ago," Sulzberger paraphrased my comments on the elections of two months earlier:

We held elections long before the Germans were ready for them. They had neither the necessary education nor the necessary background to vote intelligently. . . . we forced the process in order to turn over responsibility too fast. . . .

Many Germans who really know and like democracy feel that we are walking out on them. . . . In the too near future we shall leave and these [pro-democracy] Germans will be treated as collaborators.[2]

---

1. Two months later, on 20 May 1946, Delbert Clark reported to the *New York Times* that as a result of the cuts in military government personnel "assigned functions cannot be performed with the thoroughness necessary to assure success of the occupation mission . . . with the possible exception of the economics division."

2. Sulzberger quoted almost verbatim my observations on morale problems within military government agencies.
There is a terrible mixup in the classification of civilian employees. . . . there are gross inequalities in the pay of people doing the same job. In the Information Control Division, a number of fellows who were sergeants or second lieutenants now are getting $7,000 a year as civilians while the chiefs of their sections are getting $3,600 a year. Many of the latter are going home because of this inequality although they first had decided to stay on longer.
An application to OSS in January 1945 by Colonel Powell and Al Toombs for a raise in my Civil Service rating upon my appointment as liaison officer at Montgomery's headquarters was ignored until July, when it was rejected. Subsequent applications received no acknowledgment.
In February 1946, with the colonel and Toombs's agreement, I submitted a letter of resignation, citing complaints not only about rejection of requests for salary increase but also about problems with staffing and supplies. Toombs wrote an alarmist note, saying that intelligence operations would cease if I left, and the colonel added similar sentiments plus a warm note of commendation. General Robert McClure dispatched a cable to the State Department, requesting that I be transferred to the War Department payroll—which would have meant an immediate 25 percent raise so that my salary would match the salaries of subordinates on my staff. The general received no acknowledgment of his cable.
On 12 March I wrote home:
We haven't been paid for a while. . . . Everything is in a muddle. I have no idea how long it will be before our entire American occupation will disintegrate into chaos. . . .
More people here are expressing sympathy for the Germans and hatred for the Russians every day. After a while, you almost feel as though we ought to have a war and get it over with. We are so disorganized and have such low morale that even the Czechs could drive us into the sea.

At my suggestion Sulzberger interviewed a lieutenant colonel who held a regional MG administrative post. In his summary of this officer's remarks, Sulzberger confirmed reports ICD Intelligence was receiving from throughout the zone. He sent a pessimistic dispatch to the *Times*.[3]

Although continuing to fulfill my editorial responsibilities, I ceased drafting action memoranda. Before the imminent ICD headquarters move to Berlin, however, I prepared two valedictory documents:a report, dated 18 March, addressed to Colonel Powell and Al Toombs and headed "Criticism of the American Occupation, with Particular Emphasis on ICD Activities," and a personal aide-memoir entitled "The Significance of the Collective Guilt Theory."

Confident of a sympathetic reaction from the colonel and from Toombs, I expressed myself in the first document without compunctions, drawing upon a year and a half of personal experiences and upon insights derived from the flood of intelligence materials that passed across my desk. I alluded to the lack of clear-cut policies and long-range planning in the Zone; the failure to assemble well-trained MG personnel; and the problems arising from applying simplistic approaches to democratizing the Germans and appointing to positions of authority both Nazis and their fellow travelers instead of proven anti-Nazis. I pointed to the dangers of prematurely removing supervision of the Germans in various areas of life.[4]

Collective guilt, the topic of my second valedictory statement, encompassed fundamental issues in dispute within the American Zone:denazification, democratization, and reparations as well as attitudes toward Kzler and the KPD and toward relations among the occupation powers. The ICD daily and weekly intelligence publications had been reporting clerical attacks on the concept of collective guilt since immediately after VE Day. In a December 1945 ICD Daily Digest we published a broadside attack by Bishop Teophil Wurm of Stuttgart, a reply to an open letter addressed by the archbishop of Canterbury to the Protestant Church Council of Germany in which the British prelate called upon Germans to accept responsibility for the crimes committed in their name and to seek repentance. Wurm, the head of the council, rejected the archbishop's charges regarding German

---

3. "The military government detachments get too many directives from the Germans rather than from the American officers, who don't hand them down to the local military government detachments before the Germans receive them; military government units in the field feel that their higher echelons don't know the German people; American white soldiers and officers talk disgustingly about American Negroes in the army before the Germans, and this has a bad effect; United States personnel continually advertises its desire to pull out of Germany, which is the worst kind of propaganda" (*New York Times*, 25 March 1946).

4. See appendix 41, pp. 209-11, for the text of this memorandum. Colonel Powell returned to the States shortly after receiving this memorandum, not moving with ICD to Berlin.

collective guilt. (Wurm's son was at the time interned as an early member of the Nazi Party and as an SS officer.)

In February, emboldened by the conservative victory in the rural elections and by MG's weakening resolve in carrying out Allied war aims, Bishop Wurm issued a second, far more aggressive reply (also published in the ICD Daily Digest), advancing this time from the defensive posture of his previous statement to open defiance of the Occupation Powers. He condemned the Allied reparations policy for stripping Germany of its industrial machinery and raw materials and assailed denazification as un-Christian. He inveighed against the expulsion of Germans from the Eastern territories. Playing upon the ever more blatant Western hostility toward the Soviet Union and toward the German Communists, he echoed Goebbels's warning "of a grave danger [bolshevism] that menaces the world." Reviving another Nazi theme, he reminded the victor nations that once before the imposition of a harsh peace had made the German people receptive to National Socialism. A repetition of such a policy, he advised, would not "banish the spirit of vengeance and retribution. Nothing will be gained," he warned, "if past wrongs are surpassed by even greater wrongs." He revived the *Lebensraum* slogan Hitler had employed to justify his aggressions, insisting that confining the German people into a diminished living space and "denying them the means of survival was equivalent to Hitler's policy of exterminating the Jewish race." He went on to declare:"W e beg to point out that we suffered tremendous losses through merciless bombardment from the air. The military conquest and occupation of our country was accompanied by all the acts of brute force against the civilian population that had been committed in Allied countries and about which the Allies have rightly complained." The bishop urged revival of the prewar "anti-bolshevik" strategy Hitler pursued in courting the English pro-Nazi Clivedon set.[5]

Roman Catholic prelates matched the Lutheran bishop in audacity. In keeping with his "love thy neighbor" preachment, Cardinal Faulhaber made a pastoral visit to the Dachau concentration camp and announced that he was deeply moved by the piety of the inmates—interned SS war criminals. In a pastoral letter Archbishop Groeber of Freiburg, formerly an honorary chaplain of the SS, proclaimed, "We must unfortunately state that through the treatment of the German people generally, a poisonous seed is being sown, which to our great sorrow is already beginning to sprout and spread. . . . With hard hammer blows neither the German steel nor the German soul will become soft and yielding."

5. "It has been our misfortune and the misfortune of all Europe that Germany and England have not been able to reach an understanding despite sincere attempts on both sides during the last fifty years. If they were to do so now, their alliance would not threaten any other nation but would result in the salvation of the West."

Editors of the licensed newspapers took their cue from pronouncements by nationalistic clergyman and by politicians during the winter election campaign as well as from ICD's *Neue Zeitung*, which in a 4 January editorial announced, "That foreign countries share in the war guilt is now accepted as historical fact."[6]

"The theory of the collective guilt of a nation for crimes committed by its leaders," I observed in a prefatory statement to my summary investigation,

is new in the history of international relations, certainly novel in the scale of application attempted with the German people. According to this theory, all Germans, with the exception perhaps of an ill-defined and tiny minority, are responsible for the actions of the German government in its persecution of racial and religious minorities and of political opponents and for its policy of aggressive warfare. The basis for the theory lies in the twelve million votes received by Hitler in 1933 and in the continued support, whether active or passive, granted the Fuehrer by the German people, which enabled his government to wage a total *war of aggression.*[7]

A week after I completed the analysis of the collective guilt issue, OMGUS banned the distribution of an Easter Sunday pastoral letter promulgated by two British Zone Roman Catholic bishops, charging that it "incited resentment and unrest and possibly riot." In their epistle the bishops expressed dismay at the failure of "the new rulers of Germany . . . to restore a rule of law in the nation." They felt compelled "to take a stand against events that cried out to heaven taking place in East Germany . . . where more than ten million Germans had been brutally driven from their homelands without any investigation as to their guilt." They protested against denazification, insisting that non-Germans were incapable of judging the guilt or innocence of members of the Nazi Party. They condemned the

---

6. On 8 February the *Sueddeutsche Zeitung* editorialized:"[The Western democracies] did not understand that by [their supplying Hitler's war machine], the German opposition to Hitler was fatally weakened; in fact the backbone of the opposition was broken . . . and thus part of our current penance is to wait patiently for the hour when the others will be prepared to admit their share of the guilt." In reporting such press statements, I commented:
Of course, this approach is greeted with warmth by the readers . . . who are always looking for vindication. It is certain, however, that this is not an appropriate propaganda line at the present time. . . . the hands of the Germans are still too bloody for them to assign blame for the war to the occupying powers. . . .
   Editors who treat the question of collective guilt in this manner cannot be trusted to report objectively on the current Nuremberg trials.
7. See appendix 42, pp. 211–13, for the remainder of the memorandum. In the memorandum I sought to respond to the arguments of those who repudiated the concept and to point out how indiscriminate application of the charge of collective guilt posed a danger, how a failure in American policy impelled a vehement controversy over the guilt issue, how the intensifying hostility to the Soviet Union affected the debate about collective guilt, how rejection of collective guilt provided a rationale for attacks against the anti-Nazi left, how a measured application of the theory could facilitate the reeducation of the Germans, and, finally, how German weaseling on the issue posed a threat to denazification and democratization.

dismissal of thousands of officials and businessmen from their positions and the arrest of thousands of others as an assault on "God's justice . . . a violation of God's law." They denounced as a social and economic catastrophe the confiscation of church property in the East in the name of agrarian reform.[8]

On 26 April, with a contumacy surpassing that of the Catholic bishops in their Easter pastoral letter, the Supreme Council of the Evangelical Church published a lengthy protest against the "Act for the Liberation from National Socialism and Militarism," charging that the OMGUS directive transferring the administration of denazification to German authorities violated "all the elementary legal principles which characterize the legal structure of civilized nations and which do not ignore their ultimate dependence on God's commandments." The statement continued with a scarcely disguised threat:"The Christian church feels unable to tell the German people that this Act and its execution will in all its parts serve divine justice and truth." The churchmen objected to the application of denazification to entire categories of the population and to

the difficulties which will be caused by the Act for the Church itself in forbidding certain politically unreliable individuals to preach. Preaching is bound up with holy orders to such a degree, that the prohibition to preach is equal to a withdrawal of holy orders altogether. . . . As far as the exercise of duties based upon an ordination is concerned, the Church Council alone can make a decision.[9]

It was no longer possible to conceal the collapse of the denazification program in the American Zone. On 24 April, Raymond Daniell described conditions in the Alpine Landkreis (county) of Miesbach, "typical of those rural communities that the Nazis favored as sites for their country homes." Although noting that the daughter of Hans Frank, "the Butcher of Poland," no longer worked as secretary of the counterintelligence team at Miesbach,

---

8. A British military government spokesman declared that the letter would not be outlawed in the British Zone because "it was impossible to interfere with the liberty of the church." Besides, he added, it was not "directed specifically against British policy but against the Four-Power Control Council."

9. On 23 May, a month after the publication of the church proclamation, Gen. Lucius D. Clay delivered a vehement response:"It became in justice necessary to rid the German community of Nazism and Militarism and to assist the German people, free of these evils, to take their place eventually among the peaceful family of nations. This is a basic principle of the Berlin Protocol of 2 August 1945." Clay rejected the charge that the law imposed excessive punishments and added an implied rebuke by declaring:"It is not believed that Church authorities have thought that a minister is immune from all civil sanctions imposed for conduct condemned by a law of general application." He concluded with a firm, if, under the conditions prevailing within the American Zone, disingenuous, warning:"United States Military Government has from the first given its full support to religious freedom. It has expected the cooperation of Church authorities in removing from places of prominence in Germany those who associated themselves with a party organization which displayed utter contempt for the laws of God and trampled ruthlessly on the rights of man."

Daniell confirmed that conditions in the very area described in the August 1945 ICD Munich report persisted, asserting that Nazis were regaining their old positions and recovering their confiscated properties in Miesbach. Indeed, the former leader of the Hitler Youth in Bad Wiessee was serving as receptionist for the local MG detachment able to decide who could obtain appointments with MG officers. He himself rode about town in an MG vehicle. Daniell's comment on these developments expressed succinctly views that we had published repeatedly in the ICD Intelligence publications and in special reports:

Liberal-minded Germans are in despair for the future. They hold that, in turning the denazification over to unconverted German nationalists and opening democratic processes to an electorate [county elections were scheduled for June] still contaminated with Propaganda Minister Joseph Goebbels' poison of anti-Semitism and race superiority, the United States authorities are defeating their professed desire to establish a peaceful, democratic Germany.[10]

---

10. Raymond Daniell, "Nazis in Bavaria Regaining Position," *New York Times*, 24 April 1946.

18

Demoralized GIs

Berlin

As I recounted in *Betrayal* with fresh recollection of my first impressions upon moving to Berlin, outside the opera house emaciated Germans scrambled to retrieve cigarette butts flicked to the sidewalk by amused Americans. At the PX, GIs grinned as they tossed candy bars to desperate women who begged for food for starving children. Every evening down the block from the Titania Red Cross Club there rose a muffled hum from a long line of fraueleins whispering, "Where're you going, big boy?" "What are you doing tonight, GI?" as GIs sauntered past eying the women to pick one out for a "quickie."

But there was another, grave aspect of the breakdown in morale: a developing unconcern with problems—quite noticeable since the death of Roosevelt. Soldiers no longer discussed politics, no longer cared what was going on. Politically naive and raised in a society in which racial chauvinism and anti-Semitism were pervasive, few GIs were capable of evaluating differences between their own country and the lands they were visiting for the first time.[1] But it was the plundering frenzy that most exemplified the breakdown in the Occupation.[2] By the time I arrived in Berlin, the black market had become socially acceptable. At the dinner table people discussed prices of china, silk, jewelry, and objets d'art, all in terms of the accepted mode of exchange: cigarettes. People were having cigarettes mailed to them regularly and were accumulating all kinds of luxury goods. The cigarette exchange rate fluctuated from $180 a carton to as low as $100 (at which time people expressed indignation). It dropped precipitously when a truckload arrived from the zone or a PX train was robbed of its supply (as did happen). Fashionable blackmarketers, American and German, frequented sleek nightclubs, where for $100 one could obtain a meal with gourmet delicacies prepared by the finest chefs. Champagne was imported from France, oysters from the

---

1. "GIs fail to note," I wrote home,

that there was no great poverty to be seen any place in Germany. No poverty comparable to what we have on every hand at home. The average GI is not impressed by the fact that the cities of Germany are or were incomparably more beautiful than our own.

All over Europe people are saying that the Americans are like children. That, of course, is pleasant to hear once, but a little frightening to hear all the time. Our propaganda to our own troops has been directed toward developing smug, condescending "understanding" of other peoples, hatred of the enemy as a nation. . . . With the superficial explanations provided him for political phenomena, the GI is miserably unprepared for dealing with political issues.

2. See appendix 43, pp. 213–14.

North Sea, whipped cream from Denmark—on U.S. Army vehicles, ordinarily—and sold at fantastic prices. At one of these swanky hangouts, a GI insisted upon treating friends of mine to drinks at $20 and $30 apiece. It turned out that he was part owner of the club. He had even installed a new tiled bathroom in the club (and that in a country where plumbing supplies were unobtainable and new construction practically unthinkable). When my friends prepared to leave, the GI entrepreneur offered to drive them home. He had his own German limousine and private chauffeur. And where did this fantastic character live? Oh, he had bought his own hotel and was living there.

During the war when our Psychological Warfare detachment moved with advances at the front, we never missed more than a couple of days with our daily intelligence report. But when our Information Control HQ moved from Bad Homburg to Berlin under peacetime conditions, we had to skip two weeks of our daily bulletin and three issues of our weekly intelligence summary. Because everyone was involved in deals, there was no one to pack files and office equipment.[3] When we arrived in Berlin, we found the offices deserted with staffers out making blackmarket contacts to dispose of cigarettes and looking for good buys. So "busy" did our office become that Germans were swarming into our building throughout the day hawking cameras, binoculars, and jewelry. Finally, Al Toombs had to forbid transactions and conversations about transactions during business hours.[4]

On 16 March, while drafting the general evaluation and collective guilt documents, I received a visit from Saul Padover (coauthor of the Aachen exposé of January 1945). Saul had returned to the States after VE Day. Now he was back for a two-week stint as a lecturer in an Army orientation program. He offered to recommend me as his successor as guest lecturer, and within days I received an invitation to deliver a lecture on the German political parties at the Army Information and Education (I&E) school at Hoechst, a suburb of Frankfurt. On 27 March I wrote home that my lecture was "very successful and on that basis General Thompson, head of I&E, has requested me from General McClure for two weeks." Three days later I reported home:

I am not sure that all that I have been doing since the end of the war has been a loss, but I am certain that every day spent here now is a waste of time. Al Toombs is

---

3. One man had to find an apartment for his frauelein. Another ran to Bavaria to pick up a leather valise he had bought for a couple of cartons of cigarettes. Someone else hurried off to Strasbourg to sell clothes to obtain francs for some black-market currency transaction. Another had to pack the thirty crates of Czech cut glass he intended to sell at a fabulous profit in Berlin.

4. A 2 January 1946 headline in the *New York Times* read:"House Military Affairs Reports says 'Vast Majority of Troops Involved in Black Market.'"

in agreement that our work is finished. We both believe that the influence of people like him and me has been effective in opposing the diehard reactionaries. That time is past. . . . It is impossible for me not only to cooperate with the policies but also impossible for me not strongly to oppose these policies—and that by dissociating myself from the whole reactionary fiasco.

I was resolved, however, upon making one last effort, and on 17 April I arrived at the I&E school, where I was to lecture during the next two and a half weeks.[5] The next day I led a general discussion on "Our Job in Germany" with a group of about seventy soldiers and officers. Then at the studios of the American Forces Network radio station, with four of the students I recorded a panel discussion on German Guilt and Responsibility. I reported home:

After the general discussion yesterday, some soldiers and officers came up to me and said they were glad to know that there were people like me in Germany since they had always had the feeling that there were no people at all who had any understanding of the situation or were doing a good job. I told them that like everyone else with experience I was going home.

The sixty-six students in my two classes were, with few exceptions, newly arrived Army recruits, naive and innocent. Although they were embarrassingly respectful of the service stripes on my Eisenhower jacket, they greeted with shrugs and incredulous smiles my answers to questions like "What are we Americans here to accomplish?" "What is MG doing to fix up Germany?"

At my last session at the I&E school, seeking to test the preparation of my students for orientation responsibilities in their units and to obtain a sense of their political attitudes, I wrote on the blackboard a list of ten terms for them to define. To reassure them that they were not being judged on their responses, I instructed them not to put their names on their papers but to note the extent of their schooling and the states from which they came.

Indicative of the contempt with which some unit commanders viewed orientation programs was the selection for I&E training of ten enlisted men with no more than elementary school educations; one had not gone beyond the fourth grade and was effectively illiterate; and three had remained in school only through the seventh grade. Of the forty-seven with some high

---

5. General Thompson also asked me to write for *Stars and Stripes*, but, I wrote home, "since I know the fight needed to have any liberal material published, I declined. There is no sense using up nervous energy fighting with reactionary colonels, who may accept my articles and then revise them to render them innocuous."

school education, only thirty-four had graduated; two of the ten who had attended college had completed four years; one, a second lieutenant, had undergone a year of graduate school. A majority of the states of the union were represented among the students.

Of the ten students with only elementary school education, five failed to define any of the ten terms; the five others attempted to define only one term, "democracy." A sizable proportion of the forty-seven with some high school education proved no more knowledgeable:except for some eight or nine who responded to none of the terms, all offered a definition of democracy, most quoting or paraphrasing Lincoln's "a government of the people, by the people, and for people," evidence of their having memorized the Gettysburg Address, then a school requirement except in the former secessionist states.

Striking were the responses to terms associated with the Great Depression and the New Deal, in the dark days of struggle and ferment with, as FDR proclaimed in 1937, "one-third of a nation ill-housed, ill clad and ill-nourished." Although a small minority parroted the definition of capitalism they had memorized in civics classes or learned from Army indoctrination films—"where the individual is allowed free enterprise and profit"—the great majority of the men expressed animosity:

> *where the man who has all the money rules;*
> *government by wealthy for their own advantage;*
> *government controlled by large capitalists with the little man having no say in anything;*
> *men with the money control the government and mostly everything else;*
> *financiers have control and are able to sway opposition to their side because they have influence and a great deal of money.*

Although a minority did not recognize what "CIO" stood for, many at least knew that the letters were the initials of a labor organization. A few expressed antagonism:

> *a poor way of controlling labor;*
> *labor union which does about as much harm as it does good;*
> *labor union radical in its steps to the left;*
> *claims to work for workers but seems out to better itself.*

More representative were the following responses:

> *labor organization which has tried to better the laborer's position by collective bargaining and strikes;*

labor unions organized to unite all workers in any industry in place of craft unions;
organization of labor along democratic lines to promote security of workers;
organization honestly conscientious about the state of the working class.

I do not recall how in class discussions I handled the issue of USA-USSR relations, a sensitive topic in April 1946. In any event, I expected a radically different response to "Soviet Union" and to "Communism" from what I was certain I would have received from GIs a year earlier. In fact, only a small minority of the students expressed hostility in their definitions of Communism:

subjugation of people for an ideal;
ideal but impractical economic system;
government or system where few people tell others what to do;
fanatic form of government—people belong to state and exist for state;
government by men with absolute power, people have no choice and ruled by force and fear, shot or imprisoned if opposed.

But OMGUS and official circles in Washington would have been dismayed by the expression among a majority of these soldiers from every corner of the United States of continuing goodwill toward the Soviet ally as well as of Great Depression rancor against "the economic royalists":

government gives to workingman what he is worth, provides his needs;
government similar to democracy; they elect representatives as we do but head of government has more direct control;
all property and resources owned by government, which divides as to worth of individual, prohibits private enterprise, but sees that all who work are given a just share of profits;
form of government emphasizing opposition between capital and labor;
strong leader but with everything run on a share and share alike basis;
each according to his abilities;
government run by board of men running Communist Party for benefit in most ways of the majority of the people;
government under which everyone profits the same, and there is no one man making all the money;
giving every individual something and guaranteeing prosperity for all.

Few could differentiate between "Communism" and "Socialism." With "Socialism," once again a minority expressed antipathy:

> *close to dictatorship, not much say for anyone;*
> *government opposed to democracy;*
> *government made up of business and large concerns (!);*
> *no free enterprise and state owns industries and property and the people.*

But most responded sympathetically:

> *government ownership and control of all means of production brought about by peaceful means;*
> *advocating a more or less equal distribution of wealth and property;*
> *middle of road between capitalism and communism;*
> *economic system where free enterprise not entirely restricted but where industries and property vital to general welfare are run by the government—similar to communism, with more civil liberties;*
> *form of government that would eliminate the underclass and give power to society at large.*

Some of the soldiers associated socialism with the New Deal:

> *government ownership of public and private utilities (TVA);*
> *government control of public utilities and economic enterprises in which government control considered necessary for good of the state;*
> *economic system under which all utilities and large business are owned and controlled by government, government keeps profits and turns them back to the people in the form of public projects—roads, buildings, etc.*

Two respondents expressed pro-fascist sentiments in their definitions of nazism: "a one-man government with ideals" and "a government where everything is directed toward a better nation." It was discouraging to discover that a dozen students who attempted to enter definitions for other terms left this question blank. Others, however, expressed strong rejection, often on a class basis:

> *dictatorship where wealth is shared by the upper class;*
> *complete domination of people for gain of minority;*
> *no freedom and gives one man and his party the right to do with all persons what he desires;*
> *government by men with absolute power, people have no choice and are ruled by force and fear, shot or imprisoned if opposed;*

> *system of government with abolition of civil liberties, benefits only ruling few;*
>
> *government that takes all from the people and allows no private enterprise (!);*
>
> *the kind of government the German people were forced to endure during the Hitler regime;*
>
> *ruling the people with an iron hand and applying terror to the people.*[6]

Few students attempted to define the remaining terms: "reactionary," "liberal," "conservative," "radical," and "revolutionary." Four effectively defined "reactionary":

> *one who is opposed to change or who would like to return to some former state.*

One added: "even if harmful to the people."
Others declared:

> *oppose all new things;*
>
> *living in the past (Sen. [Burton K.] Wheeler [an ultraconservative Montana politician of the day]);*
>
> *people set in their ways and don't like new ideas.*[7]

---

6. I do not know why I did not pose a question about Hitler's treatment of the Jews. The men were taken to visit the Jewish DP community near Frankfurt with the purpose of explaining who the DPs were and what attitude the GI should take toward these people. The men were impressed with the organization of the community—the shops, infirmary, and the school.

7. About a quarter of the respondents concurred in their definitions of "liberal," declaring: "one who advocates moderate changes or improvements." Several used words like "broadminded," "fair," and "easygoing." Others stated:
   leaning toward democratic principles;
   tends toward left, toward socialism and control by the majority;
   willing to accept new and untried ideas which may benefit state and citizens;
   party upholding individual rights.
More than a third failed to respond to "conservative." Others offered mixed responses, most commonly variations of: "one who says leave well enough alone"; "treading carefully in all policies"; or "wants no change." Some were antagonistic:
   reluctant to accept anything new, United States was conservative when it didn't join the League of Nations;
   one who believes in helping himself;
   freedom for big business to operate as it pleases, favoring absolute capitalism;
   Chamberlain—lacks courage of convictions; using more discretion than necessary.
Those who responded to "revolutionary" were in general agreement that the term referred to "one who advocates extreme changes." Some expressed feelings of sympathy:
   person or idea presenting concept so new or different as to be startling—like women's suffrage;
   seeking total change to more desirable government; to fight against something you don't like, like the Revolutionary War.
   Upon leaving the I&E school at Hoechst I glanced only cursorily at the students' responses and did not look at them again until I prepared this chapter. What struck me after the passage of more than a half-

On 7 May, at the conclusion of my two and a half weeks at the school, I was offered a position as chief instructor, to lecture on Germany, Nazism, and the USSR—to begin after I took forty-five days leave in the States. I accepted tentatively, promising to inform General Thompson from the States whether I would return to Germany.[8]

A year later I presented a soberer estimate of the I&E program:

I&E . . . published bulletins on important questions concerning the occupation, disseminated educational films, trained discussion leaders and carried on what theoretically was a comprehensive orientation program . . . to make the troops well-indoctrinated bearers of democracy. Unfortunately, however, the brasshat regular Army officers didn't believe in such frills. One young fellow in one of the orientation classes complained: "In the 'Carnival' (the GI term for the Army Constabulary) they don't believe in any orientation, and if I went back and suggested more discussion periods, I'd catch it." Although they obeyed orders and scheduled orientation hours in their units, many detachment commanders sabotaged the program by openly expressing their opposition or lack of concern by appointing incapable, uninterested mess and PX officers to do orientation work "in their spare time."[9]

At a press conference on 23 April, a week after my arrival at Hoechst, General McNarney, U.S. Supreme Commander in Germany, announced a nine-point program for restoring Army discipline, including an 11 P.M. curfew for "those who do not behave." In a dispatch to the *New York Times* Dana Adams Schmidt quoted McNarney as explaining the necessity for such measures as arising from "the rapid deployment of experienced manpower and influx of inexperienced individuals." Like General Eisenhower earlier, McNarney resented press exposés of the deteriorating conditions. He complained that

---

century was not so much the lack of sophistication of the respondents in elementary political discourse (how many Americans in the Armed Services at the beginning of the twenty-first century would respond with more understanding to such a test?) but rather the unmistakable and unabashed leftist orientation of the majority of the young men, their acceptance of class differences, their hostility toward capitalism, their openness to social change, their unprejudiced attitude toward socialism, their rejection of Nazism, and their sympathetic view of the Soviet Union. Clearly, in his Iron Curtain proclamation of Cold War six weeks earlier at Fulton, Missouri, Winston Churchill did not give voice to the sentiments of these Americans. Official policy in the American Zone would have taken a different direction if motivated by the sentiments of these GIs.

8. I wrote home:"At the end of the session the students are given a chance to evaluate their experience. I had wondered why the heads of the school seemed so anxious to hire me. It appears that my lectures were adjudged far the best by the students. Really, I had a lot of success. Got applause after my lecture on Nazism from ordinary Gis."

9. Kahn, *Betrayal,* 105. In the fall of 1946 the House Military Affairs Committee debated slashing the appropriation for the I&E division. The committee objected to discussion of occupation aims and of international affairs and to the use of "communistic" literature like the Benedict-Weltfish "Races of Mankind" pamphlet, which exploded racist theories.

"certain newspaper articles calculated to decrease the prestige of the Army had contributed to the deterioration."[10]

On 18 May I submitted to Toombs the last memorandum of my overseas service: "Inasmuch as my assignment has been completed, I request acceptance of my resignation and transfer to the ZI [Zone of the Interior—the USA], effective 23 May 1946."

That very day Konnie Kellen returned from leave in the States. "Completely disgusted," I wrote home, "by conditions there," he had signed up for an indefinite stay in Germany. Disquieted by his warnings, I declared, "I have accepted the offer of the Information and Education Staff School to serve as editor of their publications for the troops and as special lecturer in their school. I must stop off in Hoechst on my way home and make all arrangements. They don't want me to stay home long since they are short of personnel and getting shorter all the time."

On 22 May 1946 I found in my in-basket a copy of a memorandum addressed by Alfred Toombs, Chief, Intelligence Branch, to Brig. Gen. Robert A. McClure, director of the Information Control Division. Noting that he had received my resignation, Toombs described my services in the PW Branch first of Third Army and then of 12th Army Group and subsequently in the ICD. General McClure responded with a memorandum to me in which he expressed regret for my resignation and protested that he had made every effort to obtain an advancement in my Civil Service rating. He wished me well in my new position.[11]

I arrived in New York in mid-June, almost precisely two years to the day since I reported for duty at OSS headquarters in London.

The director of the I&E School informed me, with regret, that the War Department had rejected his request for an order permitting my return to Germany.

---

10. In May, General McNarney admitted that despite the measures he had introduced a month earlier: "Discipline in various places and under various commands . . . has decreased to such an extent that the good reputation of our troops is generally discredited."

11. For both the Toombs and McClure memoranda, see appendix 44, pp. 214–15.

Epilogue: 1946–1947

Cold War: Attacks on the Communists

Posters throughout Berlin, articles in the press, and reports on the radio announced a conference on 26 February 1946 at which representatives of the Social Democratic and Communist parties of the Soviet Zone were to prepare for unification.

The afternoon of 25 February, someone ran down the hall at ICD headquarters in Bad Homburg throwing open office doors and calling out with exultation, "Twelve Communists have been arrested in Berlin for interfering in MG affairs." A certain Captain Kent, it appeared, had arrested two men for distributing a leaflet in a city office, thereby, Kent charged, interfering with the functioning of Military Government. Headlines and radio reports about the arrests diverted attention from the SPD-KPD unity meeting.

In a four-page appendix to the Daily Digest of 1 March, I reprinted the proclamation emerging from the Berlin meeting:"Draft of the Principles and Aims of the New Socialist Unity Party [SEP] in Germany." The document opened with a blunt declaration sharply in contrast to numerous pronouncements by churchmen and political leaders in the American Zone: "Twelve years of fascist rule, six years of Hitler war led the German people to the greatest economic, political, and moral disaster of German history." No blame was imputed to the victor states for the horrors of the previous twelve years. From my own investigations I could attest to the contention: "Of all classes of the German people, the working class has had to bear the greatest burden and misery. . . . On its shoulders rests the burden of reconstruction and reparations."

The new party urged "the unity of Germany in an anti-fascist, parliamentary democratic republic with the formation of a central government by the anti-fascist democratic parties." It recognized "the obligation to repair the damages caused by the Hitler regime to other nations," demanded an "energetic fight against racial provocations and propaganda against other nations," and called for "peaceful and friendly relations with other nations."

The party was prepared to defend a reconstituted German democracy against reactionary assaults:"The situation in Germany resulting from the collapse of the reactionary despotic government and the reorganization of a

---

Note: This chapter represents primarily a revision of a chapter in *Betrayal*, which, in turn, was based in great part on correspondence I maintained with various Germans after returning to the States as well as on articles in the *Frankfurter Rundschau*, copies of which were mailed to me into 1947.

democratic state on a new economic basis enables us to prevent the reactionary forces from hindering the liberation of the working class by force and civil war."[1]

On 3 April 1946 the Communists who had been arrested in Berlin on the charge of interfering in MG affairs were brought to trial. Details of the case now were made public. Aware of the anticommunist prejudice among many MG officers, Communist functionaries had printed a leaflet in which they urged party members employed in city agencies to see to it that only capable Communists were recommended for municipal positions and that MG directives were scrupulously obeyed. In fact, only one copy of the leaflet had been "circulated" before Captain Kent forbade distribution of leaflets in municipal offices. For their "crime" two Communist functionaries were arrested along with ten witnesses. Detained in an air-raid shelter, they were granted electric light only a few hours a day, provided meager prison rations, and for the first two weeks of their imprisonment allowed no visitors. After a month and a half of such confinement, the president of the military court Lieutenant Colonel Swoboda (the MG officer exposed a year and a half earlier by 12th Army Group PW investigators Paul Sweet and Saul Padover as responsible for appointing Nazis and Nazi sympathizers to administrative posts in Aachen) delivered "a lesson in democracy." Refusing to take into consideration the anti-Nazi activity of the defendants, one of whom had spent ten years in a Nazi prison, he stated, "After secret deliberations the court sentences you Gerhard Jurr and you Wilhelm Kammermeier to five years imprisonment." The judgment was "not so much a question of the individual case at hand," commented the military government prosecutor, "as an example to the German public."[2]

About 2:30 the morning of 22 July 1946, four American soldiers, guns at the ready, burst into the Munich home of Ludwig Ficker, a state secretary in the Bavarian cabinet and general secretary of the Bavarian Communist Party. They ordered Ficker to accompany them to the military prison at Ungererstrasse, where he found Wilhelm Specht, the former head of Freihe-

---

1. See appendix 45, pp. 215–16, for further extracts from the document. Alexi Filitov (in "Stalins Deutschlandplanung," 53) proposes that Soviet promotion of the Socialist Unity Party (SED) was merely a tactical response to Western, particularly British, intervention against the unity of the workers parties. Stalin's expression of willingness two years later, in January 1947, to permit a revival of an independent SPD in the Soviet zone, Filitov asserts, shows that the unification of the two parties was initially designed as a chess move to counter Western pressures against the unification of the workers' parties.

2. Several days after the verdict, I met one of the witnesses who had been detained in the air-raid shelter. A simple worker about thirty years of age, he was exhausted and demoralized. "We expected so much from the Americans," he declared. "Friends and relatives had told us so much about America. I have no strength to struggle any more," he assured me. He was sharing his meager rations with his sick mother, who as a nonworker was living on a "starvation ration." "My mother is frightened," he related. "Just the other day an American officer came to visit her while I was at work. He asked her why I was a Communist and told her I would get along better if I did not remain in the party."

its Aktion Bayern, and Alfred Meislinger, a Communist city councilman. Ficker was taunted and ordered to stand at attention against a wall, then locked in a toilet and violently awakened every half hour. In the afternoon he was grilled about his activities in the Communist Party and supposed espionage for the Russians. He and the two others were released at 6:30 P.M. Several others, however, were detained for further interrogation.

A few days later MG issued a statement characterizing the arrests as a "mistake." The Munich newspapers, which had carried accounts of the arrests, did not publish the MG statement.

That month also, the Social Democratic Minister President of Bavaria, Wilhelm Hoegner, replaced Heinrich Schmitt, the Communist minister of denazification, with an ultraconservative named Anton Pfeiffer.[3] Lieutenant General Clay counseled MG officers "to be careful in handling Pfeiffer. Remember, he is an old-time reactionary and a strong nationalist. If you offend him on those subjects [bungling denazification, etc.], he might resign." In October a special branch officer in charge of denazification in Munich reported to Edd Johnson, a correspondent for the New York newspaper *PM* and the *Chicago Sun*, that "a very high official from Washington . . . recently . . . told us:'You must not be too hard on these Germans or they will all turn Communists.'" On 7 November, addressing the minister-presidents of the American zone, Clay, who as deputy to Eisenhower in September 1945 had been entrusted with strict implementation of a new severe denazification directive, now pretended astonishment that "it appear[ed] that the denazification law has been used to return as many persons as possible to their former vocations, rather than to punish the guilty."[4]

---

3. A year earlier Hoegner had championed the unity of the two workers' parties, and his appointment as minister-president had been welcomed as offering the prospect of a radical turnabout in Bavarian politics. Dr. Baumgartner, the Bavarian minister of agriculture and a protégé of Cardinal Faulhaber's, had not been dismayed by Hoegner's appointment, declaring, "Dr. Hoegner is a good Social Democrat of the King's Bavaria."

Heinrich Schmitt bore primary responsibility for drafting the comprehensive zonal law for the Liberation from National Socialism and Militarism instituted with MG approval in March 1946. Of his abrupt dismissal after three months in office, Schmitt stated:

It is not by chance that the first discussion of my dismissal commenced after the sentencing of the war profiteer Leonholdt, who bought the Steinheil works in Munich for seven million Marks just two weeks before the end of the war. The day after the decision, Leonholdt's counsel complained: "The judgment shows that this law can be used against all those who made a lot of money in the last twelve years; thus the law paves the way to socialism."

After Pfeiffer took office there commenced, according to Hans Gessner, a commentator on Bavarian radio, "a conscious political game of turning followers into major offenders and major offenders into followers." For his persistence in exposing Pfeiffer's sabotage of the denazification program, Gessner was dismissed from Radio Munich. (Pfeiffer's two sons were storm troopers and his brother had been interned as a dangerous Nazi.) (*Betrayal*, 170.)

4. Under Pfeiffer's direction at least 60 percent of the Nazis automatically classified as "major offenders" were either acquitted or reclassified as "followers" and dismissed with minor fines. In addition, the Bavarian denazification courts exonerated more than three-quarters of the officials previously dismissed by MG officials from government posts on account of their Nazi associations.

Cold War: Anti-Sovietism

In a lengthy dispatch published in the *New York Times*, Cyrus L. Sulzberger quoted liberally from an interview he conducted with the commanding officer of the American unit in Wuerzburg regarding what he characterized as "one of the sharpest orders ever issued here to United States forces . . . distributed throughout the garrison stationed in Wuerzburg and the area surrounding the city." Noting that "the morale of the civilian population . . . has been greatly raised as the result of a speech in the United States by a British politician [Churchill's Iron Curtain speech at Fulton, Missouri] relative to our allies the Russian people," the colonel declared,

I have also learned that a few men from this battalion have expressed agreement with these policies to German fraueleins. This practice will stop immediately, and you may be sure that I will use great effort on the part of the counterintelligence corps and S-2 personnel to see that it stops right now. . . . Millions of Russian soldiers died to save our skins. . . . If you want to fight again, encouraging these fraueleins that we hate Russia is a good way to get things going.[5]

Sulzberger commented, "There is no doubt in the mind of this correspondent that other areas than this would benefit from similar orders."

On 20 March, a week after the Sulzberger dispatch, Florida senator Claude Pepper delivered in the Senate a sharp rebuke of the evolving American policy toward the Soviet Union, declaring:

Denied the atomic bomb, denied warm-water outlets, denied the common courtesy of economic negotiations with her greatest ally, believing that her philosophy is such that she will never be accepted by nations dominated by capitalist reactionaries or Russophobes, Russia is beset with many fears. . . .

. . . her fear is not imaginary. . . . It rises from the smoking, battered ruins of her devastated areas, from the 15 million men, women, and children—50 times our losses—she lost in the war. . . .

Russia's fear is aggravated by her memory of the past. She remembers the summer of 1919, when the armies of 14 nations, including Britain, France, China, the United States, Germany and Japan were waging war against the new Soviet Union upon Soviet soil. . . .

Russia remembers the red-baiting, the articulated and open conspiracy against her among the major capitalist powers of the world, which went on after foreign military forces were withdrawn or driven from the Soviet Union.

---

5. Sulzberger, *New York Times*, 12 March 1946. Aware that for his stance he would be denounced as "a pinko," the colonel assured his troops that he was "a conservative Southern Democrat. An ancestor of his," he related, "was killed in the war of the American Revolution."

Reacting to Churchill's call to Cold War at Fulton, Missouri, Pepper continued:

What, then, is the way out of the crisis of fear? And how can the United Nations Organization and the peace be saved?

I venture to suggest that the only way is to carry out the grand conception of Franklin Delano Roosevelt who, more than any other, is responsible for the United Nations Organization, and to reestablish the unity of Great Britain, Russia, and the United States, and to bring about a whole new mental and spiritual attitude on the part of these powers toward peace and plenty.

At a 10 July meeting in Paris of the Council of [Four] Foreign Ministers, V. I. Molotov, the Soviet foreign minister, made a plea for unification of Germany as agreed a year earlier at Potsdam. Of Soviet motives a study issued on 23 July 1946 by the Office of Research and Evaluation of the Central Intelligence Group concluded:

While the general outline of Soviet policy is based upon the conviction of a "latent and inevitable conflict" with the capitalist world, it is manifestly in the Soviet interest to avoid an overt test of strength at least until the Soviet Union has become more powerful than any possible combination of opponents." . . .

There was nothing . . . to suggest that the estimators regarded the USSR as preparing to initiate aggressive warfare against the capitalist states. On the contrary, the Soviets believed that they were the ones in peril and that they needed to acquire and maintain forces capable of ensuring Soviet security against any possible combination of foreign powers.[6]

Ignoring the findings of the Central Intelligence Group, on 6 September before a meeting in Stuttgart of Allied and German officials, in what the *New York Times* described as a response to Molotov's appeal, Secretary of State James F. Byrnes rejected a unification of the four zones. "It is not in the interest of world peace," Byrnes declared, "that Germany should become a pawn or a partner in a military struggle for power between the East and the West." On the other hand, Byrnes asserted:"The United States has formally announced that it is its intention to unify the economy of its own zone with

---

6. Matthias, *America's Strategic Blunders,* 44.
After noting Stalin's withdrawal of Soviet troops within agreed-upon borders after VE Day, Melvin P. Leffler in *Specter of Communism* asserts:
He allowed relatively free elections in Hungary, Czechoslovakia, and Berlin during late 1945 and 1946, and he cooperated in the establishment of representative governments in Finland and Austria. The Soviets seized reparations from eastern Germany and instituted major industrial and agrarian reforms, but they did not lay coherent plans either to communize their own zone or take over all of Germany. (36)

any or all of the other zones willing to participate in the unification. So far only the British Government has agreed to let its zone participate." Of the German industrial heartland, a source of contention with both the French and the Soviets, Byrnes declared that the State Department would not "favor any controls that would subject the Ruhr . . . to the political domination or manipulation of outside powers."[7]

Commented Edwin Hartrich in the *New York Herald Tribune* on 8 September 1946:"German businessmen and industrialists interpret the Byrnes speech to mean that America will virtually underwrite the recovery of at least the western zones of occupation. At the same time they believe that America and Britain have definitely decided to build up western Germany as a balance against the Russian zone."[8]

In June 1947 the British and Americans announced the formation of a bizonal Economics Council headquartered in Frankfurt. Delbert Clark reported to the *New York Times:* "There is ample reason to believe on the best authority, that it presents in effect a decision of the two Governments to shift the emphasis in Germany away from denazification and democratization toward the creation of a buffer against Russia. . . . Not since the days of Hitler has there been so much power in the hands of so few."

Indeed, the bizonal Civil Service panel overruled the decision of the bizonal communications directors to ban the employment of former Nazis. Under Director Dr. Hans Schlange-Schoeningen, 163 of the 169 appointees to the highest positions in the bizonal Food Administration were former Party members.

In April 1946 Marshal Zhukov was relieved of his post as military commandant of the Soviet Zone. Thereafter reacting to the cold war pressures deplored by Senator Pepper, the Soviets replaced Zhukov's policy of strict implementation of the Potsdam Agreement with Stalinist repression in a Soviet ratification of the Cold War.[9]

Denazification and the "Red Menace"

With the acquittal at Nuremberg in November 1946 of Nazi propagandist Hans Fritzsche, banker and industrialist Hjalmar Schacht, and Nazi diplo-

---

7. Economic unification of the British and American Zones left control of the Ruhr to these two powers; in light of the exhaustion and impoverishment of the British, however, the region fell effectively under American control.

8. A German view of American policy in Germany as proclaimed by Byrnes is expressed by Oswald Feder in *Moskau und die Deutsche Frage* (Krefeld, 1984):"With missionary conviction, [American] businessmen fell upon old Europe with a determination to assess the business potential of this part of the world and to proclaim above all 'the American way of life' as the compulsory life style for mankind. Whoever rejected this 'way' was suspect" (125).

9. "Soviet countermeasures [to Western cold war moves]," Alexei Filitov remarks, "had to lead to an

mat Franz von Papen, the theoretical basis for denazification was undermined. A few weeks later, General Clay granted a Christmas amnesty to 300 leading Nazis—former cabinet ministers and high-ranking officers of the General Staff and of the storm troopers—releasing them on parole and with immunity from the German denazification courts.

In January 1947 the *Frankfurter Rundschau* sounded an alarm regarding the future of the denazification program:

Recognition is obviously disappearing of the necessity to render the profiteers of the Nazi regime harmless, particularly since they are the only ones who combine the interest in the resurgence of this regime with the necessary financial power to sponsor it. Dozens and hundreds of so-called business leaders are in the meantime escaping with a laughable fine.[10]

In March 1947 a poll in the American Zone revealed that 60 percent of the population remained strongly anti-Semitic. In April, after a Nazi-inspired attack on the office of the Victims of Nazism in Nuremberg, the editor of the Christian Democratic periodical *Freiheit* accused Germans who condemned this act of terrorism of trying to "curry favor with the occupation powers." In Ansbach the Victims of Fascism organization petitioned the Bavarian provincial authorities for protection against amnestied Nazis who were employing all manner of intimidation including physical force to regain their jobs and homes from Kzler. The American Zone chairman of the Central Council for Distribution of Foreign Gift Packages (and head of Evangelical charities in Germany) announced that he would not distribute packages among the victims of fascism. To do so, he insisted, would represent an act of reparations and not be politically neutral, favoring, as it would, anti-Nazis over former Nazis.

In May placards were posted in the Munich railway station with caricatures of Jews, praise of Hitler, and an announcement of the founding of a new anti-Semitic political party. Public officials, including the Bavarian ministers of agriculture and economics, engaged in public anti-Semitic harangues. In Bremen, according to a *New York Times* dispatch of 17 May 1947, a German Rightist Party circulated leaflets containing such inflammatory slogans as:

---

escalation of the conflict and to a strengthening of the anti-Soviet bloc in the West, to resignation and passive resistance in the East" ("Stalins Deutschlandplanung," 54).

10. On 14 January 1947 *New York Times* correspondent Delbert Clark reported from Berlin:"A combination of [American] regular army officers, who generally are not interested in politics, and conservative economists who think only in terms of economics and not of political fitness, has operated to retain in power men who are the intellectual leaders of German fascism, whether they were Party members or not."

No compromise but war.
Bitter fighting until the decision.
This period of national humiliation.
The duty to clean the shield of the honor of the German soldiers before our own and foreign countries.

While abandoning denazification and decartellization in an effort to rebuild German industry, American officials displayed little vigor in relieving the misery of the general population. In December 1946, a member of the Hessian *Frauenausschuss* (Women's Council) summarized in a letter to me the results of a study of conditions in the Wiesbaden schools I had visited a year and a half earlier—evidence of the failure of the military government properly to prepare for the exceptionally severe winter of 1946-47. In one class of forty-eight, she reported, only seven children had any undergarments. One little boy had to wear a dress to class. Most of the children possessed only the clothing on their backs. Girls of thirteen and fourteen weighed a mere sixty to seventy pounds. Of 19,500 pupils in the Wiesbaden schools, 7,050 lacked proper footwear, 1,175 had no shoes at all; 2,000, no stockings; 3,550 owned no coats; 7,500 came to school without having eaten breakfast.

The Counterstruggle: Democratic Resistance

One segment of the German population, however, was emerging as a bulwark against the antidemocratic trend:the trade unionists. On 5 February 1946 the Associated Press quoted Brig. Gen. Frank J. McSherry, director of the manpower division of the Military Government, as advising that "the new Germany would have to be built around the working classes because virtually all German industrialists have been imbued with the twin philosophies of superiority and aggression. Even the most liberal-minded among [the industrialists] scarcely knew the meaning of the term [democracy] in the American sense."

Indeed, a month before McSherry's statement, the Frankfurt trade unions withdrew their representatives from local denazification courts, protesting that the appeal boards were exonerating 90 percent of the Nazis appearing before them. The unions also objected to Oberbuergermeister Blaum's failure to screen appointees to the denazification boards and his refusal to permit publication of denazification proceedings or of minority opinions in the decisions of investigating committees.[11]

---

11. On 12 February 1946 Sidney Hillman, president of the Amalgamated Clothing Workers of America and spokesman for a World Federation of Trade Unions commission visiting all four zones in Germany with the objective of discovering "what German workers really want in the way of the structure of their organizations as well as the part they will play in reorganizing the country on democratic lines" reported "a vigorous purge of the nazi unions in Berlin, Leipzig, Magdeburg, Hamburg, Hannover and Frankfurt."

In October 1946 delegates to a zonal trade union conference proclaimed their resolve to prevent big business leaders from exercising "special pressure on the government and the national economy and [acting] as the sponsors and instigators of fascism." The conference demanded that business and industrial associations be composed of both employers and employees (as in the Soviet Zone). On 14 December 1946, the Free German Trade Unions of Frankfurt issued a statement of principles:"The new trade union movement is based on real democracy, tolerance and humanity. It evidences this new spirit in its respect for the ideological and political convictions of its members, in its eradication of Nazi and military philosophy and its constant effort for the reconciliation of all peoples and for world peace."

At this December conference, the Frankfurt trade unions joined other workers associations in West Germany in opposition to an American attempt to discourage the formation of industrial unions (after the model of the Congress of Industrial Organizations), passing a resolution declaring that workers would "no longer permit division by politics or ideologies to waste the force of the workers."[12]

After the bombing of three Stuttgart denazification courts in the fall of 1946, some 75,000 workers marched in protest. In February 1947, upon the bombing of a Nuremberg denazification court, the local trade unions called a general strike and staged a mammoth protest demonstration.

Nor did the trade unions submit supinely to the Allied abandonment of denazification in German industry. Unions registered a complaint against the presence of sixty former Nazis among the sixty-five highest officials in the bizonal Post and Communications Administration. The railway unions protested the retention of 70 percent of the former Nazi supervisors in their industry. In March 1947 the workers in the Waterways Administration refused to recognize the authority of their administrative bizonal board because 95 percent of the officials were former Party members. The workers at the NAM plant (Nuremberg-Augsburg Machine Works) held a six-hour strike to force the dismissal of four Nazi administrators. Sympathy strikes were reported in nearby Coburg, Bamberg, Bayreuth, and Hof. In April workers protesting the retention of Nazis in high positions overturned British MG automobiles in Duesseldorf and Braunschweig and hurled stones through the windows of MG offices. A general strike of Ruhr miners was followed by strikes in factories throughout Bizonia.

12. In the fall of 1946, recalling the vehement trade union protests against the reactionary administration he had helped to establish in the city two years earlier, the bishop of Aachen complained that "the workers have not yet understood the necessity of creating a Christian trade union organization."

In January 1947 Leon Wethers of the Labor Division of Military Government declared that he opposed a unified German trade union movement because such a movement would favor the Soviet Union. When Wethers attempted to set up an independent civil service union in Berlin, however, the three leading political parties disowned the "American union."

At a meeting in May 1947, 1,000 union delegates representing two million workers in the Ruhr passed a resolution demanding action to improve food distribution. They issued a statement proclaiming:"We cannot escape the impression that the spirit of the past still has too strong an influence on the economy and the administration." They demanded the resignation of "conservative" administrators and their replacement by more aggressive, democratic individuals responsive to the will and needs of the majority and less concerned with the privileges and profits of a tiny minority. Social Democratic trade union officials advised American Military Government that they would not be able to control their membership or prevent the spread of "bolshevism" if action to resolve the food crisis was not immediately forthcoming.

Democracy in Germany in the twenty-first century owes much to the American wartime contribution to the overthrow of the Nazi regime and to the democratization efforts of individual MG officers thereafter. Education and Information Control Division staffers, particularly, carried out their responsibilities with dedication, often in face of contrary pressures from OMGUS. Confronting Cold War–American Century policies of the United States, German trade unions and democratically oriented political figures and intellectuals successfully struggled to bring Nazi leaders to justice and to outlaw advocacy of National Socialism, praise of Hitler, and denial of the Holocaust. The Germans have paid compensation to victims of Nazism, provided generous economic aid to Israel, and carried out their responsibilities in the international arena. In contrast to the United States, Germany has ratified international conventions in protection of the environment, on the establishment of an international court of justice, and on the outlawing of various weapons of war.

In "Some Concluding Observations," the concluding chapter of *Betrayal*,[13] I offered reflections on my years overseas that are applicable to the remainder of the twentieth century and into the twenty-first century:

I believe our experience in Germany demonstrates that we need to investigate and clarify the striking disparity between what our State Department officials and our president [and currently our Defense Department] publicly profess (which is frequently what the people of our country actually want) . . . and what our policymakers actually practice. . . . Their use of the word "democracy" is a good example of this hypocritical verbal jugglery. Americans sincerely desire the extension and

---

13. Kahn, *Betrayal*, 218ff.

strengthening of democracy at home and abroad. Our businessmen-banker statesmen realize the emotional power of the word and skillfully employ it to justify every kind of action.

. . . [A]bove all, our experience in Germany reveals the close connection between our political policies and the ambitions of our big monopoly interests. The old fight of the American people against the monopolies at home must apparently be waged overseas, too. . . .

The struggle for peace and international cooperation falls upon the entire American people united with all the hundreds of millions throughout the world who do not want war. Only by electing an administration responsive to the will and solicitous of the best interests of the majority of Americans can we hope to regain our self-assurance and our reputation for democratic idealism. Meanwhile we must maintain constant vigilance and unceasingly call our policymakers to account.

Appendices

APPENDIX 1

With the headline "7 July IIIrd Order to the Soviet Partisans," the paper mandated the organization of partisan detachments operating independently of the French Communist FTP. Another prescribed the maintenance of the strictest discipline in caring for the wounded and punishment for looting or misbehavior with the local population. "Remember your responsibilities to your people, flag and nation," it urged.

APPENDIX 2

In 1990, while visiting the Soviet Union upon the invitation of the Soviet Veterans of the War, I turned over to the Soviet Museum of the Armed Forces these and other documents relating to my subsequent association with Soviet PWs and forced laborers, retaining, however, photocopies. The text reads as follows:

The Fatherland knows that the Germans with their bestial criminal starvation and threat of death by firing squad or hanging have compelled you to put on a German-Fascist uniform and to join the ranks of their army. . . .

The Fatherland calls upon you to desert from the German Army immediately, taking with you weapons and supplies and fleeing at night into the forest in French territory, killing without mercy any traitors among you. . . . We will find you in time and offer you assistance, and the Fatherland will learn of your actions. . . . Further delay will not be permitted. . . .

The Hitlerites often send you into battle against the partisans. The killing of even one partisan will be punished without mercy, one hundred of you for each one of us. But the way to be restored once again as an honorable Soviet Patriot is still open.

APPENDIX 3

"Report on Soviet Refugees in France with Suggestions for American Action to Aid Them":Memorandum dated 8 October 1944, sent to SHEAF.

The administrative and supply difficulties of these two groups are probably representative of those existing in the twenty or so similar camps in Eastern France. It is probable, estimating conservatively, that in Eastern France alone there are thirty to forty thousand such refugees.

. . . experience gained in resolving their difficulties will serve in good stead in

preparing for the care of the millions of Soviet citizens to be encountered in Western and Southern Germany....

No records are kept of captured materials turned over to the French by the American Army, and most have disappeared. Local French officials are often unaware of stocks available in neighboring communities. Some of the French, hostile to the refugees, fail to contact the Americans to obtain supplementary supplies and resist instructions from their own prefects and sousprefects. In Verdun, for example, French authorities deliberately favored Polish refugees over the Soviets until Captain Middleton intervened....

Among thousands of Soviet PWs there has developed widespread suspicion of Allied intentions.... The task of eliminating this feeling might not be very difficult since the Soviets appear desirous of considering us as true allies and are ready to cooperate in resolving difficulties....

American officers are forced to work through slow military channels because of the absence of direct liaison with the French and Soviet authorities. They bear responsibility merely for the initial organization of the refugee camps, and experience shows that when they turn the refugees over to the French, conditions for the refugees often deteriorate.

APPENDIX 4
Response from Chargé d'Affaires Alexander Gusovski

I have received your letter and express my heartfelt gratitude for your kind and sympathetic relations with our Soviet citizens. I did not expect otherwise since I know that our valorous American allies are friends not only for today but for tomorrow as well.

Thanking you for your important assistance, I beg and hope that your kind cooperation will help to alleviate the suffering of Soviet people in captivity and will assist them in returning to the ranks of the Red Army for the final defeat of fascism.

APPENDIX 5
"The Evacuation Order":Memorandum describing resistance to the evacuation order in numerous rural communities around Aachen where Wehrmacht troops sided with the civilians.

In Wulselen the villagers successfully resisted a demand that they turn over their cattle to the storm troopers for transport to rear areas. Returning that evening the SA succeeded in rounding up the cattle from the fields and stables and compelled the people to depart in trucks. The Kreisleiter (local administrator), who was also the head of the local bank, ran off with the bank's deposits. Wehrmacht soldiers barricaded some of the houses, insisting that army equipment was stored within them, thereby safeguarding civilians who remained in hiding. In the confusion of the hasty evacuation women were separated from their children.

In Strass the SA fired volleys to terrorize the villagers into obeying the order to evacuate. After a Wehrmacht soldier seeking to defend the civilians was shot, a Wehrmacht officer arrested the brownshirts and threatened to pack them off to the front. Another officer was heard to remark: "It is really bad when the German population has to call on the enemy for help."

In Kohlscheidt citizens refused to obey the orders of SA officials and SS troops to abandon their homes, their cattle and fields. Wehrmacht soldiers intervened in the support of the farmers. A Wehrmacht lieutenant colonel warned a Party official that in the event of continued terrorism by the SA, he would have the Party official shot. Nevertheless, SA and SS men dragged women out of their houses by their hair and hurled them on to trucks. Children were seized out of the arms of their mothers and locked in cellars until the women agreed to leave. Scuffles broke out in the streets between the women and Party members. One civilian was shot through the arm when he refused to leave. A large portion of the population fled to the woods, where they were sheltered by Wehrmacht soldiers.

In Herzogenrath, the SA attempted to force the villagers to burn their farms. The villagers mounted such fierce resistance that the storm troopers retreated, warning, "We'll be back, you traitors!" During the night the farmers stood guard, fearing the nazis would set fire to their crops. When the SA posted a warning that anyone resisting evacuation would be shot, the villagers hid in their cellars.

APPENDIX 6

To: Chief, P & PW, 12th Army Group
Subject: The Evacuation Order

The report of 30 October on this subject which was compiled by Mr. Arthur D. Kahn, and of which a copy was sent to this Headquarters, arrived at a moment when the whole question of policy in connection with . . . was being reviewed and proved of considerable assistance in this connection. It is regarded as a highly creditable piece of work on which Mr. Kahn is to be congratulated.

Murray Gourfein
Deputy Chief of Section

APPENDIX 7

1. Many of the troops maintained a blind belief in Hitler's secret weapons. The most powerful factor in the continued resistance, however, was the fear generated by Nazi propaganda that they would be sent to Siberia and that the bolsheviks would lay waste their homes.

A large proportion of the German soldiers were carrying PASSIERSCHEINE [our PW surrender pass] "just in case." Many of them kept copies of FRONTPOST [our German frontline newspaper]. . . . As soon as leaflets began to fall from the air, the Germans cordoned off the area and prevented anyone from picking them up. . . .

2. Nuns were not allowed to wear their habits and were drafted for digging trenches. . . .

Four hundred and fifty of the 900 priests of Lorraine were expelled; 12 were sent to Dachau [concentration camp; 15 were imprisoned elsewhere in Germany; and 15, in France. . . .

All religious youth associations were dissolved. Priests were forbidden to hold meetings of young people. . . . The Nazis set Hitler Jugend and Bund der Deutschen Maedchen activities during Sunday religious services.

APPENDIX 8
Excerpts from the diary of Roger Cerf, a POW who died at Dachau

A year ago I was in Bournemouth, after an absence of two and a half years. She loves me more than she did in 1938, so she said. I believe she would feel a shock if she saw me. Since yesterday my face is swollen, so are my hands and my feet. . . . I'll have to see the doctor. . . . I wish it would rain. There is no air. It's hardly bearable. To move is a torture. What wouldn't I give for a swim? I feel dirty. There is more than a month I have had my bath. It should be my turn soon. I burned my fingers this morning but I succeeded making four matches out of one. . . .

Haven't heard anything from V these last three days. I must call him. A good thing we learned morse—I just called him, he isn't well: skin disease, he says. . . . Dinner was quite good: peas and carrots. . . .

If, as I believe, England wins the war, the danger won't be an ideology, it'll be an economical danger, I think. That means the danger will be America and not Russia. I don't think the bases loaned to the U.S.A. will ever return to their owners. . . . There'll be a lot to do in Africa after the war. Nothing proper has ever been done in Belgian Congo. . . . The factories built for the war should be torn down. A new standard of life will have to be found. . . .

V called me this morning. It is scabies. And no medicine to get rid of it. He can't be left like that, his whole body is covered. Besides, everybody here will catch it. . . . We went out this morning. My neighbor passed me some writing paper and 4 half matches. I already made 12 with them. . . . My face is almost normal again. I suppose it was my stomach. I feel very weak. I had difficult to walk. . . . By Jove, I am hungry. If I get out of here I'll devote my life to eating. No matter if I grow fat. . . . Every penny I have will be converted into food. Centuries I haven't seen a piece of meat or a potato. To eat must be the greatest comfort in life. Here I am, deprived of liberty, of everything, and what I am most craving for is a proper meal. . . .

The hairdresser came this morning and the soup was brought in while he cut my hair. Of course, it was cold when I ate it. It's disgusting how much my hair is dirty. It's impossible to wash it here. . . .

Got 3 matches from my neighbor. But what a gymnastic to get them. They were caught on the wall, and I had to climb on the bars. My hands hurt. Still I have them. Now I have had my first smoke for 5 days. Not bad, but I could easily have done without now that I have a book to read. . . . I talked a few minutes with my neighbor after lunch—about food! . . . I feel a pain in the stomach when I think of it. And I think of it all day long. . . .

When I got up this morning I was amazed to see how thin I have grown lately. I hadn't noticed it so much before. My legs are like two dry sticks. My trousers don't hang anymore from my waist but from my hips. I'll soon be able to escape through the keyhole. . . .

I have been writing to my parents. The letter is a complaint from beginning to end: no letter from them, no parcel, no visit. I wonder if they get my letters. Perhaps it would be better if they didn't get this one. I have always been careful to write them in a cheerful tone, but this one was a bad show. I shouldn't have sent it. It'll make them sadder still, as if they haven't enough grief. . . . It's terrible how much older they have grown during my absence. . . . They are pitiful shadows of what they were. My mother lost 60 pounds in less than a year. My father 40. It's my turn now. Already 12 pounds in four months. We went out. It was ever so nice. . . .

I have had a surprise just after lunch—good and bad: a letter from my father telling me he hasn't been allowed to deposit parcels for me because they don't know who's in charge of me. He's trying to find out. . . .

I'd like to hear some music, that certain prelude or that toccato or a fugue. It's odd when I can't sleep and I lay still in my bed I always hear music. It sounds soft as if played by a far away orchestra composed of 'cellos only, and the tune develops like geometry—logical and smooth, so aerial, without melody—just notes so pure, playing some heavenly mathematical game. Probably my stomach working or my head. I suppose we'll clean the rooms this afternoon. It's always a quarter of an hour gained. . . .

This time last year I was in Malvern, I think. It was beastly hot. I was sharing my time between table tennis, bathing pool and tea shops. It was a nice little place to spend a fortnight. The airy summit of the hills. It was fresh up there. But climbing was a torture in that heat and in uniform. And what a jolly good time in the tea shops: cakes, scones, butter, marmalade, lemon curd, biscuits, chocolates and that delicious raspberry jam. . . . How many cups of tea didn't I drink? . . .

Blast! Rotten luck! I went out but my neighbor was left in. . . . Once more I *have had a row with the attendant: he wants us to stand to attention for any under officer. He passed me this morning and, of course, I didn't do it. He shouted like hell and became red with indignation. And what a vocabulary. . . . The brute, he doesn't bear me in his heart. He didn't like it when I told him I couldn't see any under officer. He is so proud of his stripes. He ought to be polite with a superior, but I suppose I am a civilian here. . . .*

Lots of planes flying about today. Noisy things! I have grown an abnormal dislike for anything noisy—almost morbid. . . . Amen. Good night, my son. . . .

No wonder I left this diary so abruptly yesterday. While I was cleaning my room, I was told (hold tight, everybody!) that there was a parcel for me! And by Jove, it was true! And what a parcel . . . making up for those I haven't had. Then library came and then supper, but I can't remember what it was, for I have been eating so many different things. Of course I haven't been able to sleep, it was so hot. I was so nervy and my stomach wasn't used anymore to such feasts. . . . If we go out I'll have lots of things to pass my neighbor. I won't be able to give him everything today. My pockets would look suspicious. . . . This end of June, beginning of July, will be a date in my life, good lord! What a parcel: two breads, 2 packets of biscuits, a pound of butter and another of honey, 6 tins of liver paste, 2 of "atum," 1 of green peas, 1 of grapes, fruit juice, 1 of apple, 1 of fruit paste, 9 lemons, 1 cake, chocolates, sweets, marvelous cigarettes (of which some American), odds and ends, my laundry. It's almost a pleasure to be in jail! There was a rose, too, in good condition still. It's now in a glass on my table—just here, under my nose: pink, frail, with a smell of gardens about it—a smell of outdoors, of freedom and open spaces. My cell is full of it. . . .

Good lord, here is the answer: I'll be tried tomorrow morning, they just told me. Queer, it doesn't affect me at all. I reckon anything is better than this. What will it be? death, life, 20 years, 10 years? I'll know tomorrow night. If it's not a death sentence, I'll be sent to Germany, I expect. . . . I'll tell V. I saw him this morning. He is in better shape now. I just told him. I am eager to know what the result will be. It's a big gamble, really. I am playing my head. I hope I won't have a headache. One must be fit for such gambling. Good God! what a game! what sport! But this time I am the fox. . . . let us stick to the old habit, and not bother beforehand. . . . Have been talking with my neighbor. He bets I'll get 10 years. We'll see if he is a good prophet. Anyhow, the main thing is to save my head—5, 10 or 20 years, it's all the same. I'll get out with the end of the war. . . .

7th of July: Well, I am ready. I'll be going in about half an hour. I hope I'll have my bread by then. I just think of it: I haven't got a barrister. That's odd. . . . Half past two. I came back half an hour ago. I found my soup, which was cold, milk and a surprise—a tin of sardines which were good. My trial lasted from half past nine till half past one: the sentence is death. They even condemned me to death four times: 1. for running away from Belgium, 2. for my bad intentions towards Germany, 3. for my wireless set and 4. I don't quite remember. I nearly fainted, not when I heard the sentence but five minutes afterwards. I got over it though. A lawyer is coming to see me tomorrow to help me to write a letter to I don't know whom to try to save my head, but I don't think it's any use. What a shock it'll be to my parents, to Nesta. I am so sorry for them. If only I could eat decently during my last days. To be shot starving is not at all a nice perspective although it's not a pleasure even with a full stomach. . . . I am very much afraid Nesta won't see me back this time unless a miracle happens. Poor girl, she'll forgive and forget, I hope. Jolly good day, what a supper: cauliflower, beans and potatoes, a filchard and a piece of sausage. It's worth a death sentence.

On 3 August Roger wrote his last words in a letter addressed to "Darling Nesta":

You know roughly what job I was on; you know what the penalty would be if I were caught: I have been caught, and this is my last night. I would feel quite happy about it, shouldn't I know the shock and the pain it'll cause you and my parents. I am asking the three of you the same thing: to be strong and to be willing to try and smooth the wound. The past is passed. Look forward, you are young, life is in front of you. Remember what I told you when speaking of this eventuality; I was serious: one doesn't live with the dead. . . . it's only right; a dead weight must be cut off. I don't ask you to forget me altogether, but try and keep a smooth and happy remembrance of me. I have loved you like no one else and, believe me, I have always been faithful. Since summer 1938 my heart has been yours and no one else had had it before. . . . I only regret not to be able to give you more joy, for you'll never know how much I owe you. I would have been able to do anything with you on my side: your love was increasing my strength a thousand times. . . .

I have another thing to ask you: be kind to my parents, they had only me and they are wonderful. You must see them and comfort them; I know they'll treat you as their daughter, they'll need someone to love, take my place, it has always been a good one, but I beg you not to give anything up because of me. . . .

Darling, forgive me, but I won't write any more; you have enlightened my life and only for that I should be grateful to you, but my debt is greater; I can't express it. I would have liked to hold you once more in my arms but it can't be. Be strong, keep your chin up, life is forward. have no regret for me. I have none myself. . . . Your picture has always been present to my mind and will be till the end. It's nothing, and I don't fear it.

Author's note: Inserted in the pages of the diary, I found a poetic tribute to Roger written by Lucien André, which I translated:

> He walked lithe and strong, confident in his destiny
> And suiting his days to the rhythm of life

Ever alert, joying in beauty
Finding ample booty in sun and sky.
If death snatched him this morning
It found him pure, without rancor or jealousy
Having known how to give all without
Quenching his thirst to serve a lofty ideal.
With bravado, careless of fame,
Never doubting victory
He accepted his fate calmly.
For he was not unaware that if contrary fate
Would brutally cut short his career
The spirit of liberation would not be halted.

APPENDIX 9
"A Picture of the City as It Is Today"

The history of contemporary Mainz . . . begins 27 February, 1945, when a massive air bombardment devastated the city, leaving only a few buildings standing. Between 4:00 and 4:30 that afternoon explosions rocked the city. . . . A great cloud of black smoke hid the sky for miles. . . . The greater part of the city burned for two whole days, and some sectors for more than a week. When people emerged from the cellars, they found that almost every family had lost all its possessions. Thousands of the inhabitants, in addition, had been killed.

There had been no gas since 9 September, the day of another great attack, but now there was no electricity, no water, no bread. The NSV [Nazi welfare service] distributed food for five days—soup twice a day plus a small ration of bread at night. After three days there was a little butter. At the end of the first week it was possible to buy bread and meat—there were large quantities of burnt meat available. . . . medical supplies were not available. . . . People had to draw water either from pumps or from the Rhine. . . .

The Nazis spread word that people who had no place to live were to go to [suburban towns]. Orders were issued to the army to take civilians on their vehicles . . . and people fought to get on the trucks. The old and the weak were left behind. . . . Many who attempted to leave the city returned because no provision had been made for their care.

Before the bombardment many Party leaders in uniform were to be seen, few afterwards. One Nazi apologized for wearing a brown uniform, saying it was the only clothes he had left.

Gauleiter Springer proclaimed his determination to defend the city, and Kreisleiter Fuchs issued an order to fight to the last man. . . . The soldiers in the city garrison spent most of their time drinking. Their morale, already low, was under-

mined further by the entreaties of the population to stop fighting. A Communist [Heinrich Sohl, a pre-1933 city councilman] shouted to some Wehrmacht soldiers, "Why are you still fighting? Put down your arms. There is no sense fighting against such material superiority." The soldiers replied, "We know nothing. The SS shoot deserters."

The Volkssturm was ordered to report for duty, but their files had been destroyed in the air raid, and only a few hundred men of the four battalions answered the call to arms. . . . A VS complained to Regierungsrat Oppenheim, "I have not been taught to use the panzerfaust and my rifle has no trigger. . . . I will throw them away and go into the house, change my clothes and become a civilian again." The VS in the surrounding towns were ordered to construct tank barriers. . . . [T]heir wives, seeing the approaching American tanks, broke down the barriers in order to put an end to the senseless war. . . .

On 16 March the Nazis blew up the bridges across the Rhine. The Party bosses who had been proclaiming Goebbels' slogan, "We will hold out to the last German, to the last bullet," ran off. . . .

Indeed, the blowing up of the bridges signified the end of the connection with Berlin for the Mainzers. . . . Hardly anyone any longer gave the Hitler salute. People began to discuss foreign radio news openly. In the bunkers people talked openly against the Nazis.

On 20 March SS men went searching for men to defend the city. Arbeitsdienst [labor service] boys sixteen years of age were ordered to man posts and not to desert. Citizens took away weapons from Hitler Jugend in order to prevent unnecessary bloodshed.

On 22 March the American troops entered the city against spasmodic resistance. On 23 March a military government detachment arrived. . . . They brought the Roman Catholic bishop from his refuge twenty kilometers from the city, and with his assistance and that of the leading protestant pastor they drew up a list of potential appointees to official posts. The mayor was sworn in on 25 March; the police commissioner the next day.

The first five or six days no food was available for purchase in the city, and people were forced to rely on their own slender stores. By mid April vegetables, some fruit and potatoes were to be bought in open air markets. The bread ration was fixed at 1,500 grams a week per person. . . .

Since the Nazis had absconded with the plans of the electric lines of the city, it took a long time to repair the facilities. . . . Much of the water service and electric power was restored by 10 April. . . .

The population now had unmistakable evidence of the lying in German propaganda. A Wehrmachtsbericht [army communiqué] reported stiff fighting for the city when actually it fell after slight resistance. A further Wehrmachtsbericht announced that the Mainzers were suffering severely as a result of the outlawing of German currency, a shortage of food, the shooting of women who had unlawfully hoarded foodstuffs. . . . The MG commandant was also reported to have been shot. . . . Unaware that the Americans had disarmed mines laid by the Nazis to blow up the chief bakery, German radio announced bread riots in the city. Mainzers were further outraged by Goebbels' complaint that the Mainzers had disappointed Germany by not putting up a better defense to delay the American advance. . . . The people of the city saw American might and were astounded by it.

In Mainz, as in German cities, destruction was nearly total and seemingly irreparable. Almost all the streets had been cleared, the rubble piled neatly. Everywhere gangs of Nazi Party members were sweeping up debris. Some stores were open and conducting brisk business. People were walking to open air markets, bicycling to work or wheeling baby carriages. . . . In the square before MG HQ, GIs were playing catch with a baseball, women sat with infants in the sun, children played at the fountain, old men read newspapers. One of the big events of the day, an event that brings a near riot, is the arrival of "Die Mitteilungen" [a newspaper published by the Psychological Warfare Branch]. A line forms immediately, and very quickly all copies are gone. . . .

Citizens lined up early in the morning to present requests to the MG officers. The petitioners endured long waits, for no one of the officers had even a minimal command of German, and only one of the ten NCOs and enlisted men spoke German. (Three Dutch citizens, an American woman who had lived in Germany since 1936 and a half-Jewish woman served as interpreters and general factotums.) In their meeting with the officers, citizens called attention to a failure to take leading Nazis into custody; others brought complaints of pillaging, raping and shooting rampages by American troops.

APPENDIX 10

Poems by Hermann Butz

I

He shouts now here, he shouts now there,
Organizes the entire place,
Yes, everything for the people's defense:
Common good before private good!

Now we go out to the Volkssturm,
As German practice and custom demands,
We hurry after like loyal sheep,
Singing, "Better dead than slave!")

II

Master will I be!
And not enslaved!

Free will I be!
And not deprived of rights!

A man will I be!
And go forth righteous!
Devout will I be!
And devout perish!
German will I be!
No matter how difficult!
Human being will I be!
That above all!

III

Be united and strong!
Not much longer to hold out!
Remain loyal, be ready!
Soon the hour will summon us!

APPENDIX 11

The men described their daily routine at Buchenwald:reveille at 3:45 A.M., toilet, breakfast (cup of coffee, ten grams of margarine, 200 grams of bread); 4:30 roll call; 5:00 departure of work details; 12–12:30 P.M. rest and a glass of coffee; work until 5:30 or 6 P.M., return to camp for a liter of soup (during the last weeks a mere three-quarters of a liter).

Corpses of dead comrades had to be carried to roll call, which sometimes lasted three to four hours regardless of the weather. Often corporal punishment was meted out in the sight of all the internees—twenty blows with a rod. A public hanging was held after any attempted escape. Inmates often disappeared and were never seen again.

APPENDIX 12

The men listed as war criminals among the German camp administrators Obergruppenfuehrer Schobert, camp commandant, two SS officers in charge of roll call, Sturmfuehrer Gust and an officer named Barnewald; a certain Schwartz in charge of work details; and a Dr. Schilowski, an infirmary physician who conducted sterilization experiments. Schilowski had previously been stationed at the women's concentration camp at Ravensburg, where he experimented with artificial impregnation and carried out abortions on pregnant women and then killed the women and burned their bodies.

Adjoining the crematorium was a huge barnlike room equipped with forty-eight gallows. Men were hanged in such a way that they strangled slowly. They scratched at the wall so that finger nails were embedded in the bricks. When the bodies were taken down, the director of the crematorium performed homosexual acts on the cadavers. A Lieutenant Perkins of the U.S. Army Intelligence was hanged there a week before the arrival of the Americans.

APPENDIX 13

The arrest warrant, drafted by a German translator at the police department

The leading medical doctor of the Neubrunnenbad, a bathinghouse for medical treatment, a Nazi of the worst fame, treated everybody not a Nazi in a most cruel manner. So for instance: a jew lying with a broken arm on the floor of the Bathinghouse, was refused first medical aid by this Dr. Richter, with the remark, that he did not give any aid to jews.

During the last weeks of this Nazi regiment he pressed sick people into the "Volkssturm" in a most unhuman, rigorous manner.

Dr. Richter means a danger to public safety and is to be arrested.

Mainz, the 10th of April 1945.

(signed) The President of the Police [Jakob Steffan]

APPENDIX 14

"Wuerzburg Before and After the Arrival of the Americans"

The contemporary history of Wuerzburg begins Friday, 16 March, when at 9:30 P.M. there commenced a thirty-minute incendiary aerial bombardment of the town. . . . Fires raged for three days in the greater part of the city. In some sectors flames continued for more than a week. Not a single building in the city escaped. Preparations for an air raid had been miserably inadequate. The city had no bunkers, no adequate fire-fighting equipment and no anti-aircraft defenses.

For three or four days no bread was available. Community kitchens supplying single-dish meals were established. There was no electricity, gas or water. Where once lived some 110,000 people, only 21,000 remained. Others who survived the air raid fled to surrounding towns and villages. So far, the number of known dead has reached 3,000, though a final total of 10,000 seems likely.

The day after the disaster, the Gauleiter, who had not been present in the city at the time of the air raid, posted propaganda slogans and delivered a speech expressing his satisfaction that Wuerzburg had taken its place alongside other heroic German cities. Previously, indeed, he had declared that it was shameful that Wuerzburg remained undamaged.

On 28 March, American tank columns were reported approaching the city. The Volkssturm was called to duty. Dr. Wahl, the Kreisleiter, announced that he would defend the ruins to the last drop of blood. The majority of the men failed to report. The police were instructed under an order from Heinrich Himmler to shoot any Germans who displayed a white flag. (No white flags appeared.) In the nearby village of Zellingen a farmer was overheard to say, "The scoundrels ought all to be hanged!" That evening after a drumhead trial, he was hanged in front of his house by order of the commander of the local Volkssturm battalion. The Kreisleiter fled. The Gauleiter followed on Easter Sunday with three truckloads of furniture.

On Monday, 2 April, the half of the city on the west bank of the Main fell to the Americans. On Tuesday the Americans crossed the river in assault boats. On Wednesday a pontoon bridge was thrown across the river. An order for evacuation was transmitted from the Sturmbannfuehrer's cellar headquarters. Though warned that they would be treated as traitors, few of the citizens still in the city obeyed the order. The battle lasted until Saturday, though sniping by Hitler Jugend continued thereafter.

On 20 April, Hitler's birthday, Goebbels complained in a national broadcast that Mainfranken had defended itself badly.

The appearance of the city today;
From the distance, Wuerzburg appears still to be a beautiful city with the spires of handsome churches, the impressive dome of the cathedral and several palaces. The Main cuts through the city—broad and majestic. Strangely, numerous trees remain undamaged amidst the general devastation. Two large hills dominate the city, on one of which stands a majestic castle built for an archbishop in the sixteenth century and protected by a formidable series of ramparts. Large sections of the roof have been destroyed. On the other hill stands a chapel with walls covered with yellow stucco. Its narrow, round spires are undamaged.

Descending from these hills into the western part of the city, one finds that only shells remain of the houses, but people continue to live in the cellars, and some apartments are habitable. The two bridges spanning the river were blown up by the Nazis. The old bridge adorned with monumental statues of saints, however, was not totally destroyed, and most of the statues can be restored.

The town itself is no more. The cathedral, the palace, the churches, the university are all burned out. Most of the buildings have collapsed into heaps of rubble. Groups of people can be seen in different parts of the city repairing electric cables and water pipes. There are food queues in every quarter.

The Nazi Party headquarters at the side of the river, still usable, is occupied by the MG detachment and the new municipal administration. At the noon lunch break one can hear German young women, clerks, singing merrily on the top floor to the accompaniment of a loud piano.

APPENDIX 15

Seifert was born 9 November 1887 and was director of the local university and chief of the surgical clinic. He joined the NSDAP 1 May 1933 and the SA in November 1933, where he reached the rank of Oberstuermbannfuehrer (subject to automatic arrest under denazification regulations). He was a convinced Nazi and states that he remains one today. He admits participating actively in vandalism of Jewish property. He left the church in 1937. Subject was a physician in the German Army and sought to evade internment as a high-ranking Nazi by claiming POW status.

APPENDIX 16

I opened the description of the celebration by recounting how at a signal from Kremlin churchbells and Red Army guns heard over the camp radio, Colonel Kompanyeyets, imitating to the letter the May Day ceremony in Moscow, strode briskly about the parade grounds congratulating the men and women drawn up at attention in regiments. The regiments replied with resounding hurrahs and then marched in stiff military step past the reviewing stand to the music of the camp band. Girl gymnasts in white blouses and green skirts formed pyramids, and the crowd sang Red Army songs with lusty enthusiasm. Political Commissar Major Gregory Samolyenko, a former tractor station manager from Dnieperpetrovsk in the Ukraine, proclaimed: "This is a great day for our people. For several years we have not had the opportunity to assemble, to celebrate and to laugh. This is a new day!"

APPENDIX 17

"My Recollections" by Anatoly Epifanov

On 22 June [1941] the bestial fascist Hitler attacked our beloved homeland. . . . In September he occupied our village. . . . At once he started to wipe out the people, to hang, shoot and deport them to Germany. . . . I fell into the last group. I resisted, but the German police caught me and drove me off. They said that it would be all right for us, that we would go to school as we had at home, but in order that we should not become bolsheviks they were sending us off to Germany. . . . And so they locked us into freight cars and carted us off like chickens. . . . There was nothing to eat, it was cold, it rained, and the cars leaked. We tried to speak to the fascists, but they would not listen. We traveled around for a whole month, and during this time they gave us only four rolls of stale bread a day. Sometimes they gave us watery soup. They brought me finally to Ludwigshaven. We were not going to go to school, but to work. The camp was dirty, there was no water. . . . They gave us 200 grams of bread and some cabbage soup. The following day I was sent to work on the railroad. . . . There was an old fascist. He said, "Ah, they have brought Russians to work." They made us carry railroad ties and rails, and we worked twelve hours a day. . . . Anglo-American planes carried out raids, but the fascist women and children wouldn't let Russians into the bunkers. We ran out of the city and hid. The planes blew up the factories, the plants, and the railway lines. . . . The fascists became angry and beat us. They said that Russians were pigs, that they had no culture, that they were savages. . . . The fascists made a great mistake in saying these things. . . . And then we heard happy news. Our glorious Red Army had driven the fascists from Russian soil and was driving them into their own land . . . and the armies of our allies were advancing from the west, striking the fascists blow upon blow. And so on 25 March our dreams came true. American units liberated us and brought us to the Soviet Assembly Point. . . . The headquarters leaders immediately turned their attention to us . . . and on 13 April we went to school. For the first time in four years we saw our teachers again. For us children without parents, they organized an Internat [orphanage] where we are brought up like Soviet citizens.

APPENDIX 18
Discussions with Russians, 15 and 19 May 1945

We sincerely thank you journalist Kahn [having noted that I wore no insignia of rank and that I seemed always to be carrying a typewriter, they assumed that I was a journalist] for the attention you have shown to us Soviet citizens. Your discussions with citizens of our Assembly Center evoked great interest.

Express thanks in our name to the general for his concern for us. We will not forget that.

We promise to do everything possible in our circumstances to introduce better order in our camp and hope for his assistance and effort to improve and to render happier our life in a foreign land.

Mr. Kahn, convey to the general and to the entire American people our conviction that our friendship with you will be confirmed by the blood shed in battle by the best sons of your and our peoples and will be further strengthened with each day in the future.

Your cordial association with us and your efforts for us we will report to our people when we return to our homeland.

Author's note: This document was signed by four officers of the first regiment. The second declaration was signed by six members of the special unit of officers unassigned to regiments:

We are all former Russian prisoners of war who have undergone fascist imprisonment and liberation by our allies. At the present moment we find ourselves at the Soviet Assembly Center in Darmstadt. We thank the American journalist Mr. Kahn for his frank discussion with us.

All of us as one man wish to advance the friendship of the great Russian and American peoples.

APPENDIX 19

The mission of Psychological Warfare Branch was to play its part in making secure the peace by furthering the military and political objectives of our occupying forces, by eliminating Nazi and German militaristic influence on German information media. This was to be accomplished in three phases.

1. The prohibition of all German information services, as announced by Military Government Law 191.
2. The use of Allied information services and reconnaissance of German information services.
3. The gradual transition, varying from region to region, and from medium to medium, to German services by the Germans under Allied supervision.

APPENDIX 20

The MG-appointed mayor was assassinated under strange, never explained circumstances, but most of his appointees were left in their positions. In January 1946, the British MG detachment which had assumed control of the area dismissed the successor mayor appointed by the Americans because of prior membership in a Nazi organization which financed fifth-column groups like Henlein's Sudeten Nazis and the German-American Bund. A month later the leaders of the local trade unions and of the Social Democratic and Communist parties requested that the local technical college be shut down after students flatly refused to express their opinions on the Nuremberg trials when asked to do so by a British MG officer. Lt. Col Swoboda, the American MG commanding officer, was not cashiered for his violations of SHAEF directives. He would be heard from again.

APPENDIX 21

Letter from Captain Shrank, MG commandant in a rural county, to his wife describing his compassionate treatment of a returning Kzler, 5 June 1945.

Several veterans of Buchenwald and Dachau concentration camps have returned home to Kusel and the vicinity. I do not know how they made their way so far. These were once men. I do not believe that any care or recuperation, however solicitous and loving, can return these men to a normal state. . . . One of them is particularly vivid in my mind, a young man in spite of the deep lines of suffering on his face, leaning on two canes and his whole body from head to foot shaking as if with the ague.

A Jew returned from Buchenwald yesterday to Glan-Munschweiler. Sofsky, the Buergermeister, outdid himself in caring for this man. He threw a Nazi out of his house and gave it to him. Sofsky then arranged for the bank (did I tell you I reopened the bank with a non-Nazi director?) to loan him enough marks to get started in his old business of cattle trading. And all in one day! Incidentally, the wife of the SS major balked at obeying Sofsky's eviction order and resisted the gendarme who was doing his duty. He threw her into the clink, and when she comes before our MG court this Friday I will put her in jail for six months.

Author's note: More common was the experience of the former head of the Communist Party in the village of Lindenfels upon returning home penniless and jobless after ten years in a concentration camp. The mayor of the community, a slippery individual who had somehow never joined the Nazi Party, offered him jobs four or five miles out of town, knowing that the Kzler was too weak to walk that far daily and not strong enough, in any case, to do farm work. The anti-Nazi ended up on public charity, derided as "shiftless."

APPENDIX 22
MG's Selection of German Officials

In selecting German officials to help them "get things moving," many MG officers . . . appointed men with starched collars, good educations, the regular churchgoers, the leading citizens, the Rotary Club–Chamber of Commerce types, the kind of men "you can talk to," the men "you can trust will get the job done."

Unfortunately, some of these well-dressed, experienced administrators . . . had either been members of the Nazi Party or had closely collaborated with the Nazis. But strangely enough, after reading all the Stars and Stripes *stories of the brutality of the Nazis, many MG men found that individual Party members did not have horns; many of them were "just plain businessmen with whom it was easy to get along." . . .*

All over the zone there developed confusing and demoralizing situations where in one county an aggressive officer impervious to German flattery and whining denazified the civil administration, while in the surrounding counties other MG men retained Party members in office to assist in "getting things moving."

"Nice racket you guys got" was the laughing comment if someone told

them he was in MG, for there was more than the accepted condescension of an aircorps man for a footslugger in the attitude of the combat men toward the "chairborne" occupation officers. . . . And wasn't it a joke—typical Army snafu—that most MG officers couldn't even talk "kraut." (A few weeks of conversational German was supposed to overcome the language barrier and brief surveys of German history allegedly prepared them to tackle the complex problems involved in occupation duties.) . . .

Many GIs recalled how back in 1943 when the Provost Marshal ordered Army posts and military camps to furnish a quota of men to be trained for occupation duty many units took the opportunity to rid themselves of their duds. Word got around, too, of how the Army had given direct commissions to ex-local ward heelers, state assemblymen and county commissioners, men with "administrative experience" and political connections who wanted to do a little war. And later, men arriving in the ETO [European Theater of Operations] were dumped into MG, no matter what their training, just because the Army did not know where else to assign them.

Of a typical class of 32 men who had completed an ASTP (intensive foreign language courses) in 1943 at the University of Pennsylvania, only five ended up in MG. . . . Graduates of the advanced military government school in Brondisbury, England, who had been prepared for specific positions in specific German towns . . . found that no note whatever was taken of their specialization when they were finally assigned to MG units in Germany.

APPENDIX 23

If the change of spirit and society in the occident [Italy, Spain, Hungary and Germany and throughout Latin America] is characterized by the fact that the democratic principle of rule by the majority is being replaced by the Fuehrer principle, then this temporal development is in conformity with the tenets of the Catholic Church. In the Roman Catholic Church, the authoritarian Fuehrer principle has characterized the theory and practice of the church from its very founding. . . . The bishop in this [Nazi] state and society established on authoritarian principles is the religious leader, the spiritual Fuehrer alongside the political Fuehrer.

APPENDIX 24

Letter to the editor of *Sueddeutsche Zeitung* from Dr. Karl Ruedrich, 10 June

We did not expect any special reception. We ex-Kzler are simple and modest. . . . We were exhausted. All of us were sick. But everyone of us had to go through red tape to receive our forty marks ($4.00) and our ration points. My comrades were

running around all day attempting to buy or to obtain at least a shirt. Finally we were billeted at the Stieler school. Liberated Kzler were in charge of the billets. They did what they could, but the facilities were limited. The city administration had made no preparations for our reception. There were no washrooms or sinks. We had no towels, no messkits, no blankets, etc. That was our convalescent home in Munich!

Some city employees were helpful, others were uncooperative. The Nazi spirit has not disappeared. . . . We are always told that the directives come from higher echelons—from the Americans. I have found that the Americans show understanding when reasonable suggestions are made to them. I speak English fluently and can say that the Americans act like gentlemen, but they say that we have to help ourselves, that we must learn to administer our own country.

I remember my dead comrades. They died as martyrs for freedom. What is Munich doing for their survivors?

APPENDIX 25
"Munich, Lack of Democracy Brings Disillusionment"

The Americans want to play the anti-fascists against the fascists to keep the Germans weak. Thus Nazis remain in business and government, and the anti-fascist organizations are outlawed because they want to treat the Nazis too harshly.

The Americans talk nicely of democracy on the radio, but actually they have no intention of reeducating for democracy or of establishing political democracy.

The Americans call the old men with crucifixes to office and have no use for the anti-fascists whom they consider Communists and dangerous.

The Church and the BVP are allowed to take over everything while the anti-fascist organizations must stand outside the door and say, "May we come in?"

There can be no effective criticism of the activities of the church and the BVP or of those who sympathize with the Nazis since there are no opposition parties to do the criticizing and no organs through which to do so.

The BVP is lenient toward the Nazis because they would like to add the former Party members to their membership, thereby strengthening their position against the parties of the Left.

The Americans have come, but the swindle continues. The Nazis are still here and push us around as ever. The Americans must want the Nazis to remain, for they are still in some of the highest positions.

We have little information about what is going on in the Russian zone, but from what we hear, it seems that we feared them in vain. They, at least, are taking action against the Nazis, not relying upon the church and making preparations against the winter hardships.

APPENDIX 26
Attitudes of German Youth

The typical youth wants to continue living in Germany and considers Russia the worst place in the world in which to live. He thinks that Germans as a people are superior to the Italians, Poles, Russians and French but not to the Americans and English. He believes that the officers were justified in mounting the 20 July Putsch because it was clear that the war was already lost. It was lost primarily because of the material superiority of the Allies, especially in air power. He is ready to admit that Germany started the war although apt to add that the Jews or English or Poles were also responsible. He agrees that German Jews should be permitted to return to Germany [25 percent of those questioned, however, declared that they should not be allowed back] and that members of the Hitler Youth and BDM [Bund der deutschen Maedchen—the Nazi organization for young women] should not be permitted to hold leading positions in any new youth movements. As for women, their place is in the home, not in careers.

The majority expressed the view that Germany should become a democracy, while at the same time declaring that the idea of National Socialism was good but was badly carried out. They were unsure whether Hitler himself was bad or whether he merely had bad advisers. In any case, they were convinced that Germany needed another Fuehrer to rehabilitate it. Favoring the establishment of a free press, they also believed that newspapers should print only "what is good for the people" since they considered the average citizen to be stupid and easily misled by propaganda. They selected Roosevelt as the greatest man in history, with Bismarck and Frederick the Great as second choices. Displaying little interest in politics, they described as their chief concern getting enough to eat and worried about their personal future in regard to education and employment. Many feared that they would never be reunited with missing members of their families.

APPENDIX 27

1. complete disarmament and democratization of Germany;
2. the Nazi Party and all its institutions to be uprooted;
3. war criminals to be arrested and brought to judgment and other Nazi leaders interned;
4. German education to be controlled as to completely eliminate Nazi and militarist doctrines and to ensure the development of democratic ideals;
5. democratic political parties to be allowed and encouraged and local self-government restored on democratic principles;
6. subject to military security, freedom of speech, press and religion to be permitted.

APPENDIX 28
"Need for Propaganda on Atrocities Committed by Nazis in Occupied Countries":Memorandum

[M]any Germans express wonderment at the fact that peoples in formerly occupied lands hate them. The Germans consider the atrocities committed by their troops as ordinary excesses of war. . . .

Germans who now complain about what they consider maltreatment by the occupying powers might become more sober in their judgments if they were informed what the Wehrmacht did in other countries. . . . Information about the atrocities committed against other peoples would give them fuller understanding of the fact that the war was not waged simply over international markets, as many of them now believe. . . .

Germans often take the attitude that what Germans have done to Germans is the business of Germans. Sometimes they use the atrocity stories about the concentration camps to convince themselves that they, too, suffered at the hands of the Nazis. Thus they rationalize themselves out of guilt.

Former inmates of concentration camps protest that as a result of our propaganda about the concentration camps they are received as invalids in need of charity and are not afforded opportunities to enter the political and economic life of their communities. They regret that it is not pointed out that some of Germany's most capable leaders had been incarcerated in the camps, that these men are now available to share in the leadership of the country.

APPENDIX 29
As you know I have announced a firm policy of uprooting the whole Nazi organization regardless of the fact we may sometimes suffer from local administrative inefficiency. Reduced to its fundamentals, the United States entered this war as a foe of nazism; victory is not complete until we have eliminated from positions of responsibility and, in appropriate cases, punished every active adherent of the Nazi Party. I know that some field commanders have felt that some modification of this policy should be made. . . . We will not compromise with nazism in any way. I wish you to make particularly sure that your subordinate commanders realize that the discussion stage of this question is long past, any expressed opposition to the faithful execution of the order cannot be regarded leniently by me. I expect just as loyal execution of this and other policies applying to German occupation as I received during the war.

APPENDIX 30
We can get rid of Nazis without any trouble at all, but there is a very strong ultraconservative party in Bavaria. . . . It isn't an excrescence like the Nazi party, but it

is deeply rooted in Bavaria and particularly in the people who for years and years have been governing there and who are pretty highly respected themselves. [Bavarian Minister President] Schaeffer isn't a Nazi as much as an ultra-conservative.

APPENDIX 31

Attlee and Truman balked, for example, at Stalin's demand, reiterated daily during the weeks of the conference, that the Ruhr, the center of the German military-industrial complex, be administered jointly both to guarantee that it no longer prove the engine for German aggression and that it provide a source of reparations for nations devastated in the war.

At the Potsdam Conference . . . when President Harry S. Truman intimated the existence of a powerful new weapon, Stalin sensed that the United States was hardening its position. "They want to force us," Stalin told his associates, "to accept their plans on questions affecting Europe and the world." (Gromyko, Memoirs, 110)

"During the round-table discussions with Truman and Churchill," Zhukov recounted,

Stalin had to make several rather sharp observations on the different size of the losses borne by the Soviet Union and by its Allies in the war and on the right of our country to demand appropriate reparations. . . . Not a single bomb was dropped on American territory, not a single shell hit an American city. In the war against Germany and Japan, the United States lost 405,000 men. Britain lost 375,000 men. While Poland, for example, lost 6 million and Yugoslavia, 1,706,000 people. (Zhukov, Reminiscences and Reflections, 429–73)

APPENDIX 32

We felt that for us to be guilty of bad faith in any detail of operation or execution would defeat whatever hope we had of assisting in development of a broad basis of international cooperation. This policy of firm adherence to the pledge and word of our government was first challenged shortly after the close of hostilities. Some of my associates suddenly proposed that when so requested by the Russians I should refuse to withdraw American troops from the line of the Elbe to the area allocated to the United States area of occupation. The argument was that if we kept the troops on the Elbe, the Russians would be more likely to agree to some of our proposals, particularly as to a reasonable division of Austria. To me such an attitude seemed indefensible. I was certain and I was always supported in this attitude by the War Department that to start off in our first association with Russia on the basis of refusing to carry out an agreement in which the good faith of our government was involved would wreck the whole cooperative attempt at its very beginning. (474)

Appendices

APPENDIX 33

Reporting on his August visit to Moscow, Eisenhower recounted:

When we flew into Russia in 1945, I did not see a house standing between the western borders of the country and the area around Moscow. Through this overrun region Marshal Zhukov told me so many numbers of women, children and old men had been killed that the Russian government would never be able to estimate the total. Some of their great cities had been laid waste, and until November 1942 there seemed to be little hope that their desperate defense could hold off the enemy until their industries could be rehabilitated and Western Allies could get into the war in force. (469)

APPENDIX 34

Prewar U.S. Anti-Communism

1939
- 2 January: Dies Committee on Un-American Activities urges the unseating of Congressman Vito Marcantonio [a New York liberal].
- 14 January: Reich press assails Roosevelt policies as communistic.
- 19 May: New York State Senate urges Congress to bar members [of the Communist Party] from the ballot.
- 20 May: Kentucky borders guarded to bar entry of members.
- 1 June: Major General Mosely before Dies Committee says President should use army to prevent alleged imminent Jewish communist revolt.
- 17 July: Eleanor Roosevelt's attack on Coughlin as anti-Semitic held due to Coughlin's opposition to communism.
- 7 September: Representative J. Parnell Thomas calls New Deal a communist front.
- 29 September: American Legion urges outlawing of Communist Party.
- 3 October: Dies directs raids on Chicago Communist headquarters.
- 20 October: F. E. Beal accuses Communists of fomenting of textile strikes and formation of new unions as result of USSR orders.
- 24 October: Dies predicts deportation of 7,000,000 aliens if [his] committee gets funds to continue.
- 25 October: Eleanor Roosevelt warns curbs on isms may cut our freedoms.
- 31 October: Dies to investigate Communist influences in consumer movement.
- 24 December: Communist Party dance mobbed, building wrecked in Aberdeen, Washington.

1940:

2 February: Representative Ford offers bill to deport [Communist] affiliated aliens.

7 February: Civil Service Commission replies to J. Edgar Hoover's charge that it sent Communists to work for F.B.I.

27 May: [Communist Party] Members distributing pamphlets and soliciting petitions to place party on Illinois ballot flee to jail for protection from mob, Pekin, Ill., escorted out of town after night in jail.

29 May: Alex Rose [International Ladies Garment Workers Union] demands ban [of party].

8 June: Outlawing urged by William Green [president AFL].

20 August: Representative Dies says Roosevelt and Willkie should state whether they favor outlawing.

APPENDIX 35
Appeals for Alfred Kroth

Communist Party Statement:

1. Communists take the opportunity to declare that they consider it incomprehensible in light of the proclamation of the Supreme Commander of the American Forces in Germany General Eisenhower calling for a radical denazification of German life, a goal welcomed by the Communists, that proven anti-fascists who risked their lives against the Nazi regime should now suffer attack.

2. It is to be expected that with the publicity given to the Kroth "case" he and the Communist Party will suffer in reputation. Learning for the first time of Kroth's activity against them, former Nazis will find the means to revenge and will do everything possible to have him labelled as a "dangerous National Socialist." . . . and to see to it that he is prevented from making further contributions as a forthright opponent of Nazism. . . .

Finally, it should be noted that the underground conspiratorial struggle against Hitler on the part of active anti-fascists cost innumerable casualties and that the Kroth "case" is one of the rare instances where underground activity was carried to completion as a result of his outstanding adroitness, discipline, self-control and simple good luck. Like many others, Kroth could have ended up a victim of fascism. In that event everyone would now be mourning him. That Kroth survived the Nazi era under unimaginable hardships imposes upon us the duty to fight for him as he for twelve years fought for us, for freedom and against Hitler.

3. Appeal of a Friend:

Kroth is one of the most idealistic Communists I have ever known. I have the highest opinion and respect for him and for his hazardous struggle against the Nazis."

Perhaps this judgment of one [the woman's son] who fell in the struggle against Hitler will assist in convincing the American Military Government authorities that in the case of Dr. Kroth they are dealing with a dedicated anti-fascist who risked his life a hundredfold, a man who through his formal membership in the NSDAP provided a greater contribution to the fight against Hitler than many so-called "non-Nazis."

I note further that neither my son nor I were Communists but members of the Social Democratic party.

APPENDIX 36

I wrote this description of the manpower situation in *Betrayal*:

Because their responsibilities required a certain continuity, MG personnel had not expected to be redeployed [either to the Pacific or to the States] along with the combat troops. But as soon as word was out that they would be redeployed along with the other Americans in the theater, they, too, became agitated. . . . More and more responsibility was shifted to the frauelein secretaries and to German civil officials. Supervision decreased especially in the rural areas, where the Nazis were becoming bold again. Some detachments, like one rural MG unit north of Frankfurt with which I had dealings, practically stopped operations, and business and government activity in the towns under its control almost ceased. (99)

APPENDIX 37

"Bayonets Disperse GIs in Frankfurt" by Kathleen McLaughlin, *New York Times*, 10 January

Four thousand United States soldiers in a mutinous mood, who tried to rush headquarters of the United States Forces in the European Theatre here tonight, with the objective of forcing Gen. Joseph T. McNarney to confront them on their demand to be sent home, were stopped at bayonet point by a small group of guards.

A couple of men were roughly handled by a lieutenant in charge who refused to give his name and for a few minutes it was touch and go whether the troops would charge and try to overpower the absurdly small group. . . .

Howling down successive speakers who tried to bring order out of the chaotic situation, the disgruntled soldiers capitulated finally to an alternative proposed by T/4 Morris Cohen of Boston to restage the gathering in force in preference to dealing through nominated committees. Sergeant Cohen's contention that it would be futile to send deputies to a counsel table was obviously the consensus of the demonstrators. . . .

Yells of derision greeted reports that some officers had tried to dissuade the parti-

cipants from attending the session by declarations that it would make a bad impression on the Germans.

Charges were freely hurled that General McNarney was "too scared to face us."

APPENDIX 38

Preliminary reaction Kz movies in Bavaria: theaters filled capacity. One movie in district had queues for hours. Everybody dejected, women cried, regret expressed at portrayed conditions. However, little responsibility felt; much comment on brutality toward children; audience tense and sober. No question about authenticity.

APPENDIX 39
Report on ICD Intelligence

Preparation of the Weekly Information Control Intelligence Summary—which was praised recently by General McClure [chief of ICD] as one of the principal documents being read by high-level policy officers in Berlin—involves the combined efforts of a highly specialized staff of editors, writers, researchers, printers and interrogators working in ICD's Intelligence Branch.

Material used in the Weekly is gathered from every corner of the U.S. Zone by interrogators working directly under ICD or assigned to Information Control Branches of the three Laender. The mass of intelligence arriving in Bad Homburg is collated and evaluated here by an Editorial Section which prepares over-all reports for the publication.

The two principal sources of Intelligence material for the Weekly are the Intelligence Branch's Survey Unit and its team of Special Interrogators. The former conducts scientific polls among the Germans on a variety of subjects involving Military Government and the re-education of the German people, while the latter is concerned with interviewing German officials and other leaders in an effort to determine new trends and reactions to specific regulations.

One of the unique jobs being done by Intelligence Branch's editorial staff is the analysis of the German-language newspapers published in the French, British, Russian and American zones of occupation. This regular feature, captioned "Information Services in Germany," provides the only complete review of this type in the U.S. Zone.

In addition to the Weekly, the Editorial Section of Intelligence Branch publishes the Daily Intelligence Digest, which appears five days each week. This report includes summaries of original intelligence reports prepared by ICD interrogators, reports channeled to ICD from investigators in Information Control Branches in the three Laender and other material extracted from such sources as Land MG Summaries and Army, Corps and Division G-2 reports.

The editorial staff is under the direction of Mr. Arthur Kahn, who is assisted by

Mr. Tibor Mende, Mr. Milic Kybal, Mr. Creighton Marcott, Miss Juliette Lombard and Mrs. Frances Leishman.

APPENDIX 40

Marshal Georgi K. Zhukoff, commander of Soviet occupation forces in Germany, ordered the Germans today to turn in all Nazi publications by October 1 to speed elimination of "Nazi thought and militarism."

The order applied to publishing houses, public and private libraries, universities, schools and institutions as well as individuals.

Covered in the order are books, pamphlets, periodicals, and any other publications containing Fascist propaganda, racial theories, literature on the forceful acquisition of foreign territory, anything directed against any member of the United Nations and all war literature.

There were no reports of complaints at the Four Power Control Council about violations of the Potsdam Agreement in Soviet Zone publications or on Soviet-licensed radio stations.

APPENDIX 41

Critique of American Occupation Policies

1. It has been increasingly apparent that the lack of a clear-cut policy and of long-range planning will lead to disorganization and failure in the American occupation of Germany. The remark of an editor of a licensed newspaper that he could not tell whether the American organ Die Neue Zeitung was carrying out American policy because he did not know what that policy was is characteristic. Even if there were a policy, the employment of regular army people in positions of civil administration would not lead to best results. Indeed, there was a woeful lack of preparation for the occupation as far as advanced study of conditions and selection and training of personnel were concerned. The lack of a clear policy has led to chaos in administration, wholesale corruption in MG, and disintegration of morale among occupation personnel. In addition, American troops, uninformed as to their mission (and even highest echelons seem to be uninformed), have lost their discipline and are becoming bad representatives of their nation.

2. It must be recognized that Germany is a militarist, ultra-nationalist nation that has been sick for two hundred years. It is not going to be democratized by the institution of elections or by declaring to the German people that as a result of losing the war they have automatically become democratic. . . . In addition, failure to recognize the guilt of German indus-

trialists as the main promoters of Nazism results in an ignoring of the basic causes of the disease Americans are here to cure.

3. The current approach has resulted in (1) transferring power to unreliable Germans . . . ; and (2) a failure to develop propaganda materials appropriate to the German mentality. In addition, the rapid redeployment of American troops and the growing disaffection of American civilian officials has resulted in an ever decreasing supervision of the Germans.

4. It stands to reason that those who fought hardest against Hitler during the Nazi era would be the ones who could most be trusted in efficiently and unsentimentally eradicating remnants of Hitlerism in Germany today. Instead, American occupation forces have been impressed by well-dressed and well-educated German gentlemen with proper business, industrial and Church connections, who perhaps did not join the Nazi Party and might not have signed their letters with Heil Hitler! (an omission which they readily point to as evidence of their opposition to National Socialism). But these gentlemen did make an adjustment to Hitlerism—with all that that meant as far as making war, destroying countries and annihilating conquered peoples. Educated in German universities, steeped in German traditions, they consider themselves the defenders of the so-called German Kultur. Kultur implies not only German cultural superiority but also German imperialism, militarism and ultra-nationalism, which, brought to fulfillment, resulted in National Socialism.

5. With the weakening of American supervision and controls, German administrators are becoming belligerent and disrespectful. Minister President Geiler of Greater Hesse, for example, anticipated the transfer to the provincial governments of information control operations by announcing that Germans were to break off relations with the Information Control offices immediately and take directions from him.

6. The newspapers, subject only to post-publication scrutiny, have taken to preparing against the day when National Socialism may regain power. . . . Attacks on Allied nations appear in the press along with statements rejecting war guilt and blaming other nations for supporting Hitler as well as material aimed at dividing the occupying powers.

7. Licensed publishers are admonished not to print anything militaristic, nationalistic or national socialist. Actually they enjoy free rein, and the results are as to be expected from a people as sick as the Germans. Pamphlets have appeared defending Gestapo agents as gentlemen of culture and courtesy, asserting that the war was not of right but of might and denying the guilt of the German people for warlike aggression.

8. The inability of Americans to recognize the fundamental differences of German history, traditions and ideology from ours has resulted in our

distributing American films that are ill-adapted to our occupation goals. No consideration is taken of our reeducation responsibility. Germans are shown American comedies, detective movies and light entertainment films, many of which Americans reject as of little merit. On the other hand, films displaying the strengths of American democracy are neglected.

9. Despite the general failure to deal with Germany as a nazified, sick nation, a small number of conscientious and capable American administrators have been successful in preventing publication of Nazi propaganda. Today, however, their assignment, it appears, is adjudged finished, and it is suggested that the occupation force be cut considerably and that administration and supervision be turned over to the Germans. Because of red tape, it has been impossible to hire capable replacements for experienced American administrators who are returning home because of the unwillingness to offer attractive salaries to capable people accustomed to substantial incomes. Personnel are harried with dress regulations, lack of transport, discrimination among civilians of different civil service grades and other discouraging measures which impel capable people to resign.

10. The failures of the Americans to accept the thesis that Germany is a nazified country and their unwillingness to undertake a thorough-going rehabilitation of this nation have led to a German victory. Fifteen months ago . . . many Americans were expressing the hope that the Russians would occupy all of Germany since they considered that only the Russians would mete out the proper radical treatment necessary to revitalize this country. Since that time, however, the old Goebbels propaganda that the Western powers and the Soviet Union would inevitably come to war has been revived. Many Americans are far more concerned with opposing the Russians . . . than they are with carrying out a denazification of German life.

11. It appears that much of what the war was fought for has been forgotten and that an occupation which considers its task to be a mere policing of the German nation is doomed to fail. Two possibilities remain—either to withdraw in favor of another occupying power or fundamentally to change occupation philosophy.

APPENDIX 42
Collective Guilt

In a larger perspective, the "guilt" of the German people cannot be separated from the "guilt" of a world which provided the conditions favoring a development of fascism and failed to crush the menace at its inception. . . . The question of collective guilt, nevertheless, has become an important political and moral issue for the Germans and, indirectly, for the occupying powers.

It might seem to the uniformed observer that the preoccupation of political and church leaders and the press with the collective guilt issue represents a disproportionate expenditure of time and verbiage in a country where food shortages, lack of housing, problems of resettlement of refugees, etc. are critical issues. On the other hand, about the question . . . revolve issues of basic occupation policies-denazification, the future social order, and the rehabilitation of the German nation.

The MG officer who . . . has no use for "any of the damned krauts" and treats the ex-concentration inmate with the same indifference as he does the most ardent Nazi. Discrimination among Germans according to the guilt of individuals and recognition of the influence of world conditions on the rise of Hitler, on the other hand, emphasize the ideological character of the war. . . .

The question whether the German people as a whole is guilty and how much guilt they bear should also influence the length of time Germany is to be policed by the occupation powers.

One of the first posters posted in German public places portrayed the horrors of the concentration camps and bore the caption "Whose guilt?" . . . the introduction of denazification laws [however] implied that there was a difference in the amount of guilt borne by individual Germans. On the other hand . . . the failure of the Western powers to transfer governmental and economic controls to anti-Nazis (as differentiated from non-Nazis) has resulted in our permitting many conservative Germans who made adjustments to the Hitler regime to remain in positions of leadership. . . .

Although the initial guilt propaganda in the Russian zone was similar to that in the West, it was tempered by Stalin's reminder that "dictators come and go, but Germany remains." Exposure of the evils of the Hitler regime and of the responsibility borne by individual Germans was, in addition, accompanied by the appointment of Social Democrats and Communists and other anti-Nazis to deal with denazification and by a reorganization of the political and social structures of the zone. At the end of 1945 . . . the collective guilt propaganda had run full course and a new line was introduced—propaganda proclaiming the birth of a new democratic Germany. The first issue of the Freier Bauer [Free Farmer], *a zonal weekly, in October bore the headline "The New Era"; the publication of the Youth Council was given the title "The New Life."*

Many Germans in the Western zones (along with high officials in Military Government headquarters) have urged rejection of the collective guilt theory out of fear that its application might result in the kinds of changes in the social structure that have taken place in the Russian zone through confiscation of the wealth of Nazis and militarists and the transfer of economic and political power to proven anti-Nazis.

Kzler returned to their homes expecting that their anti-Nazi activity had earned them the right to positions of leadership. Rebuffing this claim on the basis of a rejection of collective guilt meets with the applause of a large percentage of the German people, who thereby protect their positions and property and salve their consciences.

Some conservative leaders overlook the sufferings of Communists and Social Democrats under Hitler and charge that the two left parties—nothing is said of the pre-1933 right-wing parties—share responsibility for the rise of Hitler and the present misery of the German people. Association of the collective guilt theory with the "bolsheviks" and the Soviet Union has demagogic appeal among people indoctrinated for twelve years with Goebbels' propaganda ... especially within political parties not eager to commit themselves to action on pressing issues.

Exploration of the issues involved in the collective guilt theory can lay bare the character of the Nazi regime, its goals and modes of operation and the social bases of its support and provide the rationale for the punishment of criminal elements and for the removal from positions of influence of the supporters of the Nazi system ... and their replacement by those who bear the least or, in some cases, no guilt for the Nazi crimes.

With the withdrawal of MG and decreasing American supervision of the press, radio and publications as well as of the political parties and the churches, attempts to absolve the German people of collective guilt and to incriminate other nations have become bolder. Now that German administrations have assumed charge of denazification and Germans in all areas of life are gaining independence from MG controls, it is likely that the question of collective guilt will take on increasing significance, imperiling gravely the original aims of the occupation.

APPENDIX 43

Looting Germany

During the war, there had been open hunting. A lieutenant in a tank outfit told me how after the capture of Goering's castle, he had cut out old oil paintings from their frames with his bayonet ... and wrapped them in his bedroll for safekeeping. Unfortunately, he soon lost them in a crap game and was able to send home only what he described as a "huge" tapestry. ...

We heard of a general who was sent home for selling a whole trainload of supplies on the French blackmarket. ... In Brussels there was a street where one could buy any item of GI clothing in all sizes for a good blackmarket price. ... In Luxembourg, the inhabitants of one area had a unique opportunity to stock up on American supplies when a quartermaster officer declared his depot destroyed and sold the contents after the building was slightly damaged by a V-bomb. ... After the war ... we were able to go into trade operations on a big business scale. Mess officers sold food, and the men complained of short and unvaried rations. Ration dumps sold liquor, and units went without drinks. Gas dumps sold gasoline. . . . The occupation developed into a vast bonanza. . . .

It was the dream of every BTO ["big time operator"] to go on leave, on pass, on orders or even AWOL to Berlin, where a man could get rich quick. The early comers, of course, had the advantage. They sold cigarettes at $200 a carton to the Germans. [Called "Lebensmittel"—foodstuffs—because they stifled hunger]. A tremendous traffic with Russian soldiers in watches developed with a stream of timepieces imported from Switzerland and the States for the market. Some GIs in Berlin acted as brokers for buddies in the zone. . . .

At a Wiesbaden detachment the dispatcher sold the privilege of driving the courier vehicle to Berlin for $200 to $300 a trip—two trips a week netted him up to $600. But the drivers ran no risk. They loaded up with cigarettes from their buddies (at least $150 a carton), butter ($50 a pound) and coffee ($30 a pound) taken from the mess, candy ($5 for a nickel bar), soap ($5 a bar) and watches and assorted items of clothing.

APPENDIX 44

Memoranda from Al Toombs and General McClure, May 1946

Memorandum from A. Toombs:

His first duties were in the consolidation and compilation of intelligence material on enemy forces, which was of value in the preparation of combat propaganda. He participated in the interrogation of French civilians and Russian forced laborers and soldiers. Later he participated in the preparation of the Intelligence Section's Daily Summary. Because of the outstanding ability which he demonstrated, he was placed in charge of the preparation of this Daily Summary. The Summary served as a basis for tactical propaganda carried out by Radio Luxembourg and for leaflets prepared by 12th Army Group.

During off-duty hours, Mr. Kahn improved his knowledge of the German language. In the last weeks of the war, when our forces were overrunning Germany, Mr. Kahn was assigned at the front as an interrogator. His knowledge of French, German and Russian enabled him to obtain valuable information from German civilians and soldiers, Allied prisoners of war, and displaced persons. On the basis of information gained through these interrogations, it was possible to direct effectively our propaganda designed to bring about a quick surrender of enemy forces. Information gained through these interrogations guided Military Government in decisions in these confused days.

With the cessation of hostilities and the deactivation of 12th Army Group, Mr. Kahn was transferred to the Information Control Division, U.S. Forces European

Theater. He was also transferred from the Office of Strategic Services to the Office of International Information and Cultural Affairs, State Department. He has served as Editor-in-Chief, Intelligence Branch, since that time. In this capacity, he has been charged with preparing and editing the Information Control Intelligence Summary (weekly) and the Daily Digest of Intelligence. Under his editorship, these documents have set a high standard for army Intelligence publications. As you know, both documents are highly regarded and widely read, not only in this Headquarters but by our Allies and by people in policy-making positions in Washington.

It can be said that Mr. Kahn deserves full credit for the excellent quality of our publications, which cover public opinion, the German political picture, and basic studies of the German mind.

During the time that Mr. Kahn has served with me, he has advanced from a position of small importance to become a key man in a much larger organization. This advancement has been earned by hard work, ability and intelligence. He is certainly one of the best informed men in this headquarters today on the German problem. He has an intimate knowledge of the German political picture and a true insight into the nature of the German problem. During the days of hardship and danger under combat conditions, and latterly in the face of other difficulties, he has always overcome all obstacles. I can say truly and with feeling that he will be irreplaceable in this Branch.

As you know, he accepted a comparatively low salary when he entered the Office of Stragetic Services in order to be of service to our country. Because of administrative difficulties, it has not been possible to increase his civil service standing. It is because of a better offer from another division that he is leaving this organization.

Memorandum from General McClure:

1. It is with regret that I learned of your decision to resign from the organization.

2. In spite of the fact that you were originally classified as CAF-7 [a Civil Service rating], you have been, for the past several months, filling a position which calls for a CAF-11 rating. We have done everything possible to have you reclassified to the CAF-11 which you deserve. I regret that the difficulties of getting reclassifications through the State Department for overseas personnel have stood in the way.

3. I hope that in your new assignment you will find your work congenial. May I endorse your Chief's recommendation for the valuable services you have rendered this organization.

APPENDIX 45
Socialist Unity Party Program

By the division of the working classes Fascism achieved power. With cruel terror it destroyed democratic rights and freedom and made of Germany a military prison.

The way was free for an unrestrained imperialistic militarism without scruples. German imperialism sacrificed to its desire for international power the life and existence of millions of workers, farmers, tradesmen, intellectuals, and above all the youth. . . .

Militarism, imperialistic despotism and war policies have twice led to national catastrophe.

. . . punishment of all people responsible for the war and of all war criminals, elimination of the remnants of the Hitler regime from the justice system and government, cleansing of fascist and reactionary elements from public life and official bodies . . . confiscation of industrial and commercial concerns of war criminals, fascists and war profiteers, liquidation of militarism, expropriation through land reform of the landed estates, democratic elections, and training of working people to serve as administrators, teachers, judges and managers of concerns, with special consideration being given to women.

. . . democratic taxation, freedom of the press and of religion, equality before the law without distinctions of race or sex, democratic reform of the judicial system and of the educational system, separation of church and state and cultural renewal through fostering of the arts.

In the very first few months after the end of the war the democratic bodies of self-government in Berlin, just as everywhere else in the Soviet occupation zone, effected a number of socio-economic transformations under the supervision of the Communist Party of Germany and assisted by the Soviet Command. A democratic land reform was carried out which gave land to almost a million working people. The big capitalist monopolies were abolished, and the associations of entrepreneurs were disbanded. Former Nazis were removed from top posts in various spheres of the city's economic, social and cultural life. An eight-hour working day was introduced at the factories and a single system of leaves for the workers was established.

Index

Aachen, Germany, 14–18, 36, 198
Adenauer, Konrad, 111 n. 12
Allied powers, prohibition against Germans attacking, 152–53
American Military Government. *See also* American Zone
  in Aachen, 36, 198
  anti-Communist atmosphere in, 90
  in Bavaria, 81
  clergy and, 36 n. 1
  crises facing, 80–81
  in Frankfurt, 142
  in Leipzig, 58
  in Mainz, 57–58, 66
  in Munich, 82, 83–84, 88–90, 108
  selection of German officials by, 199–200
  in Wuerzburg, 66–67
  youth and, 92, 93
American Red Cross, 12
American troops
  demoralization of, 138–39, 140, 161
  indiscipline of, 137–39
  looting by, 43
  sexually transmitted diseases among, 136
American Zone. *See also* American Military Government
  administration of, 139 n. 16
  anti-Semitism in, 177–78
  concentration camp documentary and, 144, 208
  conformity and repression in, 147
  denazification in, 132–33, 159–60
  elections in, 113–14
  political rallies in, 123
  progress in, 131–32
  Soviet critique of media in, 147
  state of at end of 1945, 135
  trade union conference in, 179
  youth in, 153–54
America's Strategic Blunders (Matthias), xi–xii

André, Lucien, 32, 189–90
anticommunism
  in America, 122 n. 11, 205–6
  in Information Control Division, 133–34 n. 7
antifascist resistance organizations (Antifa)
  disbandment of, 122
  in Leipzig, 58
  in Munich, 82
  in Soviet Zone, 126–27
  in Wuppertal, 37
Anti-Fascists of Germany, 81
anti-Nazi resistance organizations, 37, 58. *See also* Communists
anti-Semitism, 177–78
anti-Sovietism, 119, 174–76
Ardennes forest, 28–29
Arenberg, Prince von, 87–88
Army Information and Education school, 162–68, 169
assembly points
  Balts at, 67
  Darmstadt, 69–70, 71–76
  Eisenhower and, 110
  Gonsenheim Displaced Persons, 38–39
  Jewish DP community near Frankfurt, 167 n. 6
  people in, 27n. 1
Attlee, Clement, 107, 120, 204
Auschwitz, travel by inmates from to Buchenwald, 51–52
Axmann, Artur, 154 n. 4

Babcock, Colonel, 132
Bad Homburg, Germany, 92
Bad Nauheim, Germany, 69
Bad Wiessee, Germany, 108 n. 5
Balts in assembly center, 67
Bar-le-Duc, France, 7–8
Battle of the Bulge, 28–29, 35
Baumgartner, Dr., 173 n. 3

Bavaria
    antidemocratic atmosphere in, 108–9
    denazification and democratization in, 125
    dismissal of officials in, 110–11
    journalist investigation of, 136–37
Bedell Smith, Walter, 111, 203–4
Belfrage, Cedric, 116 n. 4
Berger, Wilhelm, 102
Berlin, Germany
    American troops in, 138, 161–62
    tribute to "victims of fascism" in, 126
    victory parade in, 120 n. 8
Bernstein, Bernard, 132 n. 3
Betrayal: The American Occupation of Germany (Kahn)
    manpower situation description in, 207
    publication of, ix
    "Some Concluding Observations," 180–81
    as source, xi
Betz, Dr., 55 n. 4
black market
    in Berlin, 161–62
    and looting, 161–62, 213–14
    and Al Toombs, 162
Blaum, Kurt, 115–18, 123, 124, 144, 149
Bluecherplatz elementary school, 96
BMW automobile works, 87 n. 17
Bradley, Omar, 35
Breslau, Germany, 63
British officers in Belgium, 29–31, 32
Brussels, Belgium, 29–32, 33
Buchenwald concentration camp, 51–52, 193–94
Buerckel, Gauleiter, 21, 22
Butz, Hermann
    as actor and writer, 41–42 n. 7
    on Communism, 49
    on democratization, 48
    poems by, 192–93
    on reparations, 45
    on Soviet Union, 46
    on war crimes, 44
Byrnes, James F., 139 n. 16, 175–76

capitalism, definitions of, 164, 167–68 n. 7
capture
    of Aachen, 17
    of Darmstadt, 71
    of Metz, 24–25
    of Munich, 82
Carlebach, Emil, 123, 144
Centrists, 45
Cerf, Marcelle, 32
Cerf, Roger, diary of, 32, 186–90
Christian Democratic Union (CDU), 116, 142, 151
Christian Social Union, 141
Churchill, Winston, 168 n. 7, 204
cigarette exchange rate, 161
CIO, definitions of, 164–65
Clark, Delbert, 155 n. 1, 176, 177 n. 10
Clay, Lucius B.
    amnesty granted to Nazis by, 177
    church proclamation response by, 159 n. 9
    criticism of Four Power Control Council and, 139
    denazification and, 173
    elections and, 141
    National Democratic Party and, 149
Cold War, 174–76
collective guilt
    analysis of, 156–58
    opinions on, 148
    political parties in Frankfurt and, 117
    Sevenich on, 151–52
Communism, definitions of, 165
Communist Party of Germany (KPD)
    assault on by other parties, 142
    in Bavaria, 125
    in countryside, 141
    in elections, 143
    establishment of, 122–23
    in Frankfurt, 117–18
    on land reform, 134
    opinions of, 113
    Social Democrats and, 123–24, 171
Communists
    fear of, 99

in Mainz, 57
Mainz citizens' opinions of, 48–49
public office and, 122
trials of in Berlin, 172
concentration camps
  Buchenwald, 51–52, 193–94
  documentary on, 144, 208
  Sevenich on, 151–52
  Wittig on, 57
Connell, Hollis H., 138
Crusade in Europe (Eisenhower), xi

Daniell, Raymond
  on Bavaria, 111, 125
  on denazification, 114, 123 n. 12, 159–60
  on Patton, 110
  on political parties, 123 n. 12
  on Potsdam Declaration, 120
  on transfer of authority to German officials, 131 n. 1
Danz, Christian Adam, 101, 104
Darmstadt
  capture of, 71
  clergy of, 100–105
  Displaced Persons assembly center at, 69–70, 71–76
  visit to, 79 n. 2
Degen, Valentin, 101–2, 103, 104–5
democracy
  in Germany, 180–81
  Mainz citizens' opinions of, 47–48
demoralization
  of American troops, 136, 138–39, 140, 161
  of German youth, 153–54
  of Information Control Division, 140, 145
  in Munich, 88–89
  of Wehrmacht troops, 24–25, 26, 185–86
denazification
  in American Zone, 132–33, 159–60
  in Bavaria, 125
  Clay on, 173
  clergymen on, 103, 159
  Daniell on, 123 n. 12
  Eisenhower and, 111, 114, 203
  elections and, 114

Mainz citizens' opinions of, 47
OMGUS and, 109
"Red Menace" and, 176–78
Roman Catholic bishops and, 100–101
sabotage of, 132
Sevenich on, 151
in Soviet Union, 121
trade unions and, 179
Displaced Persons (DP). *See* assembly points
Dorn, Walter L., 122 n. 11
DP (Displaced Persons). *See* assembly points
Dresden, 121
DVG (Deutsche Volksgemeinschaft), 21–22

Economics Council, bizonal, 176
Eggleston, Arthur, 147
Eisenhower, Dwight D.
  Aachen and, 36
  on Allied objectives in Germany, 14
  on American Zone, 131–32, 139 n. 16
  Crusade in Europe, xi
  denazification and, 111, 203
  elections in American Zone and, 113–14
  Haislip and, 109–10
  Patton and, 111, 112
  political parties and, 113
  Potsdam Declaration and, 109
  VE Day and, 70
  on visit to Moscow, 205
  "Whose Guilt?" posters and, 80
  Yalta and Teheran conferences and, 120, 204
elections
  in American Zone, 113–14
  in Frankfurt, 115–18
  Roman Catholic Church and, 142–43
  in rural communities, 142–43
  scheduling of, 114, 141
Epifanov, Anatoly, 72, 196–97
evacuation
  of Aachen, 15–18
  of Metz, 22–23

farmers, interviews of, 99–100
Faulhaber, Michael Cardinal von
   appointments of, 84 n. 13
   food distribution and, 87
   housing crisis and, 88
   Munich, Bavaria, and, 82–83
   Rudolph of Wittelsbach and, 134–35
   war criminals and, 157
Feder, Oswald, 176 n. 8
Ficker, Ludwig, 172–73
Filitov, Alexei, xi, 126 n. 18, 172 n. 1, 176–77 n. 9
First Army
   Battle of the Bulge and, 28–29
   German frontier and, 13–14
   POW enclosure of, 5
   at Torgau on Elbe, 69
   transfer of, 35
Fleck, Egon, 81, 84, 85, 87, 89, 90
food crisis in Munich, 87–88
forced labor
   at Buchenwald, 52
   in Metz, 22–23
Forces françaises de l'intérieur (FFI), 7–8, 9
Forster, Arnold, xvi
Four Power Control Council, 100, 107, 139
Fragebogen, 103, 110
France. *See also specific cities*
   attitudes of population of, 4
   Soviet refugees in, 6–11
   Third Army in, 4
Franc tireurs et partisan (FTP), 7
Frank, Hans, daughter of, 108, 159
Frankfurt, Germany
   demonstrations by American troops in, 138
   Economics Council, bizonal, in, 176
   Jewish DP community near, 167 n. 6
   newspaper of, 115–18
   workers parties in, 123
Frankfurter Rundschau
   Blaum and, 115–16, 118, 123, 124
   criticism of, 147
   exposure of Nazis and, 142
Frankfurter Zeitung, 117

Freedom Action Bavaria, 82
Free Germany Committee, 13
Freikorps, 82
Freudenberg, Richard, 132
Friedberg, Germany, 92
Fritzsche, Hans, 176–77
Frontpost, 3

Germany. *See also* Bavaria; Ruhr region of Germany; *specific cities*
   Allied advance into, 13–14
   democracy in, 180–81
   Four Power Control Council and, 107
   industry, reconstruction of in, 45
   surrender of, 70
   unification of, 175–76
   women in, 145–46
   youth of, 92–93, 94, 153–54, 202
Gessler, Dr., 110 n. 9
Gessner, Hans, 173 n. 3
Gestapo in Mainz, 42–43
Godin, Freiherr von, 84
Goebbels, Joseph, 56, 160
Gonsenheim Displaced Persons assembly point, 38
Gordon Walker, Patrick, 70, 71
Gourfein, Murray, 185
Greck, Lambert, 59–60, 61–62, 63
Greiner, Wilhelm, 148
Groeber, Archbishop, 157
Grohrock, Reinhardt, 104
Gromyko, Andrei, 119 n. 3, 204
Grotewohl, Otto, 127
Gusovski, Alexander, 9, 10, 184

Habe, Hans, 21, 146
Haertner, Wilhelm, 52–54
Haislip, Wayne H., 109–10
Hartrich, Edwin, 176
Herzogenrath, Germany, 185
Hickey, Doyle O., 72–74, 75, 79 n. 2
Hihn, Dr., 87 n. 16
Hilldring, John A., 132 n. 3
Hillman, Sidney, 178 n. 11
Himmler, Heinrich, 15
Hitler, Adolf
   attempt on life of, 42

attempt to overthrow, 13
Gau Cologne-Aachen and, 14
Haertner and, 53
Paulus on, 13
Seifert on, 64
"total war" decree of, 15
Hoegner, Wilhelm, 85–86, 111, 125, 173
housing issues
in Munich, 85, 88–89
in Wiesbaden, 113
Huber, Herr, 108

ICD. *See* Information Control Division (ICD)
I&E school. *See* Army Information and Education school
I.G. Farben, 132
indiscipline of American troops, 43, 137–39
industry, German, reconstruction of, 45
Information Control Division (ICD). *See also* Psychological Warfare (PW)
anti-Communist attitudes in, 133–34 n. 7
in Berlin, 162
demoralization of, 140, 145
editorial staff of, 208–9
elections and, 114
Film-Theater-Music branch of, 144
formation of, 98 n. 11
influence of, 134–35
Potsdam Declaration and, 107
praise for, 144–45, 208–9
reports of, 133, 145–46, 208–9
interviews
of Darmstadt clergy, 101–5
of farmers, 99–100
of German soldiers held by Russians, 121–22
of German workers, 91–92
of German youth, 92–93
of Mainz citizens, 40–44
of Nazi Party members, 52–57
of prisoners of war, 3, 4–5
of Soviet citizens, 5–6

Jews, German opinions of, 46–47
Jobst, Dr., 86

Johnson, Edd, 173
Jurr, Gerhard, 172

Kahn, Arthur D.
education and background of, xv–xvi, 29–30
on experience in Germany, 180–81
language competence of, xv, xvi n. 1
pay of, 155 n. 2
praise for, 185
recruitment of, xvi
resignation of, 169
Kammermeier, Wilhelm, 172
Kassel, Frieherr von, 82, 84 n. 12
Keegan, Charles, 81
Kellen, Konrad, 140, 169
Keyes, Geoffrey, 111
Kilgore, Harley M., 120–21
Kilgore Senate Subcommittee on War Mobilization, 132
Kipp, Otto, 123–24
Klopov, Tov, 72
Koenigsberg (city), 101
Kohlscheidt, Germany, 185
Kompanyeyets, Stepan Danilovich
on capture of Darmstadt, 71
on complaints about food, 72
daughter and grandson of, 76 n. 7
Hickey and, 73, 74–75
Kahn and, 70, 75–76
Krass, Boris, 5
Kriushchuk, Victor (Misha), 12, 27–28
Kroeftel, Germany, 100
Kroth, Alfred, 85, 88, 125, 206–7
Kybal, Milic, 208–9
Kzler
in Munich, 84–85
treatment of, 198–99, 200–201
welfare for, 107–8, 122

La Guardia, Fiorello, sister of, 126 n. 19
land reform, 134
Lange, Carl, 85
Leffler, Melvyn P., xi, 126 n. 18, 175 n. 6
Leipzig, 58
Leishman, Frances, 208–9

Leuschner, Wilhelm, 42
Liberal Democrats, 116–17, 142
Lindenfels, Germany, 199
Litvinov, M. M., commission of, 126 n. 18
Litzmannstadt ghetto, 61
Lombard, Juliette, 208–9
Long, Tania, 136
looting
  by American troops, 43
  black market and, 161–62, 213–14
  in Metz, 23
  trial of Germans for, 39–40
Lorraine, priests in, 186
Luxembourg, 11–12, 27
Lvovsky, Semyon (Seenya), 12, 27–28, 38 n. 4, 76 n. 7

Maas, Buergermeister, 113, 124
"Macht Schluss!" stickers, 27
Mahler, Ludwig, 12
Mainz
  Gestapo in, 42–43
  interrogation of citizens of, 40–44
  overview of, 37–39
  trial of Germans for looting in, 39–40
Maisky, I. M., commission of, 126 n. 18
Man, Paul de, 31 n. 3
Marcott, Creighton, 208–9
Matteoti, Giacomo, 42
Matthias, Willard C., xi–xii, 119
McClure, Robert A.
  Kahn and, 155 n. 2, 169, 215
  scrutiny board proposal and, 147
  Weekly Intelligence Summary and, 145, 149
McLaughlin, Kathleen, 110–11, 138, 207–8
McNarney, Joseph T., 133 n. 5, 137–38, 139, 168–69
McSherry, Frank J., 178
Meislinger, Alfred, 172–73
Meister, Dr., 86 n. 15
memorandum to OMGUS
  on German women, 145–46
  on Munich, 109, 203
  on Polish atrocity stories, 146
  on poll about *Die Neue Zeitung*, 146–47
memorandum to SHAEF
  on evacuation order, 18, 184–85
  on German revolt, 14, 15
  on Siegfried Line, 15
  on Soviet refugees in France, 11
Mende, Tibor, 208–9
Metz, Germany, 21–26
MG. *See* American Military Government
Michel, Wilhelm, 102, 103, 104, 150
Middleton, Drew
  on American troops, 138–39
  on anti-Soviet attitude, 119 n. 2
  on denazification decree, 109, 141
  Eisenhower and, 131
  on Military Government, 110 n. 7
  on transfer of authority to Germans, 139–40
Middleton, Paul E., 10–11
Miesbach, Germany, 159–60
Military Government. *See* American Military Government
Molotov, V. I., 175
Montgomery, Bernard Law, 30
Morgenthau, Henry, 126 n. 18
Mueller, Oskar, 124, 133 n. 7
Mueller, Thomas, 102, 103, 104
Muenchen-Gladbach, 35
Muhler, Emil, 83 n. 9, 89
Munich, Germany, 81–90, 107–9, 121
Munich university underground movement, 41–42 n. 7
Murphy, Robert D., 132

Naimark, Norman M., xi, 126
names in reports, ix n. 2
National Democratic Party, 149–50
Nazi influence
  in Aachen, 36
  in American counterintelligence unit, 108
  attitudes of youth toward, 93
  in countryside, 141
  in Frankfurt, 142
  in Leipzig, 58
  in Miesbach, 160

in Munich, 81–82, 83–84, 85–87, 89–90, 121
in textbooks, 95–96
in Wolfratshausen, 149
in Wuppertal, 37
Nazi Party
  clergymen members of, 102–3
  interrogation of members of, 52–57
  member interviews in Wuerzburg, 63–65
  propaganda, 185–86
Nazism, definitions of, 166–67
Die Neue Zeitung, 146–47, 149, 158
Newman, Colonel, 143
New Socialist Unity Party, 171–72, 215–16
Nik, 8
Nikolai, 67
Ninth Army, 28–29, 35
Nixon, Russell A., 132 n. 3
North Africa, 9

Oberhuber, Karl, 88 n. 19
Offenbach, Germany, 92
Office of Military Government (OMGUS). *See also* memorandum to OMGUS; Supreme Headquarters of the Allied Expeditionary Forces (SHAEF)
  clergymen and, 105
  denazification directives, 83
  Easter Sunday pastoral letter and, 158–59
  election schedule and, 114, 141
  Information Control Division of, 98 n. 11
  Internal Affairs Branch of, 109
Office of Strategic Services (OSS). *See also* Information Control Division (ICD); Psychological Warfare (PW)
  anti-Soviet atmosphere in, 119
  application to, xv
  order to report to Paris by, 69, 70
  training by, xvi
  White Russian émigré and, 27, 28
  in Wiesbaden, 79–80
Office of War Information, 98 n. 11
Only Fourteen Days, a Factual Report (Schumann), 148

Oppenheim, Michel
  on Communism, 49, 67
  on denazification, 47
  on Jews, 46
  as Regierungsrat, 42–43
  on Walther, 43
  on war crimes, 45, 105
Oradour, France, 4
"Ordnungszelle Bayern," 83
Ordway, Howard, 110
orientation program
  Army Information and Education school, 162–68, 169
  of Truscott, 135
OSS. *See* Office of Strategic Services (OSS)

Padover, Saul, 36, 162
Papen, Franz von, 176–77
Paris, France, 4
Patton, George S.
  Eisenhower and, 109–10, 112
  Faulhaber and, 83
  on *Fragebogen*, 110
  intelligence sources of, 81
  on political parties, 111
  report on, 90
  St. Malo and, 4
Paulus, Friedrich von, 13
Penzberg, Germany, 108
Pepper, Claude, 174–75
Peryegudov, Major, 71
Pfeiffer, Anton, 173
Pinkenburg, Gustav, 59, 61, 62–63, 67
Pohlgoens, Germany, 99
political parties. *See also specific parties*
  clergymen on, 104–5
  in countryside, 141
  Eisenhower and, 113
  in Frankfurt, 115–18
  Mainz citizens' opinions of, 47–48
  Patton on, 111
  in Soviet Zone, 171–72
  Wuerzburg citizens' opinions of, 63
Potsdam Declaration
  Eisenhower and, 131
  provisions of, xii, 107, 202
  Soviet Union and, 120, 175

Powell, Clifford R.
　description of, 3
　on *Die Neue Zeitung*, 146
　Kahn and, 155 n. 2
　OSS order and, 69, 70
　Patton and, 81, 90
　return to States, 156 n. 4
　son of, 69
Prediger, Herr, 95, 96–97, 113
press and radio, proposal for scrutiny board for, 147–48
Psychological Warfare (PW). *See also* Information Control Division (ICD)
　editorial staff of, 14
　German citizen interviews, 21
　German desk of, xvi–xvii
　intelligence gathering in, 40 n. 5
　in Luxembourg, 27
　mission of, xvi, 4 n. 3, 198
　morale of, 79
　in Munich, 81, 84
　prisoner of war interrogations, 3, 4–5
　reconstitution of, 69
　renaming of, 98 n. 11
　resolve of, 19, 79–80
　Soviet citizen interrogations, 5–6
　Twelfth Army Group and, 4

Rabus, Carl and Erna, 32
radio, 65, 147–48
Radio Flensberg, 70
Radio Luxembourg, program for, 69–70, 71, 196
reeducation
　of children, 96–98
　concentration camp film and, 144
　Mainz citizens' opinions of, 49–50
　publishers and, 147–48
　of teachers, 95
Regensburg, Germany, 70, 142
Reid, Charles S., 120
Reminiscences and Reflections (Zhukov), xi
reparations, 45
reports. *See also* valedictory documents
　on Darmstadt assembly center, 71
　on Frankfort, 115
　on Mainz, 40, 190–92
　on Metz, 21–22, 25–26
　on Munich, 89–90, 109, 201
　on National Democratic Party, 149–50
　on Russians in Gonsenheim assembly point, 39
　on Wuerzburg, 59, 194–96
Richman, Samuel R., 11, 59
Richter, Richard, 54–55, 194
Roman Catholic church
　collective guilt and, 157
　Easter Sunday pastoral letter, 158–59
　elections and, 142–43
　support of Nazi regime by, 83, 86–87, 100–101, 200
Roosevelt, Franklin D., xii, 38
Rudolph of Wittelsbach, 134–35
Ruedrich, Karl, 84, 200–201
Ruhr region of Germany
　administration of, 204
　assault into, 35, 37, 52–53
　trade unions in, 180
Rundstedt, Karl Rudolf Gerd von, 13, 28
Russians
　discussions with, 197–98
　farmers' opinions of, 99–100
　German POWs of, 121–22
　German propaganda and, 5–6
　opinions of, 46, 57, 62–63
Russians in Germany (Naimark), xi

Samolyenko, Gregory, 196
Saxony, journalist investigation of, 136–37
Schaab, Dr., 97
Schacht, Hjalmar, 176–77
Schaeffer, Fritz, 83–84, 85, 110, 111
Schaeffer, Stefan, 66
Schaeftlarn, Germany, 80 n. 5
Scharnagl, Karl, 118, 125
Schieffer, Gustav, 108
Schlange-Schoeningen, Hans, 176
Schmidt, Dana Adams, 168
Schmitt, Heinrich, 173
Schramm, Heinrich, 65–66

Schumann, Walter, 148
Schwerin-Krosigk, Graf von, 16
Seifert, Ernst, 63–65, 67, 196
Seisser, Obert von, 84
separatism, 45–46, 61
Sevenich, Maria, 150–53
Seventh Army, 71, 109
Seydlitz, Walther von, 13
SHAEF. *See* Supreme Headquarters of the Allied Expeditionary Forces (SHAEF)
Shorthouse, Colonel, 72, 73, 74
Shrank, Captain, 80 n. 5, 198–99
Sibert, Edward, 154 n. 4
Siegfried Line, 14, 53–54
"Sieg oder Siberien," 53–54
Sluszny, Marcel and Nicole, 31
Sluszny, Naum and Esther, 31
Social Democrats (SPD)
  in Bavaria, 85–86, 125
  Communist Party and, 123–24, 142, 171
  establishment of, 122–23
  in Frankfurt, 117
  on land reform, 134
  opinions of, 113
  opinions on, 49
socialism, definitions of, 165–66
Sohl, Heinrich
  on Communism, 48–49
  as councilman, 40–41
  on Jews, 46
  on political parties, 48
  on reeducation, 49
  on reparations, 45
  on separatism, 45–46
  on war crimes, 44
sources, ix–x, xi–xii
Soviet Partisans in France, 8, 183
Soviet refugees
  in France, 6–11
  in Luxembourg, 11–12
Soviet Repatriation Mission, 71
Soviet Union
  shift in attitude toward, 119–20
  U.S. policy toward, 174–76
Soviet Zone
  administration of, 127

  anti-fascists in, 126–27
  journalist investigation of, 136–37
  land reform in, 134
  political parties of, 114–15 n. 2, 171–72
  press policies of, 209
Specht, Wilhelm, 87, 172–73
The Specter of Communism (Leffler), xi
Speer, Albert, 65
SS
  in Aachen, 17
  Patton and, 81
  Wehrmacht troops and, 25
St. Malo, France, 4
St. Mihiel, France, 9
Stadelmayr, Fritz, 86, 88, 108, 125
Stahlhelm, 64
Stalin, Josef, 107, 120, 204
Stammler, Hans, 60–61, 62, 63
Stars and Stripes, 19
Steffan, Jakob
  arrest warrant signed by, 194
  on Communism, 49
  on democratization, 47–48
  on denazification, 47
  on Jews, 46
  as police president, 41–42
  on reconstruction, 91
  on reeducation, 49
  on reparations, 45
  on separatism, 45–46
  on Soviet Union, 46
  on war crimes, 44–45
Stenz, Ferdinand, and wife
  on Communism, 49
  on denazification, 47
  on German industry, 45
  on Jews, 46
  on Mainz, 105
  on Nazis, 54
  opinions of, 43–44
  on political parties, 48
  on Soviet Union, 46
  on war crimes, 45
Strass, Germany, 185
Stuebel, Frauelein Doktor, 96, 97
Sueddeutsche Zeitung, 84
Sulzberger, Cyrus L., 155–56, 174

Supreme Headquarters of the Allied Expeditionary Forces (SHAEF). *See also* memorandum to SHAEF; Office of Military Government (OMGUS)
  directive of on Communists, 57
  psychological warfare and, 36
  response from to "The Evacuation Order," 185
  shortage of personnel in, 80
  "we do not call upon Germans to revolt" directive, 14, 18–19, 58
Swabian People's Youth, 154
Sweet, Paul, 36
Swoboda, Lieutenant Colonel, 36, 172, 198

Teheran conference, 120
textbooks, revisions of, 95–96
themes of book, x–xi
Thiemo, Hans, 141, 149
Third Army, 4, 6–7, 35
Tiano, Anthony, 138
Todt, Fritz, 53, 133 n. 6
Toombs, Al
  black market and, 162
  description of, xvii
  German desk and, xvi
  Kahn and, 98 n. 11, 155 n. 2, 169, 214–15
  Munich reports and, 109, 119
  opinions of, 162–63
  Patton and, 90
  phone call to, 80
  return of, 144–45
Toul, France, 6
trade unionists, 178–80
transfer of authority to German officials, 131, 139–40, 207
Truman, Harry, 107, 119 n. 3, 120, 139 n. 16, 204
Truscott, Lucian K., 135–36
Tsibikov, Andrei, 7, 76 n. 7, 8, 9
Twelfth Army Group
  Battle of the Bulge and, 28–29
  First Army and, 35
  on Psychological Warfare Intelligence, 3

valedictory documents
  "Critique of American Occupation Policies," 156, 209–11
  "The Significance of the Collective Guilt Theory," 156, 211–13
Vendig, Malcolm, 81
Venedey, Hans, 124
Verdun, France, 10
Viechtach, Germany, 149
Vienna, Austria, 121, 138
Vladimir, 8–9
Vlassov, General, 5
Volkssturm, 15, 24
Voroshilov, K. V., commission of, 126 n. 18

Waldheim, Philip, 102, 103, 104
Wallenberg, Captain, 146
Walther, Rudolph, 43, 44, 46, 49–50
war crimes
  at Buchenwald concentration camp, 193–94
  Faulhaber and, 157
  Mainz citizens' opinions of, 44–45
  Schramm on, 66
  Seifert on, 64
  Wittig on, 56–57
  Wuerzburg citizens' opinions of, 61–62
War Madness (Greiner), 148
Wehrmacht troops, 24–25, 26, 185–86
Weinberger, Wilhelm, 104
Weiss, Pastor, 104
Werewolves, 37, 69, 70
Werner, Arthur, 126
Wethers, Leon, 179 n. 12
Wiedmann, Friedrich, 103, 104
Wiesbaden, Germany
  OSS headquarters in, 79
  political attitudes in, 113
  school system in, 95–99, 178
Wimmer, Thomas, 108
winter hardships, 93–94
Wittig, Georg, 55–57
Wolf, Robert, 103, 104
Wolfratshausen, Germany, 149
women in Germany, 145–46
workers, German, interviews of, 91–92

workers parties in Frankfurt, 123
Wuerzburg, Germany, 59–67
Wulselen, Germany, 184–85
Wuppertal, Germany, 37
Wurm, Teophil, 156–57

Yalta Conference, 37–38, 119, 120
Young Socialists, 86
youth
    German, attitudes of, 92–93, 153–54, 202
    living conditions of, 94

Zhukov, Gyorgy
    Nazi publications and, 209
    on Potsdam conference, 204
    relieved of post, 176
    Reminiscences and Reflections, xi
    Soviet Zone and, 127
    on U.S. policy, 119–20

www.ingramcontent.com/pod-product-compliance
Lightning Source LLC
Chambersburg PA
CBHW021401290426
44108CB00010B/339